THE BASICS OF CHRISTIAN BELIEF

THE BASICS OF CHRISTIAN BELIEF

BIBLE, THEOLOGY, AND LIFE'S BIG QUESTIONS

JOSHUA STRAHAN

a division of Baker Publishing Group
Grand Rapids, Michigan

Published by Baker Academic
a division of Baker Publishing Group
PO Box 6287, Grand Rapids, MI 49516-6287
www.bakeracademic.com

Printed in the United States of America

Library of Congress Cataloging-in-Publication Data

Names: Strahan, Joshua Marshall, author.
Title: The basics of Christian belief : Bible, theology, and life's big questions / Joshua Strahan.
Description: Grand Rapids, Michigan : Baker Academic, a division of Baker Publishing Group, 2020. | Includes bibliographical references and indexes.
Identifiers: LCCN 2019046610 | ISBN 9781540962010 (paperback)
Subjects: LCSH: Theology.
Classification: LCC BR118 .S77 2020 | DDC 230—dc23
LC record available at https://lccn.loc.gov/2019046610

ISBN 978-1-5409-6314-7 (casebound)

20 21 22 23 24 25 26 7 6 5 4 3 2 1

For Sophia, Madeline, and Josiah:
I love you three more than words can say.

Contents

Abbreviations

General

AD	after death
BC	before Christ
chap(s).	chapter(s)
cf.	compare
ed.	edition; edited by
e.g.	for example
i.e.	that is
n(n).	note(s)
NIV	New International Version
NRSV	New Revised Standard Version
repr.	reprint
trans.	translated by
v(v).	verse(s)

Old Testament

Gen.	Genesis
Exod.	Exodus
Lev.	Leviticus
Num.	Numbers
Deut.	Deuteronomy
Josh.	Joshua
Judg.	Judges
Ruth	Ruth
1 Sam.	1 Samuel
2 Sam.	2 Samuel
1 Kings	1 Kings
2 Kings	2 Kings
1 Chron.	1 Chronicles
2 Chron.	2 Chronicles
Ezra	Ezra
Neh.	Nehemiah
Esther	Esther
Job	Job
Ps(s).	Psalm(s)
Prov.	Proverbs
Eccles.	Ecclesiastes
Song	Song of Songs
Isa.	Isaiah
Jer.	Jeremiah
Lam.	Lamentations
Ezek.	Ezekiel
Dan.	Daniel
Hosea	Hosea
Joel	Joel
Amos	Amos
Obad.	Obadiah
Jon.	Jonah

Mic.	Micah
Nah.	Nahum
Hab.	Habakkuk
Zeph.	Zephaniah
Hag.	Haggai
Zech.	Zechariah
Mal.	Malachi

New Testament

Matt.	Matthew
Mark	Mark
Luke	Luke
John	John
Acts	Acts
Rom.	Romans
1 Cor.	1 Corinthians
2 Cor.	2 Corinthians
Gal.	Galatians
Eph.	Ephesians
Phil.	Philippians
Col.	Colossians
1 Thess.	1 Thessalonians
2 Thess.	2 Thessalonians
1 Tim.	1 Timothy
2 Tim.	2 Timothy
Titus	Titus
Philem.	Philemon
Heb.	Hebrews
James	James
1 Pet.	1 Peter
2 Pet.	2 Peter
1 John	1 John
2 John	2 John
3 John	3 John
Jude	Jude
Rev.	Revelation

Introduction

Why Worldview Matters

> There are some people . . . —and I am one of them—who think that the most practical and important thing about a [person] is still his [or her] view of the universe.
>
> —G. K. Chesterton, *Heretics*

If you lived in London at the turn of the twentieth century, you would probably be aware of the six-foot-four, three-hundred-pound, bushy-mustachioed, cigar-smoking, sword-cane-wielding British journalist by the name of G. K. Chesterton. This larger-than-life man had a knack for saying something that sounded unreasonable, then going on to show why, in fact, it was quite reasonable. Take Chesterton's claim above: "There are some people . . . —and I am one of them—who think that the most practical and important thing about a [person] is still his [or her] view of the universe."[1] Surely Chesterton is exaggerating, right? Could a person's view of the universe have any actual, "practical" relevance in the realm of everyday life? And sure, a person's view of the universe might be interesting, but isn't calling it "important" a bit much?

Let's consider Chesterton's bold claim by examining two "views of the universe": the worldview assumed by atheism and the worldview assumed by the Lord's Prayer. The following thought exercise will likely feel simultaneously familiar and unfamiliar. Everybody knows what atheism is. And even most people who aren't Christians have probably heard the Lord's Prayer in movies or on television. I suspect, however, that many may be unfamiliar with the "practical and important" implications of atheism and the Lord's Prayer.

I chose atheism and the Lord's Prayer because of the draw they have for me personally—in part because I believe they offer the two most intellectually satisfying systems of thought. I am a Christian who has prayed the Lord's Prayer regularly for more than fifteen years. I know firsthand the intimacy, comfort, strength, and beauty of this prayer. Sometimes, however, atheism appeals to me, especially since Christianity can feel exhausting—intellectually, emotionally, ethically. I grow tired trying to find answers to questions that don't have easy answers. I find it fatiguing to care in a world with so many broken people and broken situations. And I get worn out trying to love my neighbor as myself. So why do I stick with Christianity? There are several reasons, and one of those reasons is that I've considered the practical and important implications of both Christianity and atheism, which we'll now look at in a bit more detail.

Atheism: The Practical and Important Implications

I recently came across a fascinating book that put forward an atheistic worldview and explained its practical implications. In *The Atheist's Guide to Reality*, Alex Rosenberg, professor of philosophy at Duke University, works hard to answer life's big questions.[2] He opens the book by asking, "What is the nature of reality, the purpose of the universe, and the meaning of life? Is there any rhyme or reason to the course of human history? Why am I here? Do I have a soul? . . . What happens when we die? Do we have free will? Why should I be moral?"[3] Rosenberg is asking some great questions, and he is confident that he can provide the answers. He warns the reader, however, that the answers he offers aren't for the faint of heart: "This is a book for those who want to face up to the real answers to these questions. It's a book for people who are comfortable with the truth about reality. This is a book for atheists."[4] Rosenberg explains how we ought to answer life's big questions if we assume that there is no God. He aims to provide a view of reality that is free from all illusions and delusions. In place of this, he hopes to give the reader "an uncompromising, . . . no-nonsense, unsentimental view of the nature of reality."[5]

The Atheist's Guide to Reality gives the reader a fairly coherent and reasonable set of answers for how an atheist ought to view the world. Let's take a brief look at Rosenberg's perspective. Along the way, we'll keep in mind Chesterton's claim that the most practical and important thing about a person may indeed be his or her view of the universe. Rosenberg begins by warning the reader that these answers might seem wild, but they are the most logical answers to life's big questions (*if* one assumes God doesn't exist). He writes:

Is there a God? No.

What is the nature of reality? What physics says it is.

What is the purpose of the universe? There is none.

What is the meaning of life? Ditto.

Why am I here? Just dumb luck.

Is there a soul? Is it immortal? Are you kidding?

Is there free will? Not a chance!

What happens when we die? Everything pretty much goes on as before, except us.

What is the difference between right and wrong, good and bad? There is no moral difference between them.

Why should I be moral? Because it makes you feel better than being immoral.

Is abortion, euthanasia, suicide, paying taxes, foreign aid—or anything else you don't like—forbidden, permissible, or sometimes obligatory? Anything goes.[6]

His logic is pretty sound overall. For Rosenberg, since there is no God, reality is limited to the natural world. In other words, when we take away the supernatural or spiritual, all that's left is the natural. Therefore, all the answers to life's big questions must be limited to the material, physical world. For the consistent atheist, Rosenberg won't allow cheating by appeal to some mystical or spiritual realms, which seem to require unsubstantiated faith in something beyond the natural world. So where does that lead him? I'll summarize: *There is no purpose. There is no meaning. There is no soul. There is no objective morality. There is no free will. There is no self. There is only the illusion of these things, which we humans evolved because it aids our survival.* It's hard to quibble with Rosenberg if we play by his rules, which we'll examine in more detail in later chapters. Many atheists seem to come to the same basic conclusions—even if they are not as blunt about it as Rosenberg.

Now that we have a description of an atheistic view of the universe, let's think about its practical and important implications. One way of getting at this is to think about one's view of the universe as eyeglasses. If a person has glasses, she can look both *at* the lenses and *through* them.[7] She can look *at* the lenses, noting whether they are scratched or smudged, but she can also wear the glasses and see the world *through* the lenses. We've just taken a quick look *at* the lenses of atheism. To better understand atheism's practical and important implications, we now need to put on these glasses and see the world *through* them.

What might it be like to wear these lenses throughout a typical day? What follows is just a thought experiment. I don't propose to tell you what goes through every atheist's head on an average day. My guess is that, like most people, many atheists have a hard time looking through their worldview lenses consistently all day. But let's give it a shot anyway.

You wake up, turn off your alarm, take a shower, and then give yourself a look in the mirror. The person you see looking back at you isn't subject to pressure from any ultimate moral obligations . . . but neither does this person have a soul or lasting personhood. You're just a temporary and complex combination of molecules. You head to the kitchen for a quick bite or a cup of coffee, and there you run into a loved one. While you enjoy the bond you share with this person, your lenses help you see through this feeling, letting you know that what you're feeling isn't capital L *Love—which doesn't really exist. Instead, you're merely feeling a strong evolutionary bond that has helped our species survive by giving us the instinct to care for one another. This feeling of love is nice, but it's not pointing to some deeper reality where Love courses through the universe or some such sentimental nonsense. It's just a chemical reaction in your body.*

As you get ready for work or school, you come across a news story about some tragedy—kidnapping or terrorism or sex trafficking. Instinctively you sense the wrongness of the situation. But as you look at this more clearly through your lenses, you can see that, even though you may feel some moral outrage, it's hard to justify this feeling when you know there is no ultimate right or wrong. That's a bit disorienting, but then again, at least you don't have to feel obligated to empathize or help in any way. Of course, you can if it makes you feel good—but there's no ultimate moral pressure, just herd instinct. You then head off to work or school. Whatever your job is or whatever subject you're studying at school, it's nice knowing that you don't have to be that anxious about it, because everything is ultimately meaningless. And yet it feels kind of empty knowing that nothing you do is of any lasting importance.

Eventually the workday ends and you hopefully get to spend your evening doing what you feel like—watching television or hanging out with friends or scrolling through social media or playing music or exercising or online gaming or viewing pornography. And, if you are wondering if you had any real choice about how you spent your evening, your lenses would help you see that you probably did not (even if it feels like you did). After all, there's no spiritual or mental realm that gives you independent power over the natural world; instead, as you see it, this world inevitably follows the blind laws of nature.[8] *Free will is just another illusion that comforts the masses but not you—you see things differently. The day comes to an end, so you head to bed and fall asleep, aware that another twenty-four hours of your finite existence have ticked away.*

After looking through these lenses, we may start thinking that Chesterton is right: a person's view of the universe has practical and important implications—even in our everyday, individual lives. We just imagined how it might shape how we view ourselves, our purpose, our loved ones, our world, our responsibilities, our worth, our leisure, our freedom, and our evaluation of world events. And it's not hard to imagine how it might also inform our hopes, our fears, our victories, our regrets, our gains, and our losses. So far, we've been looking through these lenses from one individual's perspective, but we can also think about the practical importance of such lenses at a communal level. Consider the impact on a culture if everyone wore such lenses—how it might affect education, politics, economics, ethics, and the arts if a society embraced the notion that there was no ultimate purpose, objective morality, free will, soul, or lasting personhood.

Perhaps the significance of this will become clearer when we look at the worldview assumed by the Lord's Prayer. But before we turn there, we need to consider something else that our thought experiment reveals: the limitations of worldview.

Is Worldview Enough?

What Chesterton refers to as one's "view of the universe" is what we might today call one's worldview or metanarrative. It's the big picture, or overarching story, that helps us make sense of our lives. In *The Atheist's Guide to Reality*, Alex Rosenberg sketches out the worldview of atheism, offering a wide-angle perspective on life as an atheist might see it. And much of what I'll be doing in this book is offering the worldview or metanarrative of Christianity. But here's the catch: *many of us find that our self-professed worldviews don't always align with our lives.* For example, although many atheists agree with Rosenberg's worldview description, they don't maintain the unsentimental, detached perspective that Rosenberg describes. Many people don't actually "see" through these lenses consistently throughout their day. Consider the thought experiment we just went through. Does anyone—even the committed atheist—actually maintain such a detached view all day long? Instead, many atheists have moments throughout their daily lives where they act as though there *is* real love, real personhood, real morality, real free will, and real purpose.

This helps us discover that our self-professed worldviews are not all that guide us, because we humans are more than "thinking things," as philosopher James K. A. Smith likes to say.[9] Smith rightly reminds us that we don't always follow our conscious thoughts; often we follow our hearts or guts instead. We follow our hearts, not realizing that our hearts are being calibrated by things we rarely *think* about—things like our habits, our rhythms, and our culture's recurring message about what "the good life" looks like.[10]

If Smith is correct, perhaps the reason that some atheists' lives don't match their thinking is that their hearts are being shaped by a rival vision of life—a vision of the good life in which Love and free will and purpose and morality are real. But please don't hear me singling out atheists. Many Christians do the same thing. We Christians are often guilty of thinking one way and acting another. We claim to believe that mercy and compassion and humility and generosity are vital, yet we follow our hearts in another direction as they are drawn toward a vision of the good life that is materialistic and self-absorbed.

So why am I bothering to write a book on the Christian metanarrative when we humans are more than thinking things? I have three reasons:

1. Although we aren't *only* "thinking things," we *partly* are. How we think matters; and while thinking may not shape everything about us, it can profoundly impact our lives, especially when we combine right thinking with right practices. The mind matters, even if it's not the only thing that matters.
2. Paying close attention to our worldviews can help reveal a disconnect between what we claim and how we live. When a Christian notices that her worldview isn't aligning with her life, it should send a signal that something is off: perhaps she's not thinking clearly, perhaps her habits and practices are miscalibrating her heart, or perhaps she needs to question whether the Christian worldview is true and accurate. Whatever it is, it calls for us to attend to it. Similarly, when the atheist sees the disconnect between her worldview and her life, this may send a signal that something is off: perhaps she's not thinking clearly, perhaps her habits and practices are miscalibrating her heart, or perhaps she needs to question whether the atheistic worldview is true and accurate. Whatever it is, she would be wise to make sense of this disconnect.
3. Writing about the Christian worldview is not simply an intellectual exercise. The Christian metanarrative is so beautiful and so compelling

> that it speaks not only to our minds but also to our hearts, to our deepest instincts, to our gut sense of what truly is the good life. For those who think Christianity is simply boring, Dorothy Sayers writes, "The Christian faith is the most exciting drama that ever staggered the imagination of man—and the dogma *is* the drama. . . . [If] we think it dull it is because we either have never really read those amazing documents, or have recited them so often and so mechanically as to have lost all sense of their meaning."[11]

Our view of the universe matters, but we hold that view not simply in our minds but also in our hearts.

Next we turn our attention to the Lord's Prayer. In what follows, the Lord's Prayer is like a focal point, allowing me to offer a glimpse of my own personal experience of the beauty and weightiness of the Christian metanarrative. It's my firsthand account of the "practical and important" ways that the Christian worldview has shaped both my heart and my mind.

The Lord's Prayer: The Practical and Important Implications

> Our Father in heaven,
> hallowed be your name,
> your kingdom come,
> your will be done,
>   on earth as it is in heaven.
> Give us today our daily bread.
> And forgive us our debts,
>   as we also have forgiven our debtors.
> And lead us not into temptation,
>   but deliver us from the evil one.
>
> —Jesus (Matt. 6:9–13 NIV)

If I were asked what practice has impacted my life the most, I'd say it's praying the Lord's Prayer on a daily basis. The prayer isn't some magic formula: chant it three times, then God grants your requests. Instead, the prayer is like a seed that, with proper care and nourishment, can grow into something beautiful. I didn't know this when I started praying the Lord's Prayer. I simply understood that it was a good thing to do. Now, over a decade and a half later, I can speak to how God has used this simple prayer to transform my heart and mind. In what follows, don't get bogged down by what may be unfamiliar language (kingdom, debts, heaven, etc.); instead, pay attention to how this prayer has shaped my worldview, how it has taught me to see myself and the world around me. We'll get into more specific details in the following chapters.

The prayer begins with the words "Our Father."[12] It may sound strange, but for years I struggled to call God "Father." I don't have any baggage with my own dad; in fact, he's a wonderful man. But I was aware of my own sin, those stains on my soul—and it simply felt presumptuous to call God something as intimate as "Father" when I was so deeply aware of my own brokenness, faults, and repeated sins. But Jesus taught his followers to pray this prayer, so I stuck with it. Some mornings my prayer never went further than the word "Father." I'd just sit there, wrestling with this paradox: how can I, a sinful human, call the holy and divine one "Father"? Over time, though, the seed began to sprout, and the truth grew in my heart that I was a beloved child of Father God—not because I was perfect but because he was loving. God is holy and just and rightly to be feared; yet because of what Jesus has done, God is first and foremost my Father. To grasp this most basic idea was to shed so much personal baggage along with so many misconceptions about God. It was revolutionary. *I know who I am: a beloved child of God.* Everything I do can proceed from the foundation of this love.

God is not merely Father, but Father "in heaven." He is perfectly loving and good, the creator and sustainer of all things. I may call him Father, but I must also respect God as the sovereign and all-powerful Lord. When I see the world through such a lens, I see a world that is not out of control, that is not driven along by chance. It's a world governed by a loving and powerful God who is working all things for the good according to his justice and mercy.

As we continue in the prayer, we come to three closely related phrases: "hallowed be your name, your kingdom come, your will be done, on earth as it is in heaven." We could tease out the different emphases in these expressions, but for our purposes, I'll merely point out how these three phrases have together affected me. When I say, "hallowed be your name, your kingdom come, your will be done," I find that it orients my life around God and his purposes. I don't think I'm a narcissist—which is probably what a narcissist would say!—but I still find that I can default into a kind of self-centered attitude. I can become overly focused on my own wants and needs and concerns. But praying these words trains me to long for something more: to desire God's good will to take effect across the world, to hope for God's kingdom to come with peace and justice, and to yearn for God's name to be held in proper reverence (because when creatures don't acknowledge their creator, everything gets out of balance). If, as Smith argues, our hearts are steered by our vision of the good life, then this part of the prayer is a way of aligning my heart with Jesus's teaching about the good life.

The prayer continues: "Give us today our daily bread." I know that God cares for us in our totality, so I pray for God to provide for my physical, emotional, social, and spiritual needs for the day ahead. But I don't stop with my own needs. When we take notice of the "our" and "us" language in the Lord's Prayer, it reminds us to extend our concern beyond our individual selves so that it includes others. To help with this, I envision my prayer moving outward in something like concentric circles: I pray for myself, then my family, then my friends, then my nation, then the world. Praying for daily bread can produce gratitude, compassion, and humility. It helps me be grateful for the overabundance I experience. It also trains me to have compassion for those who desperately lack daily bread. And it humbles me, because I know that everything I have can ultimately be traced back to God's provision.

When I pray "forgive us our debts," I'm reminded not only that I've done wrong and that those wrongs need pardoning but also that God has anticipated this. Keep in mind, this prayer is for *daily* use. After all, we are also praying for today's daily bread. That leads me to believe that God anticipates us needing forgiveness every day. He recognizes our weakness; he knows what we're up against. God's response is not, "Oh? You're already back. You need forgiveness again? But I just pardoned you yesterday!" Instead, Jesus taught us that we can daily ask for forgiveness from our Father. This does not mean that we take sin lightly or that we presume on God's grace. To truly ask for forgiveness is to recognize the weightiness of our sin and guilt. However, we need not wallow in shame and self-loathing: God is our Father who loves us and graciously forgives us—every day.

My own instinct is to rearrange the prayer by moving this request for forgiveness to the front of the prayer rather than leaving it at the end, and sometimes that may be appropriate. But I've found comfort in resisting that instinct and keeping this request at the end of the prayer. It reminds me that God is my Father and provider of my daily needs, even before I ask pardon for my sins. God does not stop being my Father when I sin and then resume that role when I ask for forgiveness. God's bond with me is stronger and more enduring than that.

We don't pray simply "forgive us"; we pray forgive us "as we have also forgiven our debtors." For years I held on to a grudge, even though I was regularly praying this line in the prayer. I was apparently just mouthing this whole bit about forgiving others. Then one day I was praying the Lord's Prayer and found myself struggling to accept that God had forgiven me. It was wearing on me that I was struggling with the same old sins for years—asking God yet again for forgiveness. The guilt left me feeling the need to earn

God's pardon. Although I knew better, I couldn't help but feel that perhaps I needed to grovel, feel an extended period of self-loathing, or balance out my sins with some good deeds. And yet the Lord's Prayer refused to let me go there—forgiveness was God's merciful gift to me, offered freely. I merely had to ask in sincerity. As that reality slowly began to take root, I discovered that I had been unwilling to forgive a particular person because I had been waiting for that person to "earn" my forgiveness. I wanted that person to first show appropriate remorse and to take steps to change before I gave my forgiveness. When I discovered this, I was completely caught off guard. I could not continue looking to God for mercy while I myself was withholding mercy. And so the grudge I was holding began to lift.[13] I was learning to forgive as I'd been forgiven.

Last, we pray, "And lead us not into temptation, but deliver us from the evil one." As I pray this line, I am reminded that I cannot do this journey alone. I'm not strong enough by myself. I need God to walk alongside me, strengthening me through times of temptation and testing. Evil is real. But so is God—and God is stronger, so I need not live in fear or hopelessness.

I pray the Lord's Prayer in the morning; then my day begins, and the practical and important implications of this prayer go with me, shaping how I view myself, my wife, my children, my job, my enemies, my leisure, my obligations, my world, my hopes, my fears, and my longings. If you're curious how the Christian metanarrative speaks to some of the issues we mentioned earlier (like purpose, morality, personhood, free will, and the soul), we'll get there. But it seems better to start with something a bit more personal.

A Preview of What's Ahead

In the rest of the book, I will present a sketch of a Christian worldview and explain why I think it is compelling at both an intellectual and an instinctive level. First, we'll take a journey through the story line of Scripture (chaps. 1 through 3). Then, in chapters 4 through 6 we'll look closely at the Apostles' Creed, which is a statement of faith that the church has been confessing from early in its history. In the final section of the book, we'll consider what a Christian point of view might look like. Specifically, in chapter 7 we'll highlight some distinctive characteristics of the Christian faith by comparing it to a few other worldviews—sometimes a bit of contrast is needed to help us see what makes something distinctly special. Then, in chapter 8 we'll reflect on how the Christian worldview speaks to life's big questions—questions about purpose, morality, free will, the soul, and personhood. In chapter 9 we'll address some reasons that people commonly give for rejecting Christianity. Last, in chapter 10 we'll consider several reasons why Christianity is a uniquely compelling worldview. Hopefully by the end of our study it'll be clear why, in the words of Chesterton, the most practical and important thing about a person is his or her view of the universe.

PART 1

THE PLOTLINE OF SCRIPTURE

1

The Old Testament

I've worn glasses since I was eight years old. Before that, my vision was blurry enough that I had to find creative ways to get by. For example, when people weren't close enough for me to make out their faces, I learned to tell who they were by the way they walked, by their distinct gaits and strides. The odd thing is that I had no idea my vision was bad. I assumed that life was just as fuzzy for everybody else. I didn't ask to go see the optometrist because I didn't know that I needed to see the optometrist. Then came the day that someone realized I needed glasses, and soon after that I saw the world in high definition for the first time. It was life changing. Imagine seeing a tree for the first time in all its wonder—the majesty of this giant, living plant in sharp focus, top to bottom, with all the contrasts of shape and color and lighting and movement. Life with glasses was not only easier to navigate but also more beautiful, for I could really see.

I think the Christian worldview is a bit like putting on glasses that allow us to see the world in greater focus, revealing a world that is full of beauty and meaning. Over the next several chapters we will look both *at* and *through* the lenses of a Christian worldview. In chapters 1 through 6 we are primarily looking *at* the lenses. We might think of this as our way of ensuring that the lenses are free of smudges and that they're the right prescription. There are a lot of glasses on the market that are labeled "Christian," but some are knock-off products—trendy frames with cheap lenses that don't actually help one see better. So we need to take the time to look closely at the Christian lenses, primarily by studying the stories and teachings that are found in Christian

Scripture. Then, later in the book we will focus on looking *through* these lenses and consider how Christianity offers a distinct way of seeing our lives and the world we live in. Hopefully this will bring the beauty and brokenness of our world into sharper focus.

To know what Christianity is, we need to start with the Christian story. In the same way that we don't really know people until we know their stories—where they've been and what they've been through—we can't really know the Christian faith until we know the Christian story. And this story goes all the way back to the beginning. Technically, it goes back before there was a beginning.[1]

The Beginning

The first chapter of the first book of the Bible describes the creation of the universe in beautiful, near-poetic language. There is structure and symmetry and delight: God speaks, what he speaks happens, and it's declared "good." In fact, the term "good" shows up seven times in this first chapter of Genesis, making it abundantly clear that God approves of what he's made.[2] The high point of creation is humanity. Genesis tells us that humans are made in God's image, male and female. This is a way of saying that men and women have special dignity and purpose and distinction.[3] Humans are called to "image" God, representing God's benevolent care by tending and wisely ruling God's good creation. We'll have to keep reading the biblical story to learn more about what this means.

Today the Genesis account of creation seems to clash with modern science. Genesis probably sounded bizarre to its ancient audience as well, though for different reasons. We can see this when Genesis is compared with other ancient creation accounts (such as *Atrahasis* and the *Enuma Elish*).[4] Three differences stand out:

1. The Genesis account is monotheistic, which means it recognizes only one unrivaled God at a time when polytheism (multiple gods) was the standard religious view. It's not surprising that there are multiple gods in *Atrahasis* and the *Enuma Elish*; it is surprising that there is only one God in Genesis.
2. In Genesis, God simply speaks the cosmos into order and declares it good, unlike in some other ancient creation accounts where the world results from the warring and violence of the gods. For instance, in the *Enuma Elish* the bloody remains of a slain god become building blocks for creation.

3. In Genesis, humans have inherent dignity and value: they bear the image of God and are tasked with caring for and ruling over creation. In contrast, in both *Atrahasis* and the *Enuma Elish* humans lack such dignity and are tasked with doing the burdensome work of providing food for the gods—because these gods (unlike the God of Genesis) need food![5]

Although I'll visit this in more detail in chapter 7, it might be helpful to go ahead and point out how what would have seemed odd in the ancient world has become commonplace today. That is to say, in popular culture it's common to take for granted that the natural world has a "goodness" to it, that humans have inherent dignity, that monotheism is more likely than polytheism, and that a real god wouldn't need food.

The biblical story starts out promising, but things quickly go south. After presenting a wide-angle, cosmic account of creation, Genesis zooms in to focus on two humans—Adam and Eve. The setting is the garden of Eden, where Adam and Eve are dwelling in something like paradise. Two trees dominate Eden's landscape: the tree of life and the tree of knowledge of good and evil. Adam and Eve were permitted to eat from the tree of life, and as long as they ate from it, they wouldn't die. They were forbidden from eating from the other tree, though. It's never specified precisely why this was forbidden. Perhaps it was simply a way to train or test Adam's and Eve's obedience: Would they give God the obedience that was due their creator? Perhaps it was about pride and patience: Would they trust God, or would they take matters into their own hands? Perhaps it was about gratitude: Would they be content with the good life God had provided? Whatever the reason, a scheming serpent comes on the scene and successfully tempts Eve to eat the forbidden fruit. Eve, in turn, gets Adam to eat the fruit. The result of their transgression is commonly referred to as "the fall." From this point on we'll begin to see the gravitational pull of sin, which tears down the good creation that God has built up.[6]

Adam and Eve are exiled from paradise. They no longer have access to the tree of life, which means they will inevitably die. Other consequences result from their violation. In short, a pervasive corruption makes its presence felt in the world, causing damage physically, socially, and spiritually.[7]

- We see *physical brokenness*, as Genesis narrates how Adam and Eve will eventually die, how humanity's labor takes on a burdensome quality, and how the plants and soil may have become corrupted as they no longer produce vegetation as they once did. Even the nonhuman creation experiences ramifications from human disobedience.

- As for *social brokenness*, we read that man and woman will be at odds. Instead of naturally appreciating and valuing each other as partners, they will develop an unhealthy power struggle.
- Next, Genesis captures the *spiritual brokenness* that has set in: Adam and Eve no longer feel so close with God, so unashamed and vulnerable (which is symbolized by their previous nakedness in Eden); instead, they feel ashamed and distant from God (symbolized by their hiding from God and clothing themselves). Their fractured relationship with God is the overarching consequence: to be less connected with the source of life and goodness will inevitably lead to a systemic breakdown, to death—physically, socially, and spiritually.

To be clear, the physical and social and spiritual are all intertwined and perhaps inseparable. I distinguish them to draw our attention to the *holistic* consequences of sin, so that we don't think of sin as operating at only one specific level while leaving the rest of human existence and the creation untouched.

After the humans are exiled from Eden, Genesis narrates something of a downward spiral as sin and human rebellion grow more intense. This is especially captured by the narration of increasing violence: first one brother kills another (Cain and Abel); then Lamech brags of his murderous vengeance; and soon enough the earth is described as "filled with violence" (Gen. 6:11). How might God respond to this? What will he do now that his good creation is corrupted? In what seems to us an unexpected move, God sets in motion a plan to deal with the world's brokenness, and his plan will start with a seventy-five-year-old man (Abraham), his sixty-five-year-old wife (Sarah), and their infertility.

Abraham

Without any backstory or explanation, God calls Abraham and says to him:

> Go from your country, your people and your father's household to the land I will show you.
>
> I will make you into a great nation,
>   and I will bless you;
> I will make your name great,
>   and you will be a blessing.
> I will bless those who bless you,
>   and whoever curses you I will curse;
> and all peoples on earth
>   will be blessed through you. (Gen. 12:1–3 NIV)

This is an astounding promise. God is calling this seventy-five-year-old man to leave everything behind based on a promise to make his lineage great in number, blessing, renown, and impact. But isn't Abraham a bit old for this? God better hurry things up! Instead, twenty-five years pass without God delivering on his promise. Despite the delay, God again reiterates his promise: a child will be born to Abraham (now one hundred) and Sarah (now ninety), and through this child God will make good on his promise. Sure enough, God is true to his word, and Sarah gives birth to a son, Isaac.

Isaac grows up and has twin sons, the younger of which is Jacob. God chooses Jacob's lineage to fulfill the promise he earlier made to Abraham—the promise of land, numerous descendants, and to be a blessing to the world. Jacob is a fascinating and frustrating character, a bit of an antihero. He often seems more sinner than saint. For example, he exploits his hungry brother and deceives his ailing, blind father. Somewhat surprisingly, many of the Bible's heroes are not one-dimensional characters. They're not presented as perfect people who always make the right choice. Instead, their lives are often messy and complicated, sometimes showing incredible faith, sometimes showing cringeworthy doubt. Moments of sacrifice, vulnerability, and faith are followed by moments of deception, seizing control, and scandal. Even so, Jacob manages to distinguish himself as a particularly dubious character. As the story unfolds, Jacob has many children by multiple wives. This part of the narrative reads something like a dark comedy—some humorous moments played out in front of the gloomy backdrop of Jacob's polygamy. Yet God appears willing to use Jacob's broken circumstance to bring blessing, as though God realizes that if he's going to partner with humans, he has to meet them in the midst of their messiness.

The biblical story eventually shifts its focus onto Jacob's twelfth and favorite son, Joseph. In yet another head-smacking move, Jacob flaunts his favoritism for Joseph, thereby arousing envy among Joseph's brothers. The brothers grow so jealous that they seize Joseph, sell him into slavery, and feed Jacob the lie that Joseph was torn to pieces by a wild animal. Joseph is isolated from everyone—except God. God does not abandon Joseph but works through this dire situation to bring about blessing. What follows in Genesis is a series of ups and downs in Joseph's life.

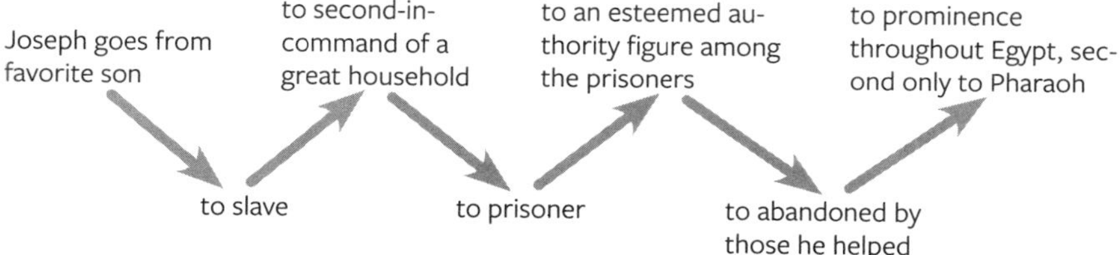

Throughout Joseph's roller coaster of a life, two things remain fairly constant: God does not abandon Joseph (even when it seems as though he has), and Joseph does not abandon God (even when it seems as though he perhaps should).

While Joseph is in Egypt, a great famine devastates the surrounding regions, which eventually brings Joseph's estranged brothers to Egypt in search of food. This results in one of the most touching reunions in Scripture. When Joseph's brothers recognize the brother whom they betrayed, they are terrified. Joseph, however, welling with tears, extends not only mercy but also an invitation to come to Egypt where they can escape the worst of the famine. And so the book of Genesis comes to an end with Joseph, his brothers, and his father all in Egypt.

At this point, the reader may be wondering how any of this fits into God's earlier promises of land, descendants, and blessing. After all, the promised land was in Canaan, not Egypt; Abraham now has many descendants but nowhere near the multitude God had promised; and while the nations have been blessed with provision during a great famine, one might wonder about the larger blessing needed in light of the pervasive corruption that we found after Eden—that physical, social, and spiritual brokenness. We need to keep reading, because the story isn't over.

Exodus

After Joseph dies, things take a turn for the worse. Jacob's descendants—who are called "Israelites" (since Jacob's other name is Israel)—become enslaved by the Egyptians. After hundreds of years of slavery, God sends a reluctant deliverer: Moses.[8] Moses and his brother, Aaron, come to Pharaoh, king of Egypt, with a warning: let the Israelites go . . . or else. Pharaoh unwisely chooses the "or else" option, which leads to a series of plagues and disasters unleashed by God. Pharaoh eventually relents; he is no match for the Israelites' powerful God. Pharaoh releases the Israelite slaves, only to quickly change his mind and chase them down, intending to re-enslave them. The Israelites find themselves trapped between a sea and the Egyptian army. God provides rescue in dramatic fashion: he parts the waters, allowing Israel to cross through the sea on dry ground. When Pharaoh charges after the Israelites, God brings the waters crashing down on Pharaoh and his army, ensuring Israel's freedom and demonstrating God's power and protection.

Having rescued the Israelites, God establishes a covenant with them. According to the terms of the covenant, God will be their God and will provide for them, and they will be God's people and follow his ways. The covenant contains a set of laws and guidelines, the most well-known of which are the Ten Commandments. The covenant guidelines, known as the law or torah, are early steps toward addressing physical, social, and spiritual brokenness. For example, we find laws dealing with animals, land, and sickness (physical restoration), laws instructing people how to wisely and justly interact with one another (social restoration), and laws teaching the people how to be in relationship with God (spiritual restoration). God is gradually bringing holistic restoration to the world. The people of Israel are to be a part of that plan, and the law will help guide them. Perhaps the pinnacle of the covenant is God's willingness to dwell with Israel in a special way, being uniquely present among them in the tabernacle, which is a kind of portable sanctuary.

Excursus

Christians and the Torah

As Christians think about the Old Testament law (torah), we should keep in mind five things. First, according to Jesus, the law is ultimately designed for shaping people to love God wholeheartedly and to love their neighbors as themselves (Matt. 22:35–40). It is not meant to be oppressive, arbitrary, or self-serving; it is meant to promote love and justice.

Second, Jesus shows that the law is, in some ways, a temporary or unfinished code. For example, Jesus points out the preliminary nature of at least some of the law, such as the guidelines related to divorce (Matt. 19:1–9). Jesus explains how God took into account the people's brokenness when he gave certain instructions, even though such instructions may fall short of God's original intent for humans (Matt. 19:8). In other words, the law may not fully meet God's standard; instead, the law is a bit like a moral steppingstone, something accessible to people who are taking early steps in their moral development. This helps explain why some laws seem problematic to us today (such as laws pertaining to slavery and women). When such laws were given, they were progressive in their ancient context, moving Israel's ethic forward from where it was. From today's viewpoint, though, such laws might seem regressive, because we forget that God was meeting an ancient people in their ancient context (and not our contemporary context).

Third, it is difficult to understand the purpose that some laws serve, especially certain dietary and purity laws. Based on the overall sensibleness of the law as a whole, those now-confusing laws likely made good ethical sense in their original setting, but that setting is now lost to us. This makes it hard to do much more than conjecture about those laws' purposes.

Fourth, humans were made in the image of God—that is, they were to represent God in their wise and benevolent caring for creation. This theme continues with Israel's story. In fact, God refers to Israel as a "kingdom and priests" (Exod. 19:6). The Israelites were to take up their kingly and priestly vocations by properly representing God's wise, loving, and just rule. It would seem, then, that the law was intended to guide Israel in carrying out that mission as they bless the nations by faithfully and accurately reflecting God's good will and wisdom to a broken and suffering world (Deut. 4:6–8).

Fifth, as Richard Middleton reminds us, "Grace comes before law; the gift of deliverance precedes the obligation of duty or obedience."[9] That is, Israel doesn't earn God's love by keeping the torah; God loves first (which means the law is itself a loving gift). The law is intended to be not burdensome but beneficial—a gift to guide the people in living wisely and justly.

Israel

Hundreds of years earlier in our story, God made Abraham several promises, one of which was to give Abraham the land of Canaan (Gen. 17:8). A lot has happened since that time. Now, after the great exodus from slavery in Egypt, God is finally preparing Abraham's descendants to enter and take the promised land. Although the Israelites will eventually receive the land, it does not result in a happily-ever-after ending. Instead, the Israelites get stuck in a repetitive cycle of God's compassionate action, followed not long after by Israel's disobedience, then by Israel receiving the consequences for their actions and repenting, before the cycle restarts with God's compassionate restoration of his people.

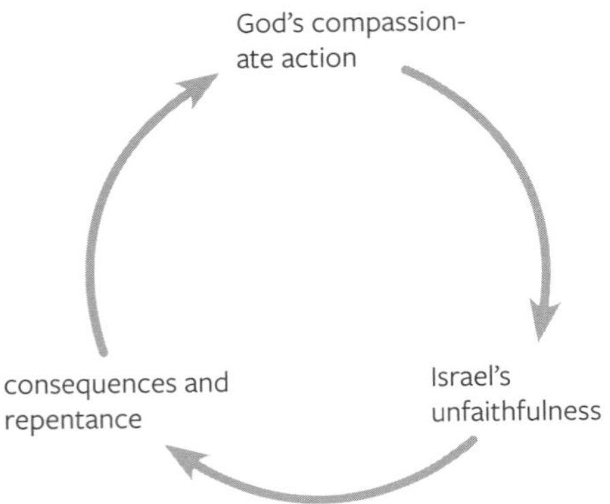

A short example may help to illustrate: after God rescues Israel out of Egyptian slavery and provides food for them in the desert (God's compassionate action), the Israelites refuse to trust that God will help drive out the Canaanites from the promised land (Israel's unfaithfulness), so the Israelites are left in limbo, wandering in the wilderness for forty years until the next generation arises and is willing to trust God (consequences and repentance), at which point God leads the people into the promised land under Moses's successor, Joshua (God's compassionate action).[10]

After the Israelites leave the desert and enter the promised land, the cycle continues. God raises up leaders ("judges") to deliver the slow-to-learn Israelites from various troubles, but these judges are often just as messed up themselves. Not surprisingly, things go awry, and God comes to the rescue—again. At some point, the Israelites get the notion that what they need is a king "like all the other nations have" (1 Sam. 8:5). If they were wise, they would have recognized that God was their true king, and they would have conducted their lives in a way that attested to this. Even God grieves about how "they've rejected me as king over them" (1 Sam. 8:7). But they are stubbornly determined to get a human king, and God grants their request.

At first, it seems as though things might turn out okay. Israel's first king, Saul, gets off to a promising start. Soon enough, though, his rule is marred by disobedience and faithlessness. Saul's life spirals downward until it comes to a tragic conclusion, ending on the point of his own sword. Saul is succeeded by Israel's most famous king—David. This is the great biblical hero who, armed with a sling and tremendous faith in his God, takes down the mighty Goliath. God delights in David, even calling him "a man after [my] own heart" (1 Sam. 13:14 NIV). God makes a promise to King David that will echo over Israel's story from this point on: "Your dynasty and your kingdom will be secured forever before me. Your throne will be established forever" (2 Sam. 7:16). Whatever God is going to do through David's lineage, it is to be of tremendous importance. It's worth pausing to notice that, although Israel goes against God by appointing a king, God chooses to partner with his people and work alongside their unwise choice.

David's reign is one of the high points in Israel's history as he leads the people in many victorious battles while demonstrating passionate devotion to God. Unfortunately, in a sad turn of events, David—this man after God's own heart—proves that even he is not immune to the persistent pull of sin. David's devotion to God turns to complacency and then to discontent—ultimately culminating with David having an affair with his soldier's wife and then having that soldier killed to cover up his wrongdoing. It's a shocking, tragic moment. All the hope and excitement seem to be slipping out of Israel's reach.[11] Even the best of kings could not be the leader that Israel truly needed.

David's son Solomon eventually takes over as king. Like his father before him, Solomon has a promising start to his reign. He shows humility, asks God for wisdom to rule justly, and practices godly devotion; he builds a magnificent temple for God—a grand, permanent dwelling to replace the portable tabernacle. Might hope be restored? Unfortunately, things take a (now predictable) turn for the worse. For example, Solomon appears to ignore the torah's instructions for the king. According to the torah, a king should not acquire too many horses (likely a reference to building a large military force), nor is he to marry numerous wives (thereby acquiring foreign alliances and foreign gods), nor is he to amass great wealth, nor is he to be overbearing toward his subjects (Deut. 17:16–20). These kingly laws appear designed, in part, to protect the king's heart and his allegiance, helping him put his trust in God rather than in military might, foreign allies, other gods, or money. And yet the "wise" King Solomon goes a different route—accumulating wives and horses while overburdening his subjects.[12]

As Solomon's reign comes to an end, the kingdom of Israel starts unraveling—a consequence of Solomon's unfaithfulness (1 Kings 11:9–13). It is clear that Israel needs a king similar to the one described in those kingly laws. Perhaps we can glimpse here a bit of foreshadowing in the law's vision of the ideal king: one who would not trust in military might, who would not seek alliance with the world powers, who would not be led astray by lust and greed, who would not be overbearing but would love his people (maybe even enough to die for them)—a king whose heart is truly, wholly, and perfectly after God's own.

Division and Exile

Solomon's son Rehoboam becomes king, and his oppressive policies are the final straw that breaks the fragile Israelite kingdom in two. The southern kingdom (referred to as Judah) will be ruled by David's lineage, and the northern kingdom (confusingly referred to as Israel) will be ruled by various dynasties. The northern kingdom is kind of a moral train wreck, consistently governed by faithless kings. Eventually the northern kingdom falls when God hands the people over to the Assyrian army in the eighth century BC.

The southern kingdom (through which Jesus's lineage is traced) is, morally speaking, something of a mixed bag, producing some faithful kings and some unfaithful kings. In the sixth century BC, the Babylonian Empire conquers the southern kingdom, destroys the temple and Jerusalem, and drives the people out of their land and into exile. Thus ends (temporally, at least) the sovereign kingdom of Israel, though a king from David's line is still alive in Babylon—a possible sign of hope.

After a while, the Israelites who were exiled are allowed to return home, but they do so in a subdued fashion. David Nienhuis sums up this stage of Israelite history: "Ultimately the Persians, under the leadership of King Cyrus, conquered the Babylonians. Cyrus allowed the people of Judah . . . to return to their ancestral land. While they were allowed to rebuild God's temple and reestablish worship, they did not possess the land God promised to them, and they were not allowed to have their own king. The [Old Testament] story of Israel ends with God's people waiting and wondering how (or if) God would complete the plan to restore the creation through the people of Israel."[13]

For centuries after this, the Israelites may have been asking themselves questions such as the following: What are we to make of God's earlier promises to Abraham, Isaac, and Jacob—promises of land, descendants, and blessing? Has Israel broken the covenant beyond repair? Will God still use Abraham's descendants to bless the nations? Has David's line become so corrupt that God's promise to him of an everlasting dynasty is now nothing more than a squandered birthright?

Prophets and Promises

To add to the uncertainties mentioned above, we might consider some mysterious references that show up in the Old Testament. Throughout Israel's ups and downs, its division, defeats, exile, and return, God continues to speak to his people through prophets. Often, the prophets are merely calling the Israelite people to keep covenant faithfulness with God. As one prophet succinctly put it, "What does the Lord require of you? To act justly and to love mercy and to walk humbly with your God" (Mic. 6:8 NIV). Sometimes, though, the prophets make references to the future. Four such prophecies are of special importance for our study.

First, the prophet Jeremiah speaks of a new covenant that God will make with his people, distinct from the covenant he made when he gave Israel the law. God declares:

> This is the covenant I will make with
> the people of Israel. . . .
> I will put my law in their minds
> and write it on their hearts.

I will be their God
    and they will be my people.
No longer will they . . . say to one another,
    "Know the Lord,"
because they will all know me,
    from the least of them to the greatest. . . .
For I will forgive their wickedness
    and remember their sins no more. (Jer. 31:33–34 NIV)

According to this new covenant, God promises a time when he will be known more intimately, when he will forgive sins in a more complete fashion, and when he will empower the people to live more faithfully. But when will this happen, and how will he accomplish it?

Second, we might consider a prophecy from Daniel, a moral exemplar known for his courage, faithfulness, and piety. Daniel has a vision of "one like a son of man . . . [who] was given authority, glory and sovereign power; all nations and peoples of every language worshiped him. His dominion is an everlasting dominion that will not pass away, and his kingdom is one that will never be destroyed" (Dan. 7:13–14 NIV). As we consider this prophecy, we should recall God's promise to King David of an everlasting dynasty. Notice that Daniel describes something that could be in conflict with God's promise to David: Daniel envisions a divine-like figure of glory and power who will have an everlasting dominion, triumphing over all other kingdoms. How will God keep his promise to David of an everlasting kingdom while also fulfilling Daniel's vision of the everlasting dominion of the divine-like Son of Man?

Third, scattered throughout the prophetic writings are glimpses of how God still plans to keep his promise to David. God will "anoint" one of David's descendants to bring restoration to Israel and perhaps the world. This mysterious, anointed figure is referred to as the "Messiah" or "Christ."[14] We catch a glimpse of this figure in the psalms:

Why do the nations rant?
    Why do the peoples rave uselessly?
The earth's rulers take their stand;
    the leaders scheme together against the Lord and
    against his *anointed* one.[15]
        "Come!" they say.
        "We will tear off their ropes and throw off their chains!"
The one who rules in heaven laughs;
    my Lord makes fun of them.

> But then God speaks to them angrily;
> then he terrifies them with his fury:
> "I hereby appoint my king on Zion, my holy mountain!"
>
> I will announce the LORD's decision:
> He said to me, "You are my son,
> today I have become your father.
> Just ask me,
> and I will make the nations your possession;
> the far corners of the earth your property." (Ps. 2:1–8)

The anointed one, the Messiah, will be opposed, but God will vindicate him and establish his rule throughout the world. This may leave us asking, "How, if at all, is God's promise of the Messiah related to Daniel's vision of the divine-like Son of Man? And what will the messianic reign look like?"

Fourth, alongside these powerful figures—the Son of Man and the Messiah—we find the humble Suffering Servant. The prophet Isaiah paints a stirring picture of this individual, as he shares God's message:

> See, my servant will act wisely;
> he will be raised and lifted up and highly exalted.
> Just as there were many who were appalled at him—
> his appearance was so disfigured beyond that of any human being
> and his form marred beyond human likeness. . . .
>
> He had no beauty or majesty to attract us to him,
> nothing in his appearance that we should desire him.
> He was despised and rejected by [humankind],
> a man of sorrows, and familiar with suffering.
> Like one from whom people hide their faces
> he was despised, and we held him in low esteem.
>
> Surely he took up our pain
> and bore our suffering,
> yet we considered him punished by God,
> stricken by him, and afflicted.
> But he was pierced for our transgressions,
> he was crushed for our iniquities;
> the punishment that brought us peace was on him,
> and by his wounds we are healed.
> We all, like sheep, have gone astray,
> each of us has turned to our own way;

> and the Lord has laid on him
> the iniquity of us all.
>
> He was oppressed and afflicted,
> yet he did not open his mouth;
> he was led like a lamb to the slaughter,
> and as a sheep before her shearers is silent,
> so he did not open his mouth.
> By oppression and judgment he was taken away. (Isa. 52:13–53:8 NIV)

Who is this mysterious figure? How, if at all, is he related to the Messiah and/or the Son of Man? And how will he bring deliverance if he is going to end up despised, oppressed, and wrongly condemned?

Summary and Observations

We'll end this chapter with a brief summary and a few observations. First, the summary. God created a world that he declared "good," and he made humans in his image to represent him and care for his creation. Humans sinned, and the corrosive power of sin made its presence known—physically, socially, and spiritually. God chooses Abraham and his descendants (the Israelites) so that they might be a blessing to the world. Abraham's descendants eventually find themselves enslaved in Egypt. God intervenes, rescues Israel, and then enters into covenant with them. God gives the Israelites the law to shape them to be a people who love God and love others. Against God's wishes, Israel appoints a king. After the checkered reigns of Saul, David, and Solomon, the kingdom divides into a northern and southern kingdom. Both kingdoms are eventually conquered by rival nations, resulting in the Israelites being exiled from the promised land. The Israelites eventually return from exile, but in a subdued fashion. Along the way, God has sent prophets who not only call Israel to faithfulness but also prophesy about a new covenant, a Son of Man, a Messiah, and a Suffering Servant.

Now a few closing observations. As a story, the Old Testament may strike the reader as incomplete. It almost begs for a "To Be Continued" notice at the end. There is so much left undone, so many questions unanswered. There's the obvious question about those shadowy figures that the prophets foretold. But there's also the sense in which the original plot is still left fairly open. How is God going to fix the large-scale brokenness that pervades the world?

Sure, God has made some progress in healing the *spiritual* brokenness—the marred relationship between humans and God. He's entered into a covenant with a group of people and given them instructions about how to be in relationship with him. Plus, he's provided a priestly and sacrificial system. But isn't this a far cry from the intimacy that Adam and Eve had in the presence of God? Is that intimacy lost for good? Consider the temple. It's a wonderful gift, the place where God is supposed to dwell most presently with his people. But access to the temple is so restrictive that it's a reminder not only of God's nearness but also of his distance. And what about the torah's sacrificial system? Can animal sacrifices restore the rift between God and humanity . . . or might they be foreshadowing a more significant sacrifice—one more appropriate for reconciling God and humans?

Or we might consider the *social* brokenness in the world. While God's law does indeed address the social brokenness in Israel, Israel's own history is a testament to how good laws are not enough to create good communities—oppression, theft, murder, adultery, and deception are still alive and well. It would seem that sin resides too deeply in the human heart for legislation alone to be the answer. And, as we're considering social brokenness, where do the Gentiles (non-Jews) fit into the picture? After all, aren't all humans God's creation, and aren't Abraham's descendants supposed to bless the world? So why does the Old Testament story focus almost exclusively on what God is doing with the people of Israel?

And what about the ongoing *physical* brokenness—suffering, war, and sickness? Plus, didn't we learn early in the biblical story that human death could have been avoided? Yet at this point death appears unavoidable, a taken-for-granted fact of life. Can this be remedied, or is death the final word, a disease caused by sin that God cannot or will not cure?

It's time now to turn to the next part of the Christian story, the life of Jesus, to see whether these issues find resolution, and if so, how.

2

The Life of Jesus

Holy Script(ure)

A theologian, a Bible scholar, and an English professor walk into a room. Sounds like the beginning of a bad joke, right? Nope, just a bad Sunday school class. Actually, it's a pretty fun class called "The Dramatic Logic of Scripture" that I teach alongside a theologian and a medieval literature scholar. I love the class's title, and I can say that because I didn't come up with it—the lit scholar did. In one sense, Scripture is "dramatic" because it's exciting: there are heroes, villains, adventure, kings, battles, sex, deception, world creating, world ending, and a God who becomes human and dies and lives again. But it's "dramatic" in another sense as well. Scripture is like a grand *drama*, an epic story, that unfolds in six acts. Here's how Craig Bartholomew and Michael Goheen arrange it:

Act 1: God Establishes His Kingdom: Creation
Act 2: Rebellion in the Kingdom: Fall
Act 3: The King Chooses Israel: Redemption Initiated
Act 4: The Coming of the King: Redemption Accomplished
Act 5: Spreading the News of the King: The Mission of the Church
Act 6: The Return of the King: Redemption Completed[1]

As we discussed earlier, humans tend to make sense of their lives according to some version of the big picture, the grand story. If we treat the Bible as merely a rule book, it's hard to see how the Bible make sense of our lives—it's just telling us what to do. But when we see how the biblical stories fit together to make one large story, then this meta-story provides a framework for making sense of life. Our own life stories find meaning and direction within the Bible's epic story. How does this work? How might we learn to see ourselves living within Scripture's story? We start by familiarizing ourselves with the Bible's "script": the Holy Script(ure).[2]

Let's return to the class title mentioned above, "The Dramatic Logic of Scripture." How do drama and logic go together? Simply put, the drama of Scripture provides its own distinct logic. That is, the biblical plotline helps us reason through life by providing a framework that tells us who we are, what our purpose is, what life is about, and so on. We learn to think and reason according to this framework. Because the drama of Scripture provides a distinct perspective on life, Christians will sometimes evaluate things differently than will their Jewish, Muslim, Hindu, atheist, or Buddhist neighbors. Each metanarrative comes with its own kind of logic—its own framework for navigating life.

To understand the logic of Christianity, we need to know the story, the drama, the script. So let's return to the grand drama of the biblical narrative as it picks back up in Act 4: The Coming of the King.

Setting the Stage: Between the Testaments

The Old Testament gave us the beginning of the Christian story, from creation to Abraham to the rise and fall of the kingdom of Israel. But the Old Testament also left us with many questions, along with a sense that the story was far from finished. We are about to turn to the New Testament, which picks the story back up a few hundred years after the Old Testament finishes. A lot has happened in the centuries between the Old and New Testaments. When the Old Testament story ends, Cyrus and the Persian Empire are in charge. Every world power comes to an end, and the Persian Empire is no exception. Eventually Alexander the Great comes onto the scene, bringing with him an ambitious goal to conquer and to spread Greek culture. Control of Israel passes to Alexander, but not for long. Alexander dies and his generals (Ptolemy and Seleucus) fight for control. In time, Seleucus gets the upper hand, but his grip on Israel is relatively short-lived. The Jews revolt and fight for independence. They are even successful, though their independence is also short-lived, lasting only about a hundred years before a new world order places Israel in its sights. The Roman Empire sweeps in and brutally takes control of Israel, killing Jews (including priests) and dishonoring and profaning the Jewish temple. To add insult to injury, the Romans even choose who will be Israel's king.

A mere sixty-some years after this, the New Testament story begins. As we enter this story, keep in mind the tension that many Jews must be feeling: on the one hand, they know God's glorious promises to Abraham, Israel, and David, and they know how God has brought down other world powers like Egypt and Babylon; on the other hand, they have just been defeated and demoralized at the hands of the very empire that is currently in authority over them. One can imagine the mixed responses this dynamic would produce—disillusionment, hope, vengefulness, sorrow, apathy, determination, religious fervor, shame, and fear. Into this messy and volatile world, a king is born.

Jesus's Birth[3]

Jesus's mother is . . . a virgin, and his father is . . . God! There is not a lot of other detail on Jesus's early life, though it appears he grew up in relative poverty and was raised in accordance with Jewish custom and law. Here we'll consider how two New Testament authors, Matthew and Luke, portray Jesus's birth as fulfilling Old Testament prophecy and promises.[4] Promise keeping and prophecy fulfillment are a bit more complex than we might at first think. Jesus is not simply fulfilling a few scattered predictions and promises, he's doing something much bigger: he's *filling full* the Old Testament promises, predictions, and story line.

For example, when telling the story of the virgin birth, Matthew mentions how Jesus's birth fulfills prophecy from the Old Testament book of Isaiah: "Look! A virgin will become pregnant and give birth to a son, and they will call him, *Emmanuel* [which] means, 'God with us'" (Matt. 1:23). When we first find this prophecy in the book of Isaiah, it represents God's promise to the king of Judah, who was then under attack, that God would soon bring both deliverance and judgment. The prophecy seems to say that God will intervene before a "virgin" (or a "young woman"—the Hebrew can mean either) becomes pregnant (presumably through the normal means) and bears a child, and that child is old enough to know right from wrong. In other words, God would intervene soon.

When we come to Jesus's birth, however, it becomes apparent that this prophecy had more robust potential. What God did previously for Judah, he's doing again, but in fuller fashion: earlier the prophesied virgin presumably became pregnant through normal means; now the prophesied virgin will remain a virgin and be impregnated by the Holy Spirit; earlier the name Emmanuel ("God with us") bore witness to God being with Judah as a deliverer from threatening neighbors; now Emmanuel bears witness to God being with Judah in the flesh to deliver the people from sin. Matthew is teaching us that Jesus's birth doesn't merely fulfill a few scattered Old Testament predictions; rather, Jesus's birth is filling to fullness Israel's story. As we consider all the hopes, promises, and failures brought to mind by our survey of the Old Testament, we might begin anticipating the other mighty ways God will *fill to the fullness* Israel's story through Jesus.

When we turn to Luke's account of Jesus's birth, we find hints that the lingering problems and promises of the Old Testament are in the early stages of finding resolution. For example, when an angel approaches Mary to announce that she will bear a special child, the angel informs her that this child will be the divine Son of God and will inherit the throne of David. In the previous chapter, we learned

- that when the Israelites asked for a human king, they were rejecting God as their king,
- that God promised David an everlasting dynasty, and
- that Israel's kings proved themselves incapable of faithfully leading Israel.

To summarize: (1) God should be Israel's king, (2) a descendant of David should *also* be Israel's king, and (3) Israel needed a king who would be fully faithful. How could all of this possibly come true? In an unexpected yet logical twist, God keeps his promise to David by *himself* becoming David's descendant and Israel's perfect king. That is, through Jesus, God will be king, David's dynasty will be established forever, *and* Israel will finally have a faithful ruler.

Perhaps we're getting ahead of ourselves a bit, so let's back up for just a moment. After the angel delivers the good news about Jesus's birth, Mary bursts into song:

> [God] has shown strength with his arm.
> He has scattered those with arrogant thoughts and proud
> inclinations.
> He has pulled the powerful down from their thrones
> and lifted up the lowly.
> He has filled the hungry with good things
> and sent the rich away empty-handed.

> He has come to the aid of his servant Israel,
> remembering his mercy,
> just as he promised to our ancestors,
> to Abraham and to Abraham's descendants forever.
> (Luke 1:51–55)

As Mary responds with praise, she indicates that what God did in the past for Israel, he will do anew through Jesus.

Israel's story attests, just as Mary sang, that God has been merciful, shown strength, pulled the powerful down from their thrones, lifted up the lowly, filled the hungry, sent the rich away empty, and been faithful to his promises to Israel. And through Jesus, God is not simply repeating himself but is instead doing something *even greater*; he's filling things full. So as we begin to look at Jesus's life, we should be asking ourselves, "How is God going to work through Jesus to reveal the depth of his mercy and the magnitude of his strength? By what mechanisms will Jesus pull down the powerful and lift up the lowly? Through what means will God fill the hungry and send the rich away empty? And how will Jesus become the way God remembers his promises to Abraham and Israel?" Let's dive in and learn more about who this Jesus is, what kind of king he's going to be, and what kind of restoration he's going to bring.

Jesus's Ministry

> The time is fulfilled, and the kingdom of God has come near; repent, and believe in the good news. (Mark 1:15 NRSV)

These are the first words we hear from Jesus in the Gospel of Mark. This is Jesus's message, which he will deliver with both words and actions as he travels from village to village and town to town, teaching and ministering to the people. Along the way, he gathers devoted followers and equally devoted adversaries. It seems as though people either love him or hate him—or are at least baffled by him. Whatever people think of Jesus, they don't find him boring. Let's consider why as we look at his ministry in more detail, using his opening words from Mark as our guide.

Good News

We'll start with the phrase "good news" (which can also be translated "gospel"). This term is pregnant with potential meaning. In the Greco-Roman world, "gospel" might refer to the good news of a king's birth or a king's victory. In the Old Testament, "gospel" can be a proclamation of peace, salvation, and the reign of God (e.g., Isa. 52:7). Interestingly, all of these possible meanings are fitting and complementary ways of understanding Jesus's message of "good news." Jesus is the coming king, he will bring some sort of victory that will accomplish peace and salvation, and he will extend God's reign over a rebellious and broken world. But this is all still vague at this point in the story—it's unclear how we are to understand peace, salvation, and the reign of God.

We can learn more about the nature of this good news if we look at Jesus's first speech in the Gospel of Luke (which Jesus delivers in a Jewish synagogue). Jesus starts by reading the Old Testament, specifically Isaiah's prophetic words: "The Spirit of the Lord is upon me, because the Lord has anointed me. He has sent me to preach *good news* to the poor, to proclaim release to the prisoners and recovery of sight to the blind, to liberate the oppressed, and to proclaim the year of the Lord's favor" (Luke 4:18–19). After reading this, Jesus shockingly declares, "Today this scripture has been fulfilled just as you heard it" (v. 21). If we want to know more about the good news Jesus is bringing, this gives us some insight. Jesus begins to define it as "good news to the poor"—which includes release for prisoners (likely a reference to debtors' prison) and liberation for the oppressed. Later in Luke, Jesus demonstrates just what he means. Through the power of the Spirit, Jesus brings release to those who are in bondage to sin, sickness, demons, and corrupt systems.[5] We will dig into this in more detail when we consider what Jesus means by the "kingdom of God." But first, we must consider the timing in which Jesus's good news will take place.

The Time Is Fulfilled

We've already seen Jesus claim that "the time is fulfilled," "the kingdom is near," and "today this is fulfilled." But we also know that Jesus's work is not complete: good news has not fully uplifted the poor, freedom is not the reality of all who are oppressed, and God's reign is clearly not established in its entirety throughout the world. Rather, we find in Jesus's ministry a tension of the *already begun* and the *not yet finished*. This tension clues us in that something is changing on a deeper level. There's another dynamic breaking into the world. A pivotal shift is occurring in and through Jesus that will change the course of human history and set in motion the inevitable completion of God's restoration of this broken world. Jesus can announce that the time has come because with his arrival the world is forever changed: to live according to the old era is to be out of step with the new reality breaking in to the present. And yet, Jesus can speak of greater things to come because the new era is not fully arrived; the old era still lingers on. Consequently, we are caught in the tension of two eras—the reign of sin and the reign of God. The war between these rival kingdoms wages on in our world, but Scripture assures us that God will win out, and we would be wise to align our lives accordingly.

The Kingdom of God

What does it mean for God to reign as king? In Jesus's most beloved prayer, we learn that God's kingdom is related to God's will being done. That is, Jesus prays, "Your *kingdom* come, your *will* be done, on earth as it is in heaven." So the "kingdom of God" is where God's kingly will is realized. What does God's will look like? We see this best in Jesus's ministry, because Jesus is the one who fully embodies God's will. From Jesus's life and teaching, we discover that God's kingdom is characterized by restoration—physical, social, and spiritual restoration. We could refer to this as "salvation," but modern usage has so spiritualized this word that it often fails to convey the wide scope of Jesus's ministry. I prefer, instead, the phrase "holistic restoration" as a better way of capturing the physical, social, and spiritual healing that Jesus brings. Notice how this plays out in Jesus's life.

For *physical restoration*, I am thinking particularly about Jesus's ministry of healing. He restores sight to the blind, dispels sickness, makes the lame able to walk, opens the ears of the deaf, and even raises the dead on more than one occasion. This helps us see that God's kingdom is not merely a "spiritual" or immaterial thing but is physical as well. This only makes sense. After all, God created the world and declared that it was good. So of course Jesus is carrying out God's will by restoring creation's goodness and wholeness, by ridding it of sickness, disease, brokenness, and especially death.

I use the term *social restoration* to refer to the consistent way in which Jesus reaches out to the marginalized—the disadvantaged, overlooked, and scorned members of society. In the first-century world, one's social status was determined by factors such as gender, age, lineage, money, and religious/ritual purity. Time and time again, Jesus breaks through these status barriers, showing compassion for those on the margins, even though it frequently exasperates and infuriates those around him. He touches the untouchables, eats meals with so-called sinners, ministers to non-Jews, befriends women with disreputable pasts, reaches out to social pariahs like tax collectors, and on and on it goes. By doing so, Jesus helps reintegrate these outcasts into society as he bears witness to their worth and dignity as persons and to their value within the community. He also reveals that the kingdom of God is available for all who will enter, that God values all humans and does not gauge a person's worth the way society does. Rather, all people are God's children, and it is his will for all to live in harmony with him and with their fellow humans.

Regarding *spiritual restoration*, I have in mind those occasions when Jesus forgives sin and casts out demons.[6] The demons are no match for Jesus; rather, they cower before him and flee at his command. Jesus's authority over the spiritual realm proves to be without equal. But what was probably most shocking to an ancient audience is Jesus's claim to have authority to forgive sins—something that is limited to God alone. Many of the religious authorities find this shocking and scandalous, yet Jesus apparently believed that he was not disrespecting God, because he himself is the divine Son of God.[7]

To summarize our understanding of the kingdom so far, we see that it is characterized by physical, social, and spiritual restoration; we also know that the kingdom has begun breaking into the world in a new and decisive way through Jesus but that the full realization of the kingdom is yet to come. Now it is time for us to return to Jesus's opening words in Mark and consider Jesus's command to "repent and believe." We are about to learn that being a citizen of the kingdom of God entails adopting a new way of life.

Repent and Believe

The word "repent" is perhaps best understood to mean "reorient." It's a call to orient one's life around God's will. If God's kingdom is breaking into the world, the wisest thing to do is to adjust one's heart, mind, and life in ways that fit this new regime.[8] Similarly, when Jesus calls people to "believe," he doesn't want them merely to acknowledge a list of facts. He wants people to both believe the truth and live accordingly. We might think of "belief" as a term that holds together several meanings: *believing* certain ideas to be true, *trusting* Jesus by following him, and *being faithful* to Jesus as one's rightful king.[9] It's not just about mentally accepting some new ideas; it's about trusting Jesus with all of one's life—heart, soul, mind, and strength.

Throughout Jesus's ministry, he teaches what this looks like by calling people to conduct themselves with compassion, humility, generosity, hope, peace, justice, and courage. We see this on display particularly in his famous Sermon on the Mount (Matt. 5–7). He calls out hypocrisy and surface-level morality, revealing in a profound way that right hearts are as important as right action. He says things like these: Don't only avoid murder; avoid hatred and contempt. Don't only avoid adultery; avoid objectifying gazes and lustful fantasies. Don't pray and fast in order to impress others, but pray and fast in a way that honors a heart-searching and gracious God. Jesus exhorts his audience to radical empathy: to love one's neighbor as oneself. Not just that; he also calls people to be merciful because God is merciful, which means that they are to give generously and even extend love toward enemies. These themes of mercy, compassion, and faithfulness show up throughout Jesus's parables too, including the well-known parables of the good Samaritan and the prodigal son (Luke 10:25–37; 15:11–30).

There is an important balance for us to recognize here: the balance of compassion and justice. Jesus preaches about a God who is both merciful and just. God is not merely a righteous and holy judge, nor is he simply a compassionate and humble, grandfatherly being. Based on Jesus's teaching, the truth is found by holding compassion and justice together. God is more righteous and holy than we can fathom, but he's also more compassionate and humble than we can imagine. Living within the kingdom of God calls for both discernment and devotion. It requires discernment because it's not always clear whether to humbly remain quiet or to courageously speak out, whether to demand justice or to extend mercy, whether to give generously or to withhold in hopes of teaching responsibility. It requires devotion because living according to the kingdom can be a challenging and costly endeavor—after all, it will lead to both Jesus's crucifixion and the early church's persecution. But this is the way of the king, and he bids his subjects to follow (Luke 9:23).

Jesus's Crucifixion

Jesus's teachings and actions eventually place him in the crosshairs of the Jewish religious leaders. Their outrage, resentment, and fear of Jesus stem from a couple of factors. First, Jesus frequently chastises the religious status quo of his day, claiming that it is far removed from God's intentions. Jesus calls out the religious leaders for being more concerned with power and status than with caring for and serving God's people. The Old Testament law was meant to promote peace and freedom, but they have wielded it as a tool of oppression and bondage. Second, Jesus has a rapidly growing popularity among the people. Not only does this threaten the religious leaders' power but it also threatens to bring unwanted attention from the Roman authorities. Israel is a volatile place: the Jews want their freedom, and they have a history of rebellion. Rome is keen to quash any Jewish rebellions. Consequently, those Jewish religious leaders who want to maintain the status quo may find themselves ironically maneuvering to keep Rome in control. A popular leader like Jesus, whom people are calling Messiah (King), could easily bring unwanted trouble on both the Jewish people and their leaders.

So a plot is hatched that brings Jesus to trial, eventually leading him before Pilate—the top Roman government official of the area. Jesus goes willingly, accepting the fate that he knows awaits him at the corrupt trial that is about to take place. Sadly, almost everyone abandons Jesus at this point, and some even turn against him. It's as if seeing Jesus bound and vulnerable is a confirmation that he cannot be the long-awaited Messiah, he cannot be the one to restore Israel. Despite all of Jesus's miracles and his teaching on humility and self-giving compassion, almost no one has the mental categories to put together what's happening. They can't see that Jesus's upcoming willing sacrifice is not his moment of shame and defeat, revealing him as a fraud. Instead, it's his moment of greatest honor and victory, revealing him as the true Son of God and Messiah. To understand all this, we may need a better grasp of what crucifixion entails.

I always feel a sense of inadequacy when it comes to discussing the cross. Part of me wants to avoid writing about it, not because I think it is unimportant, but precisely because of its immense importance. I am aware of my limited abilities, so it is intimidating to write about one of the most, if not *the* most, significant of historical events. I'm also ashamed of how little I allow my own life to be shaped by the cross. How can I tell others about the world-changing impact of the cross when I am so disappointingly aware of my own failure to take up my cross and follow Jesus? How do I tell about how the cross demands that we reevaluate the way we look at ourselves, our neighbors, our enemies, and our purpose when I so often cling to that which feels safe and comfortable?

Perhaps it's fitting then, as I am reminded of my own sense of inadequacy, that we consider the shame of the cross. This is by no means intended to downplay the physical pain and brutality of the cross. In fact, the ancient resources we have that describe crucifixion make it clear that it's excruciating. As one scholar puts it, "Crucifixion was a horribly violent, sadistic, and cruel affair. [The early Roman author Cicero] speaks of the punishment as the 'most cruel and disgusting penalty' . . . in which victims 'died in pain and agony' and suffered the 'worst extreme of the tortures inflicted on slaves.'"[10] Seneca, another Roman author, captures how the cross is a long-lasting, drawn-out torture: "Can anyone be found who would prefer wasting away in pain dying limb by limb, or letting out his life drop by drop, rather than expiring once for all? Can any man be found willing to be fastened to the accursed tree, long sickly, already deformed, swelling with ugly [welts] on shoulders and chest, and drawing the breath of life amid long drawn-out agony? He would have many excuses for dying even before [being put] on the cross."[11]

We must not downplay the physical pain and agony of crucifixion. Neither should we skip over a too-frequently overlooked aspect of the cross—its humiliation and shame. Although we may fail to notice the shame of crucifixion, the New Testament is well aware of it. Note the mockery and derision in two of the Gospel accounts:

> The governor's soldiers took Jesus into the governor's house, and they gathered the whole company of soldiers around him. They stripped him and put a red military coat on him. They twisted together a crown of thorns and put it on his head. They put a stick in his right hand. Then they bowed down in front of him and mocked him, saying, "Hey! King of the Jews!" After they spit on him, they took the stick and struck his head again and again. (Matt. 27:27–30)

> The people were standing around watching, but the leaders sneered at him, saying, "He saved others. Let him save himself if he really is the Christ sent from God, the chosen one."
>
> The soldiers also mocked him. They came up to him, offering him sour wine and saying, "If you really are the king of the Jews, save yourself." Above his head was a notice of the formal charge against him. It read "This is the king of the Jews."
>
> One of the criminals hanging next to Jesus insulted him: "Aren't you the Christ? Save yourself and us!" (Luke 23:35–39)

As another New Testament author so concisely put it, "[Jesus] endured the cross, ignoring the shame" (Heb. 12:2). Not surprisingly, Cicero referred to crucifixion as "the punishment of slaves."[12]

Utter shame and humiliation were part of Rome's intention for crucifixion. The victim was typically stripped naked—so Jesus likely was not wearing a loincloth. (Take a moment and let the indignity of that sink in.) The victim would be mocked, and often the execution was set in a visible location such as a hilltop or a popular roadway. That way, everyone could see the victim's shame. The gravity of this is hard to grasp. The man Christians call Lord, Messiah, and Son of God was beaten, tortured, mocked, spat on, stripped naked, and placed on a hill for all to see his humiliation and seeming defeat.

How might all of this have been interpreted by an ancient audience? We have one interesting take on it based on some early Roman graffiti. Scratched into some plaster are the words "Alexamenos worships his God." Along with these words is the image of a man raising his hand in worship, and what he is worshiping is a man on a cross . . . who has the head of a donkey. This graffiti artist understood the shame of crucifixion. It's as if he were saying, "Look at that moron Alexamenos! He worships a crucified god! What kind of fool would worship someone who was so clearly humiliated and overpowered?"

But this is not the perspective found in the biblical story line. According to the New Testament, the great irony of the cross of Christ is that the very instrument that was meant to disgrace Jesus becomes the means by which Jesus disgraces the powers that opposed him. But this becomes apparent only in hindsight, after the crucified Jesus is raised from the dead.

Jesus's Resurrection

If Jesus's story ended with his crucifixion, there would likely be no Christian religion. Fortunately, the story doesn't end there. Instead, God raises Jesus from death to life. Jesus appears to his followers, whole and healthy, able to eat and be touched. He's no ghost but a truly resurrected human. His new body, however, has a difference to it—he can appear and vanish in surprising ways. It's as if his earthly body has been restored not merely to its original state but to an enhanced state. His crucified body was resurrected, but it's not limited in the same ways.

Jesus's resurrection provides some foreshadowing, a glimpse of a new reality that is on the horizon. It's as if his newly resurrected body isn't fully at home in the present world, because the present world is not quite ready for it . . . yet. We are still in the tension of two eras, waiting for God's kingdom to fully arrive. Jesus's resurrection acts like a guarantee of what's to come: sin and death will be defeated, and God will carry out his will and complete his work of restoration—physically, socially, and spiritually. Elsewhere in the New Testament we catch whispers of a "new creation" or "new earth"—because something novel is looming: a new reality that will seem both expected and unexpected. We can't quite imagine what it will be like, but when it is seen, it will be as if there could be no other conclusion to the story.

When the resurrected Jesus encounters his followers, the paradigm shift in their worldview becomes apparent. Earlier, they had abandoned Jesus because they couldn't find a way to reconcile their concept of a victorious Messiah with a crucified man. What they needed was a drastic alteration in their worldview, a paradigm-shifting event that would allow them to see the world in new ways. Not surprisingly, seeing the resurrected Jesus proved to be such an event. The apparent shock of seeing someone alive and healthy who had been brutally executed just days prior was life changing. Earlier, these followers of Jesus had abandoned hope in him. They were dejected and disheartened. But after encountering the resurrected Jesus, they become so overwhelmingly convinced of his authority, of the validity of his claims, that they spend their lives as his loyal subjects, furthering his ministry, often at the cost of extreme suffering and persecution. It is to their stories that we now turn.

3

The New Testament Church

Every fall I teach a course called "The Story of Jesus." Every spring I follow that up with "The Story of the Church." Overall, students like "The Story of Jesus" more than "The Story of the Church." That's probably as it should be. Jesus is, after all, a fascinating figure who has literally impacted billions of people. The students are inspired by Jesus—this loving revolutionary who passionately speaks out against the corrupt religious and political systems and who is willing to die for a worthy cause. In "The Story of the Church" we still find loving revolutionaries who speak against corrupt religious and political systems and who are willing to die for the cause. But we also see a bit more of the daily grind of discipleship. Maybe following a loving revolutionary seems a bit less glamorous when we see what it cost the early church.

Also, in "The Story of Jesus" the bad guys are often self-righteous people, so it doesn't feel so personally convicting. After all, it's always "those folks" who are self-righteous, not us! But in "The Story of the Church" sometimes the bad guys are just too much like us—they're apathetic or self-centered or greedy or impulse-driven, or perhaps they compromise their convictions to make life easier.

Students also enter "The Story of the Church" with a bit more baggage or skepticism about this part of the biblical story. The New Testament church has been mischaracterized as dreary, domineering, and dated. Personally, this part of the New Testament took on new life when I moved from a shallow understanding of its content to a deeper understanding, when I moved from knowing about the stories to finding myself as part of the story. Whatever your previous assumptions may be, I invite you to take a closer look at the New Testament church and perhaps consider what it might be like to assume a role in this act of the biblical drama.

Prelude: Jesus's Ascension—Leaving and Remaining

After the resurrection, Jesus spends some time with his followers and then ascends to heaven to be reunited with the Father. We'll discuss Jesus's ascension more in chapter 5—it is, after all, a strange thing to try to wrap our minds around. For now, we'll simply note that Jesus's ascension stands as confirmation that he is the true Messiah and Son of God, the one who has overcome death, thereby giving us confidence in his ability to bring restoration and renewal. As we keep reading the New Testament, we soon learn that Jesus's departure is not the same as his absence. On the one hand, he is in heaven and is no longer bodily on earth; on the other hand, his presence continues on in the church, for he will send his Holy Spirit as his loving and empowering presence among his followers.

Before Jesus departs, he commissions his disciples to bear witness to the good news—of Christ and what he's achieved—throughout the world. Let's look now at how the early church carried out this charge. We'll start with a brief overview of the book of Acts, which tells the story of the early church's beginnings. Then we'll attend to the writings of a towering figure in the New Testament—the apostle Paul. We'll finish with the bizarre and beautiful book of Revelation.

Acts

As Jesus departs from his followers, he tells them two things: first, they will receive the Holy Spirit; and second, they will be his witnesses "in Jerusalem, and in all Judea and Samaria, and to the ends of the earth" (Acts 1:8). Both messages are of critical importance to the narrative of Acts. Many of Jesus's followers had abandoned him at his crucifixion, apparently giving up hope in him and his mission. Acts records a dramatic turnaround in which these same followers speak boldly about Jesus, even in the face of opposition and, sometimes, martyrdom. A major factor in this change of character is their receiving the Holy Spirit, giving them wisdom and courage to bear witness to Jesus. And whereas Jesus's ministry was primarily among the Jews, his followers are now charged with preaching the good news to Jews ("in Jerusalem and Judea"), Samaritans ("in Samaria"), and Gentiles ("to the ends of the earth"). That ancient promise that God made to Abraham, that his lineage would bless the nations, is beginning to come true in a new way as Jesus sends his followers to the nations.

His followers soon discover that Jesus may have won the war over sin and death, but the battles are far from over. In Acts, we see moments of victory: the disciples perform incredible miracles, multitudes of people give their lives to Jesus as their Lord and King, and great numbers of people pledge their allegiance to Jesus through baptism.[1] Yet we also see moments of trial and hardship: both Jews and Gentiles persecute the young church in the form of beatings, threats, imprisonment, exclusion, and even death. Ironically, this persecution seems only to enhance the church's growth, as the church's numbers continue to swell.

If persecution wasn't enough to stifle the young church's growth, the ethics of the church might have kept people away. After all, Acts narrates how Christians were selling their possessions and giving the proceeds to any who had need, and it quickly becomes apparent that falsehood and deception are not to be tolerated in the Christian community. Nonetheless, people willingly give up money, respectability, and safety to join themselves to Christ and his church. There's this great paradoxical line in Acts that reads, "No one else dared to join them. . . . Nevertheless, more and more men and women believed in the Lord and were added to their number" (5:13–14 NIV). One gets the sense that the cost of becoming a Christian was so high that "no one dared to join" except those who were wholeheartedly committed; however, a movement characterized by such sincerity and devotion could not help but attract others, so that "more and more men and women believed in the Lord and were added to their number."[2]

As we read the first several chapters of Acts, we encounter some influential early Christian leaders such as Peter, John, James, Stephen, and Philip. Perhaps most important for our study is that we notice how often these leaders' lives reflect Jesus's life. We can really see this when we lay the Gospel of Luke beside the book of Acts, both of which were authored by the same person. Someone who reads the Gospel of Luke and then reads Acts starts to see that what Jesus did in the Gospel of Luke, his followers then do in Acts. Jesus healed the lame in the Gospel of Luke; his followers heal the lame in Acts. Jesus shared meals with the lowly; his followers share meals with the lowly. Jesus spoke the truth against injustice, which led to his being persecuted; his followers speak the truth against injustice, which leads to their being persecuted. Jesus prayed that God would forgive those who were crucifying him; his follower, Stephen, prays that God will forgive those who are killing him. The implication seems clear: Christians are to follow the way of their king by extending compassion, practicing restoration, and pursuing justice.

As followers of Jesus they can expect to encounter opposition, as Jesus did. And as followers of Jesus they are expected to respond to opposition as Jesus did. One noted scholar, Kavin Rowe, sums up this inevitable "collision" of Christianity and the world with the phrase "new culture, yes—coup, no."[3]

- *New culture, yes.* The Christian way of life results in an alternative culture—a new way of seeing and being in the world, a new value system with new practices. The Christian way of life is supposed to carry with it a certain kind of culture. This culture should naturally stem from a distinctly Christian worldview so that it is characterized by such things as compassion, monotheism, and the recognized dignity of all persons. And this way of life will inevitably clash with cultures that are based on a different worldview, such as the dominant Greco-Roman worldview, which was characterized by competition, polytheism, and the unequal worth of all persons.
- *Coup, no.* Precisely because Christianity is a Christ-following movement, it will not be a movement of violence, revolt, and sedition. The way of Jesus is the way of peace. Christians are to pursue *what* Jesus pursued *how* he pursued it. They are to spend their energy seeking restoration and justice, and they are to do so with lives of compassion, peacefulness, honesty, and courage.

The second half of Acts focuses on Paul. When he first enters the narrative, we see Paul approving of the stoning of Stephen, the first Christian martyr. The reader soon finds out that Paul has been "spewing out murderous threats against the Lord's disciples" (9:1). While Paul is on his way to Damascus, intent on rooting out these Christian deviants, a blinding light blazes around him, and a voice asks, "Why do you persecute me?" (9:4 NIV; cf. 22:7; 26:14). We soon learn that this is the voice of Jesus.[4] Paul leaves this encounter blind and humbled, but not without hope. Jesus does not smite him but sends him to a man named Ananias, who will pray for his sight to be restored. When Paul regains his sight, he is a new man with a new mission. He is baptized, pledging his allegiance to Jesus and having his sins washed away. He receives the Holy Spirit along with a new mission—a royal summons from Jesus that will leave its mark on the world forever after. Jesus declares, "This man is my chosen instrument to proclaim my name to the Gentiles and their kings and to the people of Israel" (9:15 NIV). And so begins a new chapter in Paul's life; he will go on to become perhaps the most influential follower of Jesus ever.

Paul travels throughout the vast Roman Empire proclaiming the good news of Jesus, planting churches, and encountering the same kind of persecution to which he had previously subjected others. Paul's influence as a missionary is enhanced by his influence as a writer. Of the twenty-seven books of the New Testament, an astounding thirteen are attributed to Paul.[5] As Paul moved from town to town proclaiming the good news, he kept in touch with his young churches through letter writing. He also wrote letters to churches he hadn't visited, the most important being his monumental letter to the Romans. To better understand the Christian worldview, one must have some familiarity with Paul's writings, to which we now turn.

Paul

Any serious student of the New Testament soon discovers that Paul is not always easy to understand. This is the case for a few reasons. First, Paul's letters often deal with specific issues that a particular church is facing. Thus we only have access to one side of a larger conversation, and because it's not always clear exactly what issue Paul is addressing, it's not always clear how to make sense of his teachings. Second, even though Paul writes extremely long letters in comparison to typical ancient letter writing, he doesn't always explain himself clearly. His writing style can be dense and peppered with ambiguous words and phrases. Nonetheless, a close reading of Paul's letters can reveal certain themes and ideas that are central to Paul's teaching. Though we must remain humble about our ability to fully understand Paul's writings, we can have a certain degree of confidence that we can hear the main gist of his teaching coming through. To demonstrate this, I will give a brief overview of some of his central ideas by looking at three of Paul's writings: Romans, 2 Corinthians 5:14–21, and Philippians. (For more on Paul's theology, see appendix A.)

As we study Paul's writings, let us bear in mind that his teaching and ministry have come with great sacrifice. He is not the kind of minister who's in it for the power and prestige.

> I've been beaten more times than I can count. I've faced death many times. I received the "forty lashes minus one" from the Jews five times. I was beaten with rods three times. I was stoned once. I was shipwrecked three times. I spent a day and a night on the open sea. I've been on many journeys. I faced dangers from rivers, robbers, my people, and Gentiles. I faced dangers in the city, in the desert, on the sea, and from false brothers and sisters. I faced these dangers with hard work and heavy labor, many sleepless nights, hunger and thirst, often without food, and in the cold without enough clothes.

> Besides all the other things I could mention, there's my daily stress because I'm concerned about all the churches. Who is weak without me being weak? Who is led astray without me being furious about it? (2 Cor. 11:23–29)

Romans

Paul's letter to the church in Rome is arguably his masterpiece, giving us the most extensive look at his theology and worldview. We'll focus on a few key passages, starting with his opening words, because they provide a framework for what follows.

> From Paul, a slave of *Christ* Jesus, called to be an apostle and set apart for God's *good news*. God promised this good news about his *Son* ahead of time through his prophets in the *holy scriptures*. His *Son* was descended from David. He was publicly identified as God's *Son* with power through his *resurrection* from the dead, which was based on the *Spirit* of holiness. This *Son* is Jesus *Christ* our *Lord*. Through him we have received God's *grace* and our appointment to be apostles. This was to bring all *Gentiles* to *faithful obedience* for his name's sake. You who are called by Jesus *Christ* are also included among these *Gentiles*.
>
> To those in Rome who are dearly loved by God and called to be God's people.
>
> *Grace* to you and *peace* from God our *Father* and the *Lord* Jesus *Christ*. (1:1–7)

It's so easy to skip over these introductory words, but if we do we may end up missing the framework for understanding Paul. It's like putting together a puzzle: we need to start with the border before moving to the interior. So let's pay attention to several words and phrases that Paul uses in the opening of this letter, which make up the "border." These include "Christ," "good news," "holy scriptures," "Spirit," "Gentiles," "faithful obedience," "Lord," "Father," "Son," "grace," "peace," and "resurrection." Paul will repeat many of these same terms at the end of Romans, which is a clue that everything he says in the middle of the letter fits within the border assumed by these terms.

- Christ: We've already discussed what it means to call Jesus the *Christ* (or Messiah); in short, Jesus is the long-awaited king of Israel who has come to bring restoration.
- Good news: We've also learned how the *good news* (or gospel) can reference both a king winning a victory and God reigning. Both seem to fit Paul's writings, as King Jesus has defeated sin and death, bringing in a new era of God's rule.

- Holy scriptures: When we looked at Jesus's life in chapter 2, we noticed how Jesus was portrayed as "filling full" the Old Testament story. In a similar way, Paul sees Jesus as filling full Israel's *holy scriptures*—and Paul here specifically references the prophets, David, and the Messiah. Jesus is not simply fulfilling some predictions but is also bringing to fullness Israel's hopes and calling and story.
- Spirit: The Holy Spirit plays a vital role not only in Jesus's life but also in the church's, freeing and empowering the church to embody Christ's love and faithfulness, while also giving assurance that God will complete the work he's begun in Christ.
- Gentiles: Here we might recall both that Paul was sent as a missionary among the *Gentiles* (non-Jews) and that the promises to Abraham were always meant to extend beyond Israel, thereby blessing the nations.
- Faithful obedience: The spread of the good news will ultimately call people to *faithful obedience*. Belief that Jesus is the true Christ should lead one to faithful obedience, an offering of fealty to this messianic king.
- Lord: Jesus is not only Christ but also *Lord*. Although "lord" can carry the more generic meaning of "master," it becomes clear from Paul's writings that it also means "Lord" in the capital *L* sense—Jesus is Lord God. Further, Jesus's lordship trumps any allegiance one might have for Lord Caesar.
- Father and Son: Somehow Jesus is God the *Son*, who is distinct from God the *Father*. Based on his writings, Paul is monotheistic (he believes in one God). Consequently, for Paul, God is somehow one while also being distinctly two: Father and Son. We'll dig into this more in the next chapters (where we see that God is, in fact, three in one: Father, Son, Spirit), but for now we will note that "Father" might bring to mind how God is creator and compassionate and close. (Paul's God is not a raging tyrant but is better understood as a holy and loving father.)
- Grace and peace: Because God is who he is, and because Jesus is who he is, Paul can speak the blessing of *grace and peace* over the church. "Peace" picks up the Jewish blessing of shalom, the expectant hope of holistic restoration on earth. "Grace" brings in the Christian emphasis on the sacrificial love that was especially displayed in Jesus's willing death. This combination of grace and peace functions as a reminder that God's grace is necessary for achieving true and lasting shalom.
- Resurrection: Foundational to all of these ideas is the *resurrection* of Jesus. By the resurrection, we know that Jesus is Christ and Lord and

> God's Son, that sin and death are defeated, that grace secured this victory, that God has looked on his people with compassion, that God is in the process of bringing restoration, and that we would be foolish not to respond to this hope and grace with faithful obedience.

Having put together the border, let's work on the rest of the puzzle. We'll start with what some regard as the thesis of Paul's letter to the Romans. Whether or not it is the thesis, it is undeniably an important part of the letter: "I'm not ashamed of the gospel: it is God's own power for salvation to all who have faith in God, to the Jew first and also to the Greek. God's righteousness is being revealed in the gospel, from faithfulness for faith, as it is written, *The righteous person will live by faith*" (1:16–17). This is one of those passages where Paul's language is a bit ambiguous. One example is the word "faith." This could mean something like "belief" or something like "faithfulness." And it's not always clear whose faith is being referred to—Jesus's or the Christian's. I will not pretend to solve this issue, though it is helpful to keep in mind our need for humility when studying Scripture. Some things are simply confusing. Nevertheless, I think when we pay attention to the "border" discussed above, we realize that we may not have to know precisely how to translate this passage to get at Paul's main ideas. In fact, I think the best way to proceed is to think "both/and" rather than "either/or." It is not *either* belief *or* faithfulness; instead, it is *both* belief *and* faithfulness. The one who believes the truth should respond with faithful obedience. Similarly, it is not *either* Jesus's faith *or* our faith; instead, it is *both* Jesus's faith *and* our faith. Jesus demonstrated his faith in God (both his belief and faithfulness) and made possible our salvation, and so we respond with faith (both belief and faithfulness).

There's also some confusion about what the term "righteousness" means. Once again, the conversation often includes a lot of unnecessary either/or-ing. A close reading of Romans reveals that God's righteousness is no simplistic idea able to be narrowed down to some single formula. Rather, God's righteousness is far-reaching and awe-inspiring, which is only appropriate to anything so centrally attributed to God. In Romans, we learn how God's righteousness is revealed in at least three ways.

First, we see God's righteousness in his doing right with regard to sin.[6] God's righteousness means that he cannot ignore or overlook sin but must respond to it. In some cases, this takes the form of God's righteous wrath—his holy indignation whereby he deals appropriately with injustice. In some cases, God's righteousness takes the form of forgiveness of sin, as Jesus's death becomes a means of atoning for sin.[7] In some cases, God's righteousness takes the form of setting right what has become broken, through restoration and renewal.

This naturally leads to the second way God's righteousness is revealed in Romans: the holistic and cosmic sense. In Romans we see that God is not only restoring humans but also restoring creation, setting it "free from slavery to decay" (8:21). This seems to refer to the cancerous corruption of sin that pervades the world. Something is wrong in the created order, God is planning on healing it, and he will enlist humans to help. God not only forgives his people but also liberates them from the enslaving influence of sin, thereby freeing humans to more effectively live into their original calling to love God, love others, and care for creation. Under sin's enslavement, humans "fall short of God's glory" (3:23)—which means that we fall short both in our sinfulness and in our failure to live up to our calling. The enslaving power of sin holds humans back from our vocation to care for creation. As Paul tells us, the created order itself "waits breathless with anticipation for the revelation of God's sons and daughters" (8:19)—because, apparently, we humans have a role to play in fixing a world that we have helped break.

Third, God's righteousness is revealed in his doing right with regard to his covenant with Abraham and Israel. God is showing himself faithful to his ancient promise of (a) descendants, (b) land, and (c) being a blessing to the nations. But God is going to keep his promise in unexpected ways. Abraham's descendants will include not only the people of Israel but also Christians from all over the world. What about the promise of land? It is no longer limited to Canaan but will include the fully restored earth. And blessing? God has chosen Abraham's lineage to bring forth the Messiah, who has broken sin and death and who has sent forth his people to expand and prepare for the full restoration of all things. We see how God is "filling full" Israel's story. We could draw even more parallels that show God filling full Israel's story:

- God rescued Israel out of slavery in Egypt → God calls Israel to lives of faithfulness and holiness according to the old covenant → Israel should represent God to a broken world through its wisdom, justice, goodness, and compassion.
- God rescues the church out of the slavery of sin and death → God calls the church to lives of faithfulness and holiness according to the new covenant → the church, empowered by the Holy Spirit, should more clearly represent God to a broken world through its increased wisdom, justice, goodness, and compassion.

As we continue through Paul's letter to the Roman church, we find Paul comparing Jesus with Adam. As we saw earlier, Genesis presents Adam as triggering a downward spiral in which the world and humanity experienced increasing brokenness. Jesus represents someone both like and unlike Adam. Jesus is ushering in a new kind of humanity—one that is free from the corruption of sin and death. Adam's descendants all know the brokenness that resulted from Adam's disobedience (and the brokenness resulting from their own disobedience). Jesus's "descendants" will know the wholeness resulting from Jesus's obedience. In Adam's wounds we find our own wounds; in Jesus's wounds we find our healing.

In Romans 6 Paul helps us see that sin is more than disobedient actions. Paul personifies it, treating it as though it's a force. According to Paul, it enslaves, masters, shapes one's desires, makes one its instrument, and leads to death. For Paul, sin is ultimately stronger than the human will; it can manipulate us into acting in ways that are contrary to our desires, and worse, it can even shape our desires so that we begin to want those things that dehumanize us. Jesus, however, did what no human could do—he conquered sin. For those who will submit to him, Jesus will be united with them in such a way that his strength will be their strength, his wholeness will be their wholeness: they can find freedom from sin's manipulation. This leads to "new life"—which isn't only about life after death but is also about life now and living as an "instrument of righteousness" (6:4, 13 NIV). In the language of Romans, Christians die to sin and live by the Spirit; they are no longer slaves to sin but are now slaves to righteousness. Not surprisingly, the ethics of this new life are the ethics of Christ: "Love should be shown without pretending. Hate evil, and hold on to what is good. Love each other like the members of your family. Be the best at showing honor to each other. . . . Contribute to the needs of God's people, and welcome strangers into your home. Bless people who harass you—bless and don't curse them" (12:9–14).

Finally, to make sense of all of this, we must give a bit more attention to Paul's idea of grace. John Barclay has written an incredibly helpful book on this topic titled *Paul and the Gift*.[8] In it he gives a nice, thick description of what "grace" means in the first century and how Paul molds that first-century concept of grace in such a way that it takes on a distinctly Christian nuance. First, though, we must recognize grace as a gift of God that reaches its zenith in Jesus's willingness to become human, suffer, and die on behalf of his creation. This gift of grace includes forgiveness of sin, freedom from sin's enslavement, and empowerment to new life. Barclay then helps us understand that God's grace is *initiated*, *extravagant*, *unrepayable*, *unrelated to status or achievements*, and *calls for response*.

- God's grace is *initiated*, meaning that God is the first to act. God initiates out of his own love. Humans cannot initiate; they can only respond.
- God's grace is *extravagant* because it is extraordinary, an overwhelming expression of generosity, demonstrated in God becoming human and dying to save even those who killed him.
- God's grace is *unrepayable*, for the size of the gift is too immense to ever pay back. No human could ever reimburse God for what he's given.
- God's grace is *unrelated to status or achievements*. That is, God's grace is not based on any accomplishments, good deeds, or virtue, nor is it based on any status markers (which in the first century were things like gender, age, power, owning land, family, ethnicity, and religious purity).
- God's grace *calls for response* from the recipient. To be clear, this isn't a response that leads to repayment, for we've already established that it can't be repaid. It's more like a response that should naturally arise out of recognition of this amazing gift. The appropriate response could never be apathy or indifference. Rather, the appropriate response is to pledge one's allegiance to this gracious God, trusting him with one's everything—to use Paul's words, to become a "slave to God" and a "living sacrifice" (Rom. 6:22; 12:1).

One final note on Romans. It would be easy to misunderstand Paul as saying that this new reality is fully available now. However, when we pay attention to Paul's writings, we discover that he is working with an already/not-yet framework, like we saw with Jesus's teaching on the kingdom. What does this look like? On the one hand, we are no longer enslaved to sin; on the other hand, we find that sin still trips us up and sometimes seems stronger than we are. On the one hand, we are children of God who are united with Christ; on the other hand, we find that God and Christ can seem quite distant. Hence, we live in a kind of limbo. We are restored by grace, yet we struggle to live out that reality in our daily lives. As a result, we wait with expectation for the time when we will experience God's renewal in its fullness.

2 Corinthians 5:14–21

In a letter to the church in Corinth, Paul writes the following:

> For Christ's love compels us, because we are convinced that one died for all, and therefore all died. And he died for all, that those who live should no longer live for themselves but for him who died for them and was raised again.

> So from now on we regard no one from a worldly point of view. Though we once regarded Christ in this way, we do so no longer. Therefore, if anyone is in Christ, the new creation has come: The old has gone, the new is here! All this is from God, who reconciled us to himself through Christ and gave us the ministry of reconciliation: that God was reconciling the world to himself in Christ, not counting people's sins against them. And he has committed to us the message of reconciliation. We are therefore Christ's ambassadors, as though God were making his appeal through us. We implore you on Christ's behalf: Be reconciled to God. God made him who had no sin to be sin for us, so that in him we might become the righteousness of God. (2 Cor. 5:14–21 NIV)

As Paul here explains the shape of his ministry, he also gives us insight into the Christian worldview. We'll start with his declaration, "Christ's love compels us." To miss this is to misunderstand Christianity: Christians don't do good *in order to* make God love them; Christians do good *because* God loves them. And God's love isn't just good vibes; it's cruciform love, the kind of love wherein "one died for all." Compelled by love, Christians should "no longer live for themselves, but for him who died and was raised again." To not live for oneself isn't about self-loathing; it's about living for something (and someone) that's truly worthy of our lives. This isn't supposed to be a begrudging response; instead, we know that anyone who has loved us as Christ loves us will call us to the kind of life and service that we were created for.

Experiencing such grace and mercy, we discover that our old value system no longer suffices. If God looks at us and sees objects worthy of his sacrificial love, then we must look at ourselves and others from that perspective too: consequently, "from now on we regard no one from a worldly point of view." We put aside a worldly value system that measures people according to shallow cultural standards, and we take up a kingdom value system that measures people according to Christ's standards. Paul reminds us that we used to wrongly regard Christ. But Jesus has turned our worldly perspective upside down. If we judge based on the world's perspective, Christ might seem insignificant—having no wealth and being crucified like a slave. But, as we learn elsewhere in Paul's letters, Christ "became wisdom from God for us" (1 Cor. 1:30). Hence, we reevaluate what truly matters, which means that we recognize the inherent value of every person. The central truth about every person's worth is not found in money, beauty, or power; rather, the central truth is that every individual is of such immense worth to God that he took on flesh, suffered, and died for all of them. Such a perspective leaves absolutely no room for Christians to participate in oppressing, marginalizing, or objectifying another human.

Paul also declares that "if anyone is in Christ, the new creation has come." With the phrase "new creation," Paul might be referring to one's new identity (indwelt and loved by Christ), one's new community (a community that transcends the divisions that are arbitrarily based on ethnicity, gender, and social status), and/or one's new humanity (a people who will one day be completely at home in the kingdom of God, living free from the brokenness of sin and death).[9] We know, however, that new creation is also an already/not-yet reality—it has broken into the present world through Jesus ("the old has gone, the new is here"), yet we are waiting for its consummation when Jesus returns and finishes what he began. As part of this new reality, Christians are reconciled to God through Christ. The broken relationship between God and humans is restored through Christ, who makes it possible that people's sins are not counted against them. The obvious implication is that humans can't repair this relationship on their own—they can't adequately deal with their own sin—so God sent Christ to do for humans what humans can't do for themselves.

Within this framework, Paul regards himself as an "ambassador for Christ"—that is, one who represents God "as though God were making his appeal through [him]." Paul puts it another way by calling himself a "minister of reconciliation." Although Paul is more specifically speaking of his own calling and mission,[10] what he's describing rings true for all Christians. That is, all Christians have been reconciled to God and therefore have the calling to engage in the work of reconciliation as Christ's representatives. For each Christian this work will look different. In fact, several New Testament letters speak to the diversity of giftedness among church members, leading us to recognize that reconciliation is a far-reaching project. This makes perfect sense when we recall sin's pervasive, far-reaching impact. Naturally, restoration and reconciliation are needed across all levels—personal, spiritual, social, economic, political, environmental, and so on.

All of this comes to a dramatic point when Paul declares, "God made him who had no sin to be sin for us, so that in him we might become the righteousness of God." To paraphrase the great Christian theologian Irenaeus, Paul is saying that Christ joined himself to humanity's brokenness in order that humans might join themselves to Christ's wholeness.[11] Christ took on our sin so that we might take on his righteousness. The incarnation makes possible new creation. Last, when Paul writes that Christians become "the righteousness of God," this seems to imply two things: First, it calls to mind our right standing as those who have been forgiven, whose sins are not counted against us. Jesus Christ is righteous, and we are made righteous by being united with him. Second, it reminds us of our vocation as Christians, as those who participate in God's project of putting things right, living out our roles as ambassadors of Christ and ministers of reconciliation. We are to embody God's righteousness in our lives.

Philippians

Paul's letter to the Philippians starts out with language similar to what we've seen earlier, showing us that the same worldview framework is still in mind: "May the grace and peace from God our Father and the Lord Jesus Christ be with you" (1:2). So what we learn from Philippians builds on what we've already learned from Romans about grace, peace, God as Father, and Jesus as Christ. The beating heart of Philippians is found in the second chapter, where we get a songlike description of Jesus:

> Adopt the attitude that was in Christ Jesus:
> Though he was in the form of God,
> he did not consider being equal with God something to exploit.
> But he emptied himself
> by taking the form of a slave
> and by becoming like human beings.
> When he found himself in the form of a human,
> he humbled himself by becoming obedient to the point of death,
> even death on a cross.
> Therefore, God highly honored him
> and gave him a name above all names,
> so that at the name of Jesus everyone
> in heaven, on earth, and under the earth might bow
> and every tongue confess
> that Jesus Christ is Lord, to the glory of God the Father.
> (2:5–11)

Any commentary on such a beautiful passage will inevitably seem a bit homely, but let's notice a few important ideas. First, we see how Paul holds in tension that Jesus is both God ("in the form of God") and human ("in the form of a human"). Second, as both God and human Jesus reveals who God is and who humans are to be. God certainly revealed himself to his creatures before the incarnation, but he had never revealed himself in such a clear, distinct, and accessible way. Through Jesus it becomes especially apparent that God is merciful, self-giving, and good beyond anything humans could have guessed. Jesus gave up more than anyone ever could—more peace, more power, more security. He gave up the invulnerability of divine existence when he became human. Yet he didn't only make the humble step from divine to human; he also entered his own creation as a child of poor parents of little status. As if that weren't humble enough, the immortal deity gave up his immortality and experienced death. Even more, he suffered the humiliating and agonizing death of crucifixion. If Jesus truly reveals God, then we must abandon notions of God as a tyrant, as some uncaring, violent, and oppressive being. When Jesus "empties himself," he does not become less divine; rather, he unveils the true nature of the divine—one willing to limit his own power for the sake of his creatures. Through Jesus we see a God who is supremely gracious and self-giving. Third, from this passage we learn how the resurrection vindicates Jesus, proving that he truly is God, that he's rightfully honored and given the "name above all names, so that at the name of Jesus everyone in heaven, on earth, and under the earth might bow and every tongue confess that Jesus Christ is Lord."[12]

Since we've learned that humans are made in the image of God, it's not surprising that Jesus is set forth as the model for humans to imitate. That is, when Jesus perfectly imaged God to us, he exemplified how humans might bear the image of God. As Michael Gorman puts it, "*Becoming more Christ-like means both becoming more Godlike and becoming more fully human.*"[13] Of course, there's an understanding that no human can do what Jesus did, nor does this imply some sort of overliteral imitation, as though Christians need to try to get crucified by Roman authorities. Rather, as we learn from Paul, this is about taking on the virtues or value system of Christ—in whatever society and situation we find ourselves. So Paul calls the Philippians to "adopt the attitude that was in Christ Jesus." Or, as he says earlier, "Don't do anything for selfish purposes but with humility think of others as better than yourselves" (2:3). Christ, then, is our example of what it looks like when humans fully embrace their purpose to bear the image of God. "Paul did not want [his readers] . . . merely to *believe* the gospel, but also to *become* the gospel—to faithfully embody the gospel narrative."[14]

To embody this narrative requires a partnership between God and humans. Just after Paul's beautiful description of Jesus, he tells the Philippians to "carry out your own salvation" while "God is the one who enables you both to want and to actually live out his good purposes" (2:12–13). Notice the God-and-human dynamic: humans play a role in carrying out their salvation, but they don't do so on their own steam; God gives them the strength and desire to carry out their salvation. What, exactly, does it mean to "carry out your own salvation"? As should be clear by now, it cannot mean "earn" your salvation or "repay" God. Paul would never say that. Instead, this means something more like "live out" or "embody" your salvation. As Paul writes earlier in this same letter, "live together in a manner worthy of Christ's gospel" (1:27). So if we keep in mind that "salvation" refers to God's holistic-restoration project, and if we keep in mind that "gospel" refers to a king winning a victory and God reigning, then we get a sense of what it means to live out one's *salvation* or to live in a way worthy of the *gospel*. Specifically, it is to live in such a way that is consistent with being united to the victorious king Jesus, to strive to live as though sin and death are defeated and no longer control us, and to join with God's mission of bringing restoration and reconciliation.

Paul captures this idea when he reminds his readers that their "citizenship is in heaven" (Phil. 3:20). As well-known scholar N. T. Wright cleverly explains, "When Paul says 'our citizenship is in heaven,' . . . he does not mean, 'Therefore that is where we go when we die.' That is not how citizenship worked. Roman citizens living in Philippi would not expect to return to Rome upon retirement, but to be agents of Roman civilization in Philippi and the surrounding countryside."[15] Citizenship is about values and allegiance. A Roman citizen adopts Roman values and allegiances, whereas a "citizen of heaven" adopts the values and allegiances of the kingdom of heaven, where God reigns. Lest we forget, this is not something humans are able to do independently; they need the power of the Holy Spirit to aid them. For Paul, when we give ourselves wholeheartedly to King Jesus, when we allow God's Spirit to transform our hearts and minds, we will find true life. Nothing else compares: "Everything [is] a loss in comparison with the superior value of knowing Christ Jesus my Lord" (3:8).

Summarizing Paul

Paul can be dense, so let's summarize the main points we've covered from this survey of Paul's letters. We'll organize this summary around some of the questions from Alex Rosenberg we encountered in the introduction. Here's how Paul might respond.

Is there a God? Yes. This God is revealed as Father, the creator and compassionate one. God is also revealed as Jesus, the one who is the image of the invisible God, the embodiment of true humanity, the conqueror of sin and death, the Christ. God is even revealed as the Holy Spirit, who unites us with Christ's love and strength and goodness.

What is the nature of reality? Reality is an eternal God who created a good world that sin has corrupted. Thus we should expect to see great beauty in the world—and great tragedy. Further, a decisive victory has been won over sin and death, the effects of which are felt now in part but not yet in full.

What is the purpose of the universe? The purpose of the universe is to love God and be loved by God, which we surmise not only on the basis of God's initial act of creating but also on the basis of his great efforts to restore and be reconciled to his creation.

What is the meaning of life? This answer is similar to the previous answer: the meaning of life is found in being restored to God and in partnering with him to extend his restorative mission.

Why am I here? The original human calling was to bear God's image (by caring for creation) and to be in faithful relationship with God and loving relationship with others. As sin has distorted creation, the original human calling has shifted so that humans are to represent God not only by caring for creation but also by helping restore the sin-damaged world—physically, socially, and spiritually. This is entailed in being ambassadors of Christ and ministers of reconciliation. Such a mission is characterized by grace and by cruciform love.

Is there a soul? There is something soulish about humans, but not as some Greeks thought, where our souls/spirits are separate from and superior to our bodies. Humans are more like embodied souls. What one does in the body affects one's soul. The new creation will not be merely spiritual but will also be physical.

Is there free will? Free will is implied in those places where explicit commands are given ("work out your salvation" [Phil. 2:12 NIV]), which would make little sense if people had no choice. It's also implied in the references to human guilt (How could a just God hold people guilty if they had no free will in their decisions?). Yet this is a soft "yes," because it recognizes that human choices are not completely wide open, which is seen especially in the concept of the enslavement to sin as well as in the reality of our embodied existence—wherein our choices are limited by our bodies, communities, and environments.

What happens when we die? What happens between our death and the final restoration of all things is not fully clear, though Christians can refer to this period as "sleep" or being "with Christ" (1 Thess. 4:13; Phil. 1:23). However, at some future point God will restore all things, at which time those who are in Christ will receive bodies that are made whole, no longer subject to sin and death.

What is the difference between right and wrong, good and bad? To put it simply, "good" is that which is characteristic of and aligned with God, which means that "bad" is that which is contrary to and opposed to God. God's goodness is characterized by grace, justice, truth, and self-giving—or as Paul describes the fruit of God's Holy Spirit: "love, joy, peace, patience, kindness, goodness, faithfulness, gentleness, and self-control" (Gal. 5:22–23). Badness, then, is characterized by miserliness, injustice, falsehood, and selfishness—or as sin is characterized: "hatred, discord, jealousy, fits of rage, selfish ambition, dissensions, factions and envy" (Gal. 5:20–21 NIV). Another angle would be to consider the nature of wisdom—that is, the way to think and live rightly. For Paul, Christ is like "wisdom from God for us" (1 Cor. 1:30)—he demonstrates what it means to think and live rightly.

What is love? Love is at the center of reality, it flows from God to his creation, and in its purest form it looks like a divine being who gave up his peace and invulnerability, became truly human, lived a life of humble service in solidarity with even the poorest and lowest of society, and submitted himself not only to death but also to the agonizing and shameful death of crucifixion, all so that he might redeem a broken and rebellious world. As humans embrace such love, they are to love one another in similar fashion—regardless of whether they are rich or poor, slave or master, Jew or Gentile, male or female.

Revelation

Finally, we close our survey with what may be the strangest and most misinterpreted book of the Bible: Revelation. According to tradition, this book was written by the apostle John while he was in exile. The primary genre of this book is referred to as "apocalyptic." James K. A. Smith does a nice job explaining this genre, describing how apocalyptic literature helps reveal things "for what they *really* are." He writes, "Unfortunately, we associate apocalyptic literature with 'end-times' literature, as if its goal were a matter of prediction. But this is a misunderstanding of the biblical genre. The point of apocalyptic literature is not prediction but *unmasking*—unveiling the realities around us for what they really are. . . . [It] tries to get us to see the world on a slant, and thus see through the spin. . . . Apocalyptic literature is *revealing* precisely because it gives us a new perspective to see *through* this beguiling misrepresentation."[16] I love his analogy: *seeing the world on a slant*. As Smith explains, if we think about vertical blinds, we can both look *at* and look *beyond* them. If blinds are partially open, from one angle all we can see is the blinds. If, however, we adjust our position, we can see at a "slant" through the blinds to the reality beyond them. This is what apocalyptic literature can do with its gripping imagery and symbolism. It offers an invitation to change perspective so that we don't look at the surface of things but look beyond them to a deeper reality.

Around the time that John wrote Revelation, Rome looked unstoppable; it seemed as though coercion and violence were where ultimate power lies, and it appeared that Christians were an insignificant group of misfits, rejects, and social deviants. At least that's how things looked on the surface. But what if we look at a slant to the reality beyond? Revelation invites us to consider a different perspective, something like a God's-eye view of things. From this vantage point—"slantage point"?—it is God who is in control, not Rome . . . and Rome doesn't appear so invincible from God's view. Through the slant we see that real power is found not in violence and oppression but in sacrificial love, and we discover that the seemingly insignificant Christians will one day be rulers themselves (finally taking up their God-given roles as image bearers who are to care for and properly rule over creation).

To give one striking example of the apocalyptic genre teaching us to see the world on a slant, let's look at a vision described in Revelation 5:

> "See, the Lion of the tribe of Judah, the Root of David, has triumphed. He is able to open the scroll and its seven seals."
>
> Then I saw a Lamb, looking as if it had been slain, standing at the center of the throne. . . . The Lamb had seven horns and seven eyes. . . . The four living creatures and the twenty-four elders fell down before the Lamb. . . . And they sang a new song, saying:
>
> "You are worthy to take the scroll
> and to open its seals,
> because you were slain,
> and with your blood you purchased for God
> persons from every tribe and language and people and nation.
> You have made them to be a kingdom and priests to serve our God,
> and they will reign on the earth."
>
> Then I looked and heard the voice of many angels, numbering thousands upon thousands, and ten thousand times ten thousand. They encircled the throne and the living creatures and the elders. In a loud voice they were saying:
>
> "Worthy is the Lamb, who was slain,
> to receive power and wealth and wisdom and strength
> and honor and glory and praise!"
>
> Then I heard every creature in heaven and on earth and under the earth and on the sea, and all that is in them, saying:
>
> "To him who sits on the throne and to the Lamb
> be praise and honor and glory and power,
> for ever and ever!" (vv. 5–13 NIV)

Admittedly, this all can seem a bit bizarre, but a closer inspection reveals that it is both bizarre *and* beautiful. The apocalyptic imagery takes us beyond the surface-level propaganda and invites us to consider a different perspective, to discover the true reality. Let's start with the opening proclamation that "the Lion of the tribe of Judah, the Root of David, has triumphed." This contains powerful imagery (lion) combined with deeply rooted symbolism from the Old Testament (the references to the "tribe of Judah" and the "Root of David" point to the hopes of the promised and long-awaited Messiah who will bring victory). Language about a lion and a great king leads the reader to expect a warrior figure. But that may be because we're thinking more like Rome and less like God. What Revelation reveals to us is not a warrior but "a Lamb, looking as if it had been slain." Surely this can't be right, the reader may think. Can a slaughtered lamb really be the lion of Judah, the Messiah? But the symbolism leaves little doubt, as this lamb has "seven horns"—a symbol of total power. The Roman perspective on reality is that total power is demonstrated through coercion and violence. But if we view this from Revelation's slant, the God's-eye point of view, we see a vivid scene in which total power is demonstrated through Jesus's cruciform love. (Though, in the future, God's Messiah may very well use force to subdue the rebellious and resistant who align themselves with evil; see Rev. 19:11–21.)

As the vision continues, thousands upon thousands of angels fall down and worship the slain lamb—a stirring image of the crucified Jesus. The angels sing, "You are worthy . . . because you were slain." Notice the word "because." It is not, "You are worthy *even though* you were slain." Rather, the lamb's worth is rooted in his sacrifice. Once again we are seeing reality at a slant. From a Roman perspective, Jesus's crucifixion proved that he was unworthy of honor. After all, to their untrained eyes Jesus was a powerless man subjected to the humiliating death of a criminal at the mighty hands of Roman officials. But the heavenly perspective sees *beyond* to a different reality, where Jesus's death confirms his worth, honor, and power. He is not defeated at the cross; instead, the cross is where he wins a victory that no one else has, could, or will. He redeems humanity "with [his] blood" and unites people from "every tribe and language and people and nation." He makes possible a new community with a "kingdom and priests" who will "reign on the earth." The contrast between the Roman perspective and the heavenly perspective is striking: those rejected by their empire are now rulers of a new kingdom; those who are regarded as spiritual parasites, God regards as priests; those who are oppressed will reign on the earth. As a kingdom and as priests they are to represent (image) God to the world, for they "reign on the earth" by extending the gracious rule of God (in contrast to the corruption and tyranny that characterize so many rulers).

Last, consider how the camera pans back on this vision, bringing into view angels who can't be numbered: "thousands upon thousands, and ten thousand times ten thousand." It doesn't stop with angels but includes all of creation: "every creature in heaven and on earth and under the earth and on the sea, and all that is in them." What are they doing? They're singing! "Worthy is the Lamb, who was slain. . . . To the Lamb be praise and honor and glory and power, for ever." To the untrained eye, Rome might have seemed so powerful, so impressive, so vast—but Revelation reveals how vulnerable, insignificant, and little Rome truly is. The vast empire of Rome all of a sudden appears tiny when compared with the reality of millions of angels and the whole created order worshiping their true king, Jesus.

This brings us to the last two chapters of Revelation, which also happen to be the last two chapters of the Bible. Here we catch a glimpse of the restoration the Bible has been pointing to all along:

> Then I saw "a new heaven and a new earth," for the first heaven and the first earth had passed away, and there was no longer any sea. I saw the Holy City, the new Jerusalem, coming down out of heaven from God, prepared as a bride beautifully dressed for her husband. And I heard a loud voice from the throne saying, "Look! God's dwelling place is now among the people, and he will dwell with them. They will be his people, and God himself will be with them and be their God. 'He will wipe every tear from their eyes. There will be no more death' or mourning or crying or pain, for the old order of things has passed away."
>
> He who was seated on the throne said, "I am making everything new!" (21:1–5 NIV)

> I did not see a temple in the city, because the Lord God Almighty and the Lamb are its temple. The city does not need the sun or the moon to shine on it, for the glory of God gives it light, and the Lamb is its lamp. The nations will walk by its light, and the kings of the earth will bring their splendor into it. (21:22–24 NIV)

> Then the angel showed me the river of the water of life. . . . On each side of the river stood the tree of life, bearing twelve crops of fruit, yielding its fruit every month. And the leaves of the tree are for the healing of the nations. No longer will there be any curse. The throne of God and of the Lamb will be in the city, and his servants will serve him. They will see his face, and his name will be on their foreheads. There will be no more night. They will not need the light of a lamp or the light of the sun, for the Lord God will give them light. And they will reign forever and ever. (22:1–5 NIV)

> "Look, I am coming soon! My reward is with me, and I will give to each person according to what they have done. I am the Alpha and the Omega, the First and the Last, the Beginning and the End." (22:12–13 NIV)

I cannot possibly explain all that is going on in these verses (nor can I pretend to even *know* all that is going on). However, I am confident that we can pick out four important ideas. First, God's renewal of creation will be a major overhaul, not simply a few minor tweaks and adjustments. John reveals this with language such as "I saw 'a new heaven and a new earth'" and "the first heaven and the first earth had passed away." If people were not reading closely or were only reading bits and pieces of the New Testament, they could easily misread John as saying that all the created order was completely destroyed. However, those who have been paying attention to the whole biblical story know that God's project was not to destroy his good creation and start over from scratch; rather, his plan was to renew and restore his good creation. We should remember from Romans how creation "waits in eager expectation" (8:19 NIV) for a time when it will be "liberated from its bondage to decay" (8:21 NIV) (or, as we read in Colossians 1:20, how God is reconciling "all things" to himself through Jesus). Here in Revelation we don't see a picture of destruction but rather a radical overhaul and judgment.[17] Notice, for example, that some of God's original good creation (such as the tree of life) is still around. Also notice that "the Holy City, the New Jerusalem" is "coming down." The "coming down" language envisions something like God's realm coming down to overlap with a restored (not discarded) earth. Even as we acknowledge that creation is redeemed and not scrapped, we also must bear in mind that John describes a radical transformation of the created order. The contamination of sin is so deep and pervasive that every inch of creation needs purification and renewal.

Second, this renewal can be described as holistic restoration. As we've learned, sin has broken things physically, socially, and spiritually. There is physical brokenness—sickness, death, and a groaning creation. There is spiritual brokenness—the guilt and unholiness of sin has fractured the relationship between God and humans. And there is social brokenness—violence and greed and selfishness have left their devastating marks on marriages, families, societies, politics, and all forms of culture. We recall how the Messiah, Jesus, launched his kingdom by bringing holistic restoration: physical (healing the sick, raising the dead), social (ministering to the marginalized, such as lepers and tax collectors), and spiritual (forgiving sins and casting out demons). So when we come to this vision at the end of Revelation, we discover what the biblical story has led us to anticipate: the kingdom fully present, where things are completely restored—physically, socially, and spiritually.

- There will be *physical wholeness*. This is true not just for humans: "'There will be no more death' or mourning or crying or pain." It is also true for creation itself: "there was no longer any sea." (Here the "sea" functions as a symbol of chaos within the created world.)

- There will be *social wholeness*. The nations will "walk by [the glory of God's] light," and the leaves of the tree of life will be for the "healing of the nations."
- There will be *spiritual wholeness*. "God's dwelling place is now among the people, and he will dwell with them. They will be his people, and God himself will be with them and be their God." When sin is dealt with, people can once again be in true intimate friendship with God, for they "will see his face." There won't even be a need for a temple, "because the Lord God Almighty and the Lamb are [the] temple."

Third, as restored humans in a restored world, humans can finally do what they were always made to do: bear God's image to the world while enjoying loving relationship with God and fellow humans. Notice the odd combination of verbs that describe what humans will be doing: they will both "serve" and "reign." Only in a world that is truly free of sin can serving and reigning fully go hand in hand. Yet that's the picture: "his servants will serve him. . . . And they will reign forever." To serve the king is to accept the dignified status of bearing God's image, gratefully carrying out his will for our lives, wherein humans are to rule the earth with goodness and care and humility.

Fourth, the fullness of restoration will happen when Jesus returns to finish what he began. In this life, Christians partner with Jesus's ongoing work of restoration and reconciliation, but we also realize that we are incapable of fully healing the world on our own. We cannot achieve utopia. Sin runs too deep in the human heart and in the created order. The work we do now, however, still matters: it prepares us for our vocation in the renewed world to come, it demonstrates our allegiance to Jesus's kingdom, it bears witness to the world of a truer reality and a hope to come, and it is somehow mysteriously related to future reward and responsibility.[18]

Let's return to the concept of Scripture as a six-act drama. We've just finished going through this epic story, familiarizing ourselves with the Holy Script(ure). N. T. Wright invites us to envision ourselves as participants within this biblical drama.[19] If we think about the six acts listed earlier, where do we find ourselves today? We would be somewhere in Act 5: Spreading the News of the King: The Mission of the Church. Wise Christians ought to live in ways that fit this particular stage of the drama. If we know where the story has been (acts 1–4), and if we know where the story is going (act 6), then we have a better idea about how to wisely and faithfully play our current role in this part of the drama (act 5).

Let's finish with a brief recap of the biblical drama, noting some prominent themes while paying attention to how Scripture's plotline moves from conflict to resolution:[20]

- In the beginning, God creates a good world with humans bearing God's image and where things are physically, socially, and spiritually whole.
- Sin comes on the scene like a cancer, spreading its corruption across God's good world, rendering humans less capable of fulfilling their roles as image bearers and leaving brokenness in its wake—physically, socially, and spiritually.
- God redeems a people (Israel) and provides them with a good land and the dignified status to be a kingdom and priests, where the brokenness is being partially mended—physically, socially, and spiritually.
- After Israel's failure, the Son—the perfect image of God—enters our world as a human, and through his life, death, resurrection, and ascension, he inaugurates a new reality that will break the power of sin and will make possible a total restoration and renewal: physically, socially, and spiritually.
- The church—made up of those who have pledged their faith in Jesus—is united with Christ, and thereby all who make up the church are forgiven, justified, reconciled, and empowered by the Spirit to be ministers of reconciliation and restoration: physically, socially, and spiritually.
- At some future point, God will finish the work that Christ achieved, fully destroying sin, renewing his good world, enabling humans to faithfully bear God's image as they serve and reign, and finalizing his will to bring holistic restoration—physically, socially, and spiritually.

PART 2

THE APOSTLES' CREED

4

God the Father

Introducing the Apostles' Creed

In the next three chapters, we'll be going line by line through the Apostles' Creed, a confession of Christian faith that succinctly states the basic framework of Christianity. It's helpful for our study because it offers a nice, basic representation of the Christian metanarrative and because Christians have recognized the central truths of this confession across the centuries, across continents, and across denominational differences. That is, even though Christians have disagreed with one another about various teachings and ideas, almost all Christians of all times and places can confidently confess the following:

> I believe in God, the Father almighty,
> creator of heaven and earth.
>
> I believe in Jesus Christ, his only Son, our Lord.
> He was conceived by the power of the Holy Spirit
> and born of the Virgin Mary.
>
> He suffered under Pontius Pilate,
> was crucified, died, and was buried.
>
> He descended to the dead.
> On the third day he rose again.
> He ascended into heaven,
> and is seated at the right hand of the Father.
> He will come again to judge the living and the dead.

> I believe in the Holy Spirit,
> the holy catholic Church,
> the communion of saints,
> the forgiveness of sins,
> the resurrection of the body,
> and the life everlasting.
> Amen.[1]

As we work our way through this ancient creed, I hope to show how such a confession ought to shape a Christian's worldview. Along the way, I will make occasional reference to another early and widespread creed, the Nicene Creed. The Nicene Creed is like a longer, more-detailed version of the Apostles' Creed, making it a bit too extensive for us to study in detail, although we will occasionally look to it for insight.

The precise origin of the Apostles' Creed is not known, though its roots are clearly evident from early on. For example, in the New Testament we find Paul making creed-like statements (1 Cor. 15:3–8). Early Christian writers like Irenaeus (second century) and Tertullian (early third century) train Christians in what's called the "rule of faith"—a concise statement about the core of Christian teaching.[2] From church history, we discover how the rule of faith played an important role for the church: clarifying important details, centering the faith, and distinguishing what is orthodox from what is unorthodox.[3] We can think of the Apostles' Creed as a standardized version of the early church's rule of faith. With such introductory matters in mind, we move forward to the opening words of the Apostles' Creed.

I Believe

Because the Apostles' Creed distills what we find in Scripture, we need to understand "belief" in light of Scripture. In other words, as we study this ancient creed that is rooted in the Bible, it is wise for us to seek its meaning in the Bible rather than in *Wiktionary* or *Merriam-Webster's Collegiate Dictionary*. Based on our study so far, we have learned that both *content* and *embodiment* matter for belief. That is, it matters both *what* we believe and *how* we put that belief into practice.

Content matters: Israelites must believe that God is one; Christians must believe that Jesus rose from the dead. Embodiment matters: Israelites must embody their belief that God is one by worshiping him only, by going where he calls and keeping his commandments, trusting that he is their creator who knows what is best for them. Christians must embody their belief that Jesus rose from the dead by trusting that a new reality has broken into the world; by maintaining a faithful witness even when persecuted, because they know that all will be made right; and by living according to Jesus's teachings, because they trust that such is the path of true wisdom and reconciliation. As one New Testament author puts it, "faith without actions is dead" (James 2:26). Belief that is not embodied is not Christian belief. When the Apostles' Creed opens with "I believe," it expects us to make this confession not only with our mouths but with our lives as well.

In God

To say "I believe *in God*" is to open a door to a realm of possibilities that would otherwise be unlikely or impossible. If Alex Rosenberg is correct, to deny the existence of God is to deny the possibility of ultimate purpose, objective morality, free will, lasting personhood, and life after death. In contrast, if God exists then all of these are possible: God can provide the foundation for real purpose, for genuine morality, for freedom of the will, for lasting personhood, and for life beyond death. Let me be clear: belief in God does not guarantee this; it simply opens the door to these possibilities. If God created the world on a whim, then there's still no purpose; if God is not good, then there is no objective morality; if God is a cosmic puppet master, then there is no free will; and if God does not enable his creatures to survive beyond death, then there is no hope of life after death. Thus the claim "I believe *in God*" informs one's worldview by opening up a range of possibilities. How it *specifically* shapes one's worldview, though, depends on the nature and/or character of God. In other words, it matters just as much *what* one believes *about* God as it does *that* one believes *in* God.

As we will see, certain ancient and contemporary views of God cannot sustain a belief in purpose, morality, free will, and life after death. In fact, many pop-culture views of God are too flimsy and insubstantial to speak with much substance to life's big questions. This is not to say that people haven't tried to connect such flimsy views of God with big questions about morality and purpose. But when one actually starts to ask some logical questions, it becomes clear that there are major gaps in the worldview.

I find it frustrating when such worldviews borrow Judeo-Christian elements without realizing that such elements make sense only within certain frameworks. For example, as a Christian it makes sense to believe that "all humans have dignity and purpose," because this idea stems from the biblical doctrine that all humans are created in God's image. In contrast, some popular worldviews seem to assume human dignity and purpose without providing some foundation on which to base the claim. Does it make sense to say that the world is a big accident, humans are merely highly evolved animals, and yet every person has objective worth and dignity and purpose? The math doesn't add up for me: accidental universe + evolved animals = objective worth, dignity, and purpose. That kind of framework can only account for *subjective* (not *objective*) worth, dignity, and purpose. Related to this, the claim that "God is love" makes sense in a Christian framework where God exists in a trinitarian community of love (which we'll explore later) and where God expresses that love by becoming human and dying to rescue his people. Apart from this framework, what does it mean to claim that "God is love," and what is the claim based on?

One further note: the Nicene Creed makes explicit what is implicit in the Apostles' Creed—namely, that God is "one." Within a Christian worldview, the oneness of God provides a helpful foundation for morality and purpose and hope. We can see this when we compare monotheism with a cosmic dualistic worldview that supposes two equal powers—one good and one evil.[4] When we think about such a dualistic worldview, it doesn't take much mental work to discover that "good" and "evil" are arbitrary, just a matter of perspective. In other words, what is good according to one power is evil according to the other, and vice versa. There is no standard above these two powers to help one determine which is good and which is evil. With no ultimate standard for good, there's no clear purpose to pursue. What should humans do with their lives? Pursue the good. But what is "good" when you're in a system with two equal powers that disagree? Further, if there are two equal and opposing powers, what is the basis for hope? Can one have any hope that good will triumph in the end? Is there any reason to hope that wrongs will be made right when good and evil are deadlocked as equals? In the Christian framework, however, the oneness of God is capable of providing a basis for morality, purpose, and hope. This is particularly true when, as the Apostles' Creed claims, that one God is revealed as "Father almighty, creator of heaven and earth."

The Father

To call God "Father" is not to claim that God is male—as though he had a physical body with male reproductive organs. In fact, Scripture at times uses feminine imagery to describe God's relationship to his people (e.g., Isa. 49:15). All titles and descriptors for God are ultimately inadequate because they are attempts to put into words something that is essentially inexpressible. Every title or description of God carries with it a potential for misunderstanding or abuse. In this case, "Father" could mistakenly call to mind abusive and negligent fathers; similarly, calling God "Father" could be twisted to suggest that males are inherently superior to females. That's why it's always necessary to look to Scripture to learn what these titles mean.

What might we learn from Scripture? To refer to God as "Father" is to point to (1) God's role as creator, (2) God's relationship with the Son, (3) God's relationship with his people, and (4) God's character. We'll discuss God's role as creator in more detail later. For now, we'll take the other three ideas in turn.

Father to the Son

The title "Father" implies relationship. To be a father, you must be father to someone. And through a thoughtful reading of the New Testament, one discovers that God the Father has always been in relationship with the Son. This is captured in the disorienting language of the prologue of the Gospel of John: "In the beginning was the Word, and the Word was with God, and the Word was God" (1:1). For John, the "Word" can refer to the Son, and "God" can refer to the Father (though not always). In other words, we might read this as follows: "In the beginning was the Son, and the Son was with Father God, and the Son was God." This may seem like nonsense. Didn't we just learn that God is one? Then how can God also be two—Father and Son? There is no simplistic way to grasp this concept. We will get into this more later on, but for now it's understandable to feel some confusion.

Leaving this conundrum for a moment, we learn three things from the doctrine that God is *Father to the Son*. First, this testifies to a unique, intimate bond between God the Father and God the Son. From a time beyond time, there have been two persons (Father and Son) who are confessed as "one God." The Nicene Creed makes this even more explicit, confessing Jesus as "true God from true God." Every other relationship we know—friends, lovers, families—is at best a faint shadow of the relationship that is at the center of all reality, a relationship that is so deeply connected that two persons are one. And if we object that such a concept seems nonsensical, we should stop to realize that, if our concept of God is easy to fit into our reality, then our concept of God is probably too small. After all, can anyone fully grasp how God could be eternal, immortal, all-powerful, all-knowing, or not bound by time? If not, then why should we be able to fully grasp his unique oneness?

Second, if the center of all reality is a being who exists in a relationship of such closeness, then we discover that love is at the center of all reality. In a traditional monotheistic system like that of Judaism or Islam, God is one being and one person. In such a framework, love would seem to be something peripheral to who God is. After all, if God were one person, how would he love? Whom would he love? There would be nothing or no one to love, which would mean that love would be a secondary characteristic of God.[5] The Christian monotheistic framework is unique. It holds that there is one God but two persons—Father and Son. (Later, we'll see that God is actually three persons.) If God has always been both Father and Son, then for all eternity God has been in a relationship of love. In a surprising twist, we begin to see that what at first seems contradictory (one God, two persons) starts to make sense on a deep, intuitive level—that instinctive level where we sense in our gut that capital *L* Love is real.

For atheists like Rosenberg, love is ultimately an illusion—an evolutionary survival strategy to create family and social bonds. For the traditional monotheists, love is less than central to God: a singular God might be many things—omnipotent, omniscient, eternal—but that God would not have love at the core of his nature. For the Christian, however, love is central. God has existed for all eternity in a community of oneness; such a God is a being of eternal love—forever before and forever after.

Perhaps we should stop to notice that the Christian has the difficult job of accepting that God is both one and more than one—a strange, almost nonsensical notion. The trade-off, though, is that the Christian has a solid reason to believe that God is love and therefore that love is at the center of reality. The non-Christian is free from trying to make sense of the notion of God being one and more than one. The downside is that this seems to commit the non-Christian to an equally or more difficult belief—namely, that love either is nothing more than an illusion or is less than central to reality.

Third, the relationship between Father and Son is not identical to the relationship between the Father and his human creatures. In the Gospels we discern a unique intimacy that the Father and Son share. Not only does Jesus hint at this by repeatedly referring to God as "Father" and "my Father" but he also makes it particularly clear when he talks about their closeness. For example, he can claim, "No one knows the Son except the Father, and no one knows the Father except the Son" (Matt. 11:27 NIV), and, "Anyone who has seen me has seen the Father. . . . I am in the Father and the Father is in me" (John 14:9, 11 NIV).[6]

Father to His Children

Jesus is God's Son in a unique and special way, but Jesus also makes it possible for Christians to become daughters and sons of God. Paul writes in

Ephesians that we are God's "adopted children through Jesus Christ because of his love" (1:5). And John writes, "See what kind of love the Father has given to us in that we should be called God's children" (1 John 3:1). Recall that when Jesus teaches his disciples how to pray, he starts with the words "Our Father."

For the Christian, to confess God as "Father" is to confess one's identity and mission. To know who God is (Father) is to know one's identity (child of God), which is to know one's purpose (to embody the love and mercy of God). For example, we learn from Jesus to "be compassionate just as your Father is compassionate," and again, to "love your enemies . . . [and] you will be acting the way children of the Most High act, for he is kind to ungrateful and wicked people" (Luke 6:35–36). The children of God are to reflect the mercy of their Father in heaven. If we return to the prayer Jesus taught his disciples, we learn that to call on God as Father is to be a people who desire God's name to be made holy, who hope for God's kingdom to come on earth as in heaven, who trust God to provide for our daily needs, and who are dependent on God to deliver us from evil. Thus, to call God "Father" is to say that "we are his people, who trust him to care for us, and who devote our hearts and energies to his good purposes." Once again, the Apostles' Creed is to be confessed with both one's mouth and one's life.

Father as Character Trait

To confess God as Father is to confess one's belief about God's character.[7] To those who have had abusive, absent, reckless, or foolish fathers, it may never be easy to consider God the Father as good and loving. Even Jesus contrasts earthly fathers with the heavenly Father, drawing attention to "how much more" the heavenly Father can be trusted to be good to his children (Luke 11:11–13). A few examples can help us see how confessing God as Father is meant to be a confession of God's good and merciful character. We saw above Jesus's concise statement, "Be compassionate just as your Father is compassionate." And to this we might add biblical descriptions of God as "father to the fatherless" (Ps. 68:5 NIV). In Romans, Paul writes that as God's children we can cry out to God as "Abba," an Aramaic term for "father" that conveys intimacy, perhaps better translated as "Dad." Paul goes on to explain how, as God's children, we are like heirs, who will one day receive our full inheritance (Rom. 8:14–17). Paul seems to have in mind how we'll inherit our rightful place as caretakers of a restored earth, where we will live in harmony with God and our neighbors, free from sin, sickness, and death.

Interestingly, in both the Apostles' Creed and the Lord's Prayer, God is called Father before any other descriptor or title. In the Apostles' Creed the confession "Father" precedes the confession that God is "almighty" and "creator." And in the Lord's Prayer the words "Our Father" precede the descriptor "in heaven." This teaches Christians that our primary relationship to God is to be understood as a parent-child relationship. Viewing God first as a loving parent is one of Christianity's distinctive traits. In fact, according to Michael Bird, "Crying out to God as Father would be irreverent for Jews, blasphemy to Muslims, weird for Buddhists, and mean something entirely different for Hindus."[8] Bird might overstate this a bit, but I don't believe he's too far off.

Almighty

God relates to his people as Father first, but we must be careful not to press this description so far that God begins to look more like Father Christmas than Father Almighty. God is almighty, all-powerful. He has made all things, sustains all things, and can unmake all things. He is without equal, unrivaled in his authority, strength, and control. He is not bound by time or space. Nothing is so large as to be beyond his control, nor is anything so small as to be hidden from him. He has the power to create and destroy, to split the sea and to bring it crashing down, to install rulers and to dethrone kings, to prosper a nation and to bring a nation to its knees, to cause leprosy and to cleanse leprosy, to create storms and to calm storms, to command angels and to cast out demons, to harden hearts and to soften hearts, to defeat death and to resurrect the righteous, to overcome sin and to make the broken whole.

What can God not do? Perhaps only two things.[9] First, he cannot go against his nature. For example, because God is good he cannot do evil. As we consider God's power, it may arouse feelings of suspicion or fear, because we know of example after example of persons of great power who started out corrupt or became corrupt. With God, though, we need not fear that he will use his power arbitrarily, capriciously, or vindictively. Everything he does will be consistent with his goodness, mercy, and justice. What else might God not be able to do? He most likely cannot do what C. S. Lewis labels the "intrinsically impossible"—something that "carries its impossibility within itself."[10] Examples of this might include creating a square circle or a four-sided triangle. As Lewis goes on to say, "Meaningless combinations of words [such as "square circle"] do not suddenly acquire meaning simply because we prefix to them the two other words 'God can.' It remains true that all *things* are possible with God: the intrinsic impossibilities are not things but nonentities. . . . Nonsense remains nonsense even when we talk it about God."[11]

Creator of Heaven and Earth

To claim that God is "creator of heaven and earth" is to claim that God has created everything. Only God is unmade. Only God has no beginning. Everything else, material or spiritual, was made by God.[12] All things depend on God for their existence, whereas God exists on his own. Without God, nothing would exist; God, however, still exists even if nothing else does. To confess God as creator is to claim that God is distinct from his creation—he is over, beyond, outside, superior, and separate. (This trait is sometimes labeled "transcendence.")

The Bible also teaches that not only are all things *created* by God but they are also *continuously sustained* by God (Col. 1:15–23). This balances the picture, for it means that God is not only beyond his creation but also within his creation. If all creation finds its origin in God, then to some degree all creation has a godly aspect to it. Similarly, if all creation is sustained by God, then to some degree God is present throughout all creation. (This is what we might call God's "immanence.") This suggests that God has a self-limiting ability, whereby he is able to create something that derives from him but is nonetheless not him. The cosmos arises from God, but it is not God. God is both transcendent and immanent, both distinct from his creation and present in it. (This self-limiting ability of God might also give us a clue about how God can create beings who have some degree of free will—even the ability to rebel.)

Genesis 1 describes creation as "good," with humans invested with the special status as God's image bearers. So to confess God as "creator" is to confess that the material world was made good (even if it has become broken) and that humans have inherent dignity and purpose and distinction. The Christian worldview rejects any notion of the universe as a mere accident (as we might find in atheism). It is also at odds with Platonic-like views, wherein the physical realm is inferior and the spiritual realm is superior. (In many such worldviews, salvation tends to look like escape from the material world and entrance into a purely spiritual world—a notion we find reflected in Buddhism and Gnosticism.)

Excursus
Creation and Science

What are we to do with the supposed conflict between science and the biblical accounts of creation? Four observations can help us navigate this issue. First, the Apostles' Creed itself doesn't commit the Christian to any particulars about the mechanics or time line of creation. That is, the creed does not confess that God created in six twenty-four-hour days or that God created instantaneously rather than through the long process of evolution. According to the Apostles' Creed, the central issue is *that* God created, not *how* God created.

Second, the Christian understanding on the matter is not limited to the creed but is also informed by Scripture. Christians are committed to the notion that the biblical accounts of creation bear witness to the truth. This commitment to Scripture leads to our next observation.

Third, it's not entirely clear how to interpret the biblical creation accounts. Yes, the accounts are teaching truths, but what truths are they teaching? This is where it becomes necessary to interpret Scripture with wisdom and discernment. One thing we discover is that the Bible can discuss creation using different genres or styles of literature: sometimes the genre resembles ancient historiography, other times something closer to poetry, other times something like an ancient origin story, and still other times like wisdom literature. To give an example of each, we find references to creation in the poetry of Psalms (24:1–2; 136:5–9), in the wisdom literature of Proverbs (8:22–31), in the ancient origin mythology Job adapts to artfully describe God's power over creation (26:7–13), and in the ancient historiographical book of Genesis.[13]

When Christians read about creation in the Bible's poetic or mythological passages, we have little trouble recognizing the nonscientific language. For instance, when we read in the Bible about things like the "pillars of the deep" or the "four corners of the earth" or the earth's "cornerstone," we don't assume this is a scientific view of the world but understand that it is something more like a poetic description or a concept that was common at that time. The biblical truth in such texts is not that the earth is square or rests on an actual cornerstone. Even today we speak of the "sun rising" although we don't believe the sun literally rises. It's everyday language that we use with no intention of making scientific truth claims about the movement of the sun.

The real confusion comes when we turn to Genesis 1–2. Here things get a bit tricky, mostly because it's not clear what genre of literature we're dealing with. Sometimes Genesis seems as though it's offering a straightforward description, especially when specific rivers are mentioned (Tigris and Euphrates) or when the first human (Adam) shows up in later genealogies. At many other places, though, Genesis seems to be closer to poetry, wisdom literature, or an ancient origin story.

Like poetry, there is recurring rhythm and structure (six times we see this pattern: God said, "Let there be . . ." → and it was so → and it was good → and there was . . .). Also similar to poetry, Genesis has parallelism (what God creates on day one corresponds with what he creates on day four, what he creates on day two with day five, and day three with day six). Like wisdom literature, the Genesis account shows that Adam and Eve can either follow God's instruction or they can foolishly go their own way and ignore wisdom—which Proverbs interestingly describes as "a tree of life" (3:18).[14]

Genesis also resembles some ancient origin stories. In chapter 1 we highlighted parallels between Genesis and other ancient origin stories like the *Enuma Elish* and *Atrahasis*. We could add even more similarities: in Genesis, humans are made from both dirt and God's breath; in *Atrahasis*, they are made from both clay and the blood of a god. In another ancient story, the *Gilgamesh Epic*, there's even a snake who tricks a man out of life-prolonging fruit, which sounds a bit like the sly serpent we meet in Genesis. Such parallels lead scholars such as Tremper Longman to believe that Genesis is not attempting to give a scientific account of origins.[15] It might be better to see how Genesis is, in part, teaching by way of contrast. The message of Genesis to its ancient audience might be something like this: "You may have heard that creation was the result of violence between the gods and that humans were created as slaves, but here's how we would tell the story: In the beginning, one God (not many) created something good (not bad) by the power of his word (not through violence). This God gave a dignified calling to all humans (not just the king) to bear his image by properly caring for the earth (not to be slaves tasked with menial labor)."[16]

On top of all of this, when we read Genesis 1–2 closely we find several clues that the details are probably not all meant to be taken as literal history or science.[17] For example, there is evening and morning on days one through three of creation, even though there's no sun until day four (by which to mark evening and morning). Or we see in Genesis 1 that plants were created before humans; then in Genesis 2 it appears that humans have preceded plants. Additionally, there's a talking snake, God's footsteps are audible (even though God presumably doesn't have a body), God somehow breathes into Adam (even though God is not a physical being with lungs), and the man and woman have names that sound like something we'd find in fables: Adam means "human," and Eve means "life." There are even hints that Adam, Eve, and their children are not the only humans around (Gen. 4:14–17).

Fourth, Christians should not fear scientific research. Instead, they should expect that God's general revelation in his creation is reconcilable with God's special revelation in Scripture. If God is the creator of all things, then the scientific study of his creation has something to tell us about the world we live in. Christians throughout the centuries have recognized this as they sought to understand how God has revealed himself in both Scripture and the creation. (This, of course, means that Christians do not think that science can provide all the answers; after all, science can only describe the natural world, and Christians believe that the natural world is only a portion of reality.) The Christian acknowledges that there are truths about the natural world that are not mentioned in the Bible—truths about atoms and energy and DNA and disease.

What might scientific study teach Christians about the world we live in? The majority scientific consensus about our universe is that it is around fourteen billion years old, and the majority scientific consensus is that DNA and fossil records support the theory of the evolutionary development of species. As a biblical scholar with little training in science, I cannot speak to the data behind this. As one with much training in Scripture, however, I don't see any compelling reasons that force Christians to reject either an old universe or evolution (though I can respect those Christians who disagree with me). The ambiguities about how to read the Bible's creation references are too great to divide the church over the matters of the mechanics and time line of creation. Having said that, Christians must maintain belief in God as the transcendent and immanent creator, along with belief that humans are created in God's image. Such ideas seem foundational throughout the biblical witness, regardless of genre.

I think of Genesis 1–2 similarly to how I think of a parable—it reveals truth but is not a precise historical account.[18] We could think of it in comparison with the parable of the prodigal son (Luke 15:11–32). This parable reveals truth about God, sin, and humanity; however, that truth is not dependent on there being an actual, historical prodigal-son event. Similarly, the Genesis creation account reveals truth, but that truth may not be dependent on a literal six-day creation in which evening and morning occur without a sun, God seems to have lungs to breathe with and feet to make footsteps, and species appear instantaneously and distinct from one another. Genesis is teaching truths about God, creation, sin, and humanity; it is (probably) not trying to give its ancient audience a scientific description of the mechanics and time line of creation.

5

Jesus Christ

Who is Jesus? What is Jesus? Where is Jesus? When is Jesus? Why is Jesus? These questions have no simple answers. Jesus doesn't fit into any of our normal categories. He is truly unique. The Apostles' Creed acts to protect Jesus's uniqueness, even though the culture pressured the early church to do otherwise. Rather than making things simplistic, the creed holds many ideas in tension: Jesus is both human and divine; he is both killed and resurrected; he endured injustice and will bring justice; he departed and will return. Once again, we'll go through the Apostles' Creed line by line as we consider what makes the Christian metanarrative both distinct and compelling.

> I believe in Jesus Christ, his only Son, our Lord. He was conceived by the power of the Holy Spirit and born of the Virgin Mary. He suffered under Pontius Pilate, was crucified, died, and was buried. He descended to the dead. On the third day he rose again. He ascended into heaven, and is seated at the right hand of the Father. He will come again to judge the living and the dead.

I Believe in Jesus Christ, His Only Son, Our Lord

We've discussed some of this material in the previous chapters, so we'll just do a brief summary of what it means to confess Jesus as Christ, Son, and Lord. To claim that Jesus is "Christ" is to believe that he is the long-awaited, promised king of Israel who will bring restoration and whose kingdom will have no end. As the Christ, Jesus "fills to the full" the Old Testament story line and covenants. We've seen numerous examples of this in earlier chapters, so I'll point out only one more here. In the next line of the creed we see that Jesus was "conceived by the power of the Holy Spirit." This links Jesus to Israel's hopes for the Messiah—God's Servant—who will be empowered by the Spirit to rule with wisdom and justice, to bring good news to the poor along with restoration.[1]

To claim that Jesus is God's "only Son" is to believe that Jesus and the Father have a unique relationship: they are separate persons (Father and Son) yet one being (the one God). Although God's people are also called God's children, they do not share the same unity as the Father and Son, who have been in loving, united relationship for all eternity. As we saw earlier, when God created humans he created something distinct from himself, something of a different kind or substance. In contrast, the Father and Son are of the same kind or substance. When Christians confess Jesus as the Father's "only Son," they are stating that Jesus is the definitive revelation of God. As Jesus himself claims, "Whoever has seen me has seen the Father. . . . I am in the Father and the Father is in me" (John 14:9–10). Jesus reveals the distinct character of the Christian God—a God of self-giving love whose compassion is so immense that he takes upon himself humanity's frailty, suffering, and death in order to bring them healing.

To claim Jesus as "Lord" is to claim he is God, Ruler, and Master.[2] As we've already seen, the New Testament can speak of Jesus as Lord God—one who is worthy of our reverence and worship (John 1:1–3; Phil. 2:5–11). This conviction that Jesus is God shows up in the New Testament, in early church writings, and in the major Christian creeds.[3] To claim Jesus as Lord is also to claim that he is one's sovereign Ruler. Confessing Jesus as Lord is a political statement—a declaration that one's primary allegiance is to Lord Jesus and not anyone else, including Lord Caesar. Recall Paul's words to the Philippians that their "citizenship is in heaven" (3:20), which means that their loyalty is not ultimately with Caesar as citizens of Rome but with Jesus as citizens of the kingdom of heaven.[4] The heavenly citizen adopts the values and commitments of the kingdom of heaven, where King (Christ) Jesus reigns.

In the New Testament we can also discern a master-slave nuance that goes with the confession that Jesus is "Lord." Christians are to view themselves as servants, with Jesus as their master. This is not portrayed as a demeaning relationship; instead, Christians are called to partner with their master in his work of setting the world right. As Paul puts it, Christians are "slaves of righteousness" (Rom. 6:18–19), a status that, ironically, is the only life of true freedom—freedom from the manipulative, enslaving influence of sin, and freedom to be the people we were meant to be.

To speak of Jesus as Christ, only Son, and Lord is to make a claim not only about who Jesus is but also about who Christians are in relationship to him. If we confess that Jesus is the Christ, we are confessing that we are subjects of the king. We are committing to live as faithful citizens of his kingdom, working for restoration by embodying goodness and sacrificial love, motivated by the hope that the ultimate victory has been won. If we confess that Jesus is God's only Son, we are confessing that we know the character of God by looking to Jesus. We discover that we are loved in ways that surpass the imagination, because God took on flesh and suffered and died in order that we might be reconciled to him and one another. If we confess that Jesus is Lord (God, Ruler, Master), we are confessing that we are his creatures, who owe him our reverence and worship; we are his subjects, pledging him the allegiance of our hearts, minds, and bodies; we are his servants, ready to carry out his work of righteousness; and we are ministers of reconciliation, who are bringing holistic restoration to our neighbors. The creed is both a confession of faith and a commitment to faithfulness.

He Was Conceived by the Power of the Holy Spirit and Born of the Virgin Mary

To add a little clarity to the next line of the Apostles' Creed, we'll bring in another early confession, the Chalcedonian Creed (AD 451). The Chalcedonian Creed makes explicit what is implicit in the Apostles' Creed—namely, Jesus is both truly God and truly human. He is truly God ("conceived by the power of the Holy Spirit") and truly human ("born of the virgin Mary"). We see this idea captured beautifully in John's Gospel: "In the beginning was the Word [Jesus] and the Word was with God and the Word was God. The Word was with God in the beginning. . . . The Word became flesh and made his home among us" (1:1–2, 14). Thus Jesus is truly God ("the Word was God") and truly human ("the Word became flesh"). He's not half God, half human; nor is he truly God while pretending to be human; nor is he truly human while pretending to be God. Instead, the Chalcedonian Creed's balanced statement—truly God, truly human—concisely and accurately captures the New Testament's witness to the mystery of Jesus as the only one to be both truly human and truly divine.[5] He is both the eternal creator and a first-century Jew.

But what does any of this have to do with confessing that Mary was a virgin? Specifying that Mary was a virgin is, in part, a way of highlighting Jesus's divine nature. Jesus is not simply a human with two human parents.

God didn't look down at the human Jesus and decide to grant him a special status and superpowers. We do find some specially gifted humans in Scripture (like Samson or Elisha or John the Baptist), but they are not portrayed as God. Jesus is. In some mysterious way, a virgin gives birth to a human child, and that human child is simultaneously her son and the always-existing Son of the Father. The uncreated Creator enters his creation as a human creature!

In chapter 7 we'll look at certain heresies that arose in the early church. When we do so, we'll learn more about why this concept of Jesus's true humanity and true divinity was sometimes difficult to come to terms with. When we understand the ancient cultural setting, it's not surprising that some came to reject Jesus's divinity (claiming he was only human) and others rejected Jesus's humanity (claiming he was only divine and just appeared to be human). What might be surprising is that the church, despite cultural pressures, maintained belief that Jesus was an unprecedented, unique being who did not neatly fit into anyone's categories and whose nature could not be fully grasped.

Confessional statements like the Apostles' Creed help the church navigate confusing topics like the nature of Jesus. In this way the creed acts as a standard or rule. In fact, sometimes the Apostles' Creed is called the "rule of faith." In today's world we tend to view such rules with suspicion—arbitrary standards enforced by the powerful elites to serve their own purposes. However, such a picture doesn't fit the church's early rule of faith (although it may sometimes fit the later church's doctrines and practices). The earliest churches, after all, didn't wield much power. In addition, the rule of faith often made Christians look like misfits within the dominant culture—hardly a wise power play. For early Christians, the rule of faith basically formalized what was already the standard teaching and practice of the early churches. The rule was not a late imposition but more like a recognition of what was already reflected in early Christian worship, Scripture, and tradition.

Why might we need such a rule anyway? Is this just for eggheads in ivory towers? Does Jesus's true divinity and true humanity matter? Luke Timothy Johnson expertly explains the profound implications of this doctrine:

> If salvation were simply a matter of correcting some mistaken ideas that humans held, then Jesus need be no more than a good teacher sent by God in the manner of Moses. If salvation were simply a question of rectifying social structures that were oppressing people, then Jesus need be no more than a faithful prophet sent by God. . . . If salvation, in short, were simply a human matter, then Jesus needed be only a human being.
>
> But what if the New Testament speaks about salvation in terms quite other than didactic or political? What if the witness of the New Testament—and

> the life and practice of the church from the beginning—regarded salvation as something far more than the adjustment of thought or of social structures? Then the agent of salvation must fit the nature of salvation. If the salvation witnessed by the Scripture and experienced by the church could come only from God, then the agent of that salvation, Jesus Christ, must be considered fully divine (because we have received from him what only God could give) just as he is fully human (because we have seen and heard him as a human like us). And this is exactly what the earliest witnesses to the experience of Jesus tell us.[6]

The nature of Jesus reveals the nature of our problem. If Jesus is merely human, then the solution to our problem must be better thinking, better government, better education, and so on. But if Jesus is divine, then it tells us that the problem runs deeper, that we humans cannot fix ourselves. For the Christian worldview, this is pivotal. The claim that humans are not capable of saving themselves sets Christianity apart from many other worldview systems. For some, this will be off-putting; for others, it will ring true, accurately describing the situation one finds when looking inside at the brokenness of the self and when looking outside to the brokenness of our world.

The quotation above focuses on the implications of Jesus's divinity. What about Jesus's humanity? Why does it matter? In Michael Bird's excellent chapter on this topic, he explains how God becoming human makes it possible for humans to become like God: "The Son who knew no sin became sin to make sinners righteous. He took on mortality in order to make humans immortal."[7] You may need to read that twice. Bird is describing an important, though mysterious, interchange. As we learned from our study of Paul, Christ shared in what we are in order that we might share in what Christ is (2 Cor. 5:21).[8] Christ took on our brokenness so that we might take on his wholeness.

Jesus's true humanity and divinity tells us something else, which is spelled out in the New Testament book of Hebrews: "Since the children have flesh and blood, [Jesus] too shared in their humanity so that by his death he might break the power of him who holds the power of death—that is, the devil. . . . For this reason he had to be made like [them] in every way, in order that he might become a merciful and faithful high priest in service to God, and that he might make atonement for the sins of the people" (2:14, 17 NIV). The author of Hebrews uses the analogy of a high priest to portray how Jesus not only rescues his people but also intercedes and makes atonement on their behalf. For Christians, Jesus is the perfect mediator between God the Father and humanity. Because he is truly human, Jesus can perfectly relate to humans; because he is truly God, Jesus can perfectly relate to the Father.[9] What more could we hope for? In prayer, we speak to someone who is both empathetic and omnipotent.

He Suffered under Pontius Pilate and Was Crucified

In chapter 2 we saw that the cross was designed to bring both pain and shame. The Roman world looked at the cross and saw defeat, foolishness, curse, rejection, shame, isolation, and unrighteousness. In contrast, early Christians looked at the cross and saw the opposite: not defeat but victory, not foolishness but wisdom, not curse but forgiveness, not rejection but reconciliation, not shame but honor, not isolation but mediation, not unrighteousness but righteousness.

- They saw *victory*, for the cross is where Jesus defeated sin and death.
- They saw *wisdom*, for the true path to life is the way not of grasping but of giving.
- They saw *forgiveness*, for through the cross forgiveness is made available and extended in a new and far-reaching way.
- They saw *reconciliation*, for "God was reconciling the world to himself through Christ" (2 Cor. 5:19).
- They saw *honor*, for the cross epitomizes what makes Jesus so worthy of honor, glory, and praise.
- They saw *mediation*, for Jesus is not only the sacrifice but also the high priest who offers the sacrifice—the true high priest who, as truly God and truly human, can best intercede between humans and God.
- They saw *righteousness*, for the cross not only revealed Jesus's righteousness but also revealed how God is making things right.[10]

Perhaps above all, they saw *love*, for the cross declared in no uncertain terms that God loved the world enough to send his only Son to suffer and die to make it whole.

I like Scot McKnight's concise description of how Jesus dies "with us," "instead of us," and "for us": "We see the achievement of the cross in three expressions: Jesus dies 'with us'—entering into our evil and our sin and our suffering to subvert it and create a new way; Jesus dies 'instead of us'—he enters into *our* sin, *our* wrath, and *our* death; and Jesus dies 'for us'—his death forgives our sin, 'declares us right,' absorbs the wrath of God against us, and creates new life where there was once only death."[11] We might add to this description the way in which Johnson nicely captures the paradoxical nature of Jesus's death: "Blessing can come through one cursed (Gal. 3:6–14), freedom through a slave (Gal. 5:1), righteousness through one made sin (2 Cor. 5:21), wealth through one made poor (2 Cor. 8:9), wisdom through such obvious foolishness (1 Cor. 1:25), strength through weakness (2 Cor. 13:4), and life for all through one man's death (Rom. 5:12–21)."[12]

The Apostles' Creed does not specify which of these numerous descriptions is the primary way to understand the cross. Given the diversity of biblical descriptions, it's probably unwise to make any one the "main" achievement of the cross.[13] The cross of Christ is too large, too far-reaching, too oddly beautiful to be constrained by one description, accomplishment, or metaphor.

Plus there are more metaphors to consider. For example, when Jesus refers to his upcoming death, he speaks of his spilled blood as "the new covenant by my blood" (Luke 22:20). The language of "new covenant" picks up on a prophecy from the Old Testament book of Jeremiah, which we looked at earlier. God foretells the time of a new covenant, when he will be known more intimately, forgive sins in a more complete fashion, and empower his people to live more faithfully. When Jesus frames his own death in new-covenant terms, he characterizes his death as the beginning of a new order, a decisive shift in how humans relate to God. Because a covenant is two-sided, it entails a commitment from both parties—in this case, a commitment from both God and humans. By grace, God commits to making people right through Jesus. Those who enter into the grace of this new covenant are thereby pledging (covenanting) to live according to the norms of this sacred contract. The cross of Jesus, therefore, marks both the gateway into the new covenant and the path beyond the gateway. By entering the new covenant, Christians are committing to walk this path with Jesus and to do so willingly rather than being dragged limply or belligerently. Christians believe that, by grace, they do not walk this cross-shaped path alone. Instead, God has given us new hearts, his Holy Spirit, and fellow travelers to help us on our way.

He Died and Was Buried

I doubt anyone in the ancient world who knew of the brutality and public nature of crucifixion would have imagined that anyone could survive the cross. So why does the creed specify that Jesus *died*? This was likely intended to correct (or prevent) the belief that Jesus was not truly human and therefore only appeared to die. According to the creed, God became human and died. He didn't fake his death but truly died. And to drive this point home, the creed confesses that Jesus "was buried." The burial is further confirmation that Jesus was dead, placed in a guarded tomb from Friday evening to Sunday morning.[14]

As a side note, the reference to Pontius Pilate—"he suffered under Pontius Pilate"—offers a clear statement that the crucifixion was a historical event, not a fable or parable.[15] It's a confession that Jesus truly suffered death by crucifixion under the Roman governor Pilate. The historicity of the crucifixion is firmly established. References to Jesus's crucifixion are found not only throughout the New Testament (such as in the Gospels and the writings of Paul) but also in non-Christian Roman authors (such as Tacitus and Josephus).[16] Such evidence leads most historians to agree that the crucifixion of Jesus was a historical event (even if they disagree on its significance).[17]

He Descended to the Dead (or Hades)[18]

I must admit that this strikes me as one of the strangest lines in the Apostles' Creed. Would anything really be lost by leaving out this confession that Jesus "descended to the dead"? I'm not sure. The Nicene Creed doesn't include this bit, and Jesus's descent is only vaguely referenced in the New Testament. However, this claim about Jesus's descent has some biblical support (1 Pet. 3:19–20; 4:6; Eph. 4:8–10), along with some early Christian backing, and has been deemed worthy of inclusion for hundreds and hundreds of years.[19] Although this part of the confession may be less central to the Christian faith, it may nonetheless point us to some important aspects of Jesus's death. I'll mention three insights offered by three different scholars.

According to Alister McGrath, Jesus's descent to the dead is important because it underscores that Jesus "really did die"—that he shared in our humanity even to the point of death.[20] Luke Timothy Johnson suggests that Jesus's descent to the dead bears witness to "God's universal will for salvation" and his "cosmic victory."[21] That is, the good news of Jesus is relevant not only to those who live *after* the crucifixion but also in some mysterious way to those who died *before* the crucifixion. Last, Michael Bird points out the connection between Jesus's descent to the dead and his victory over death. For example, in Revelation 1:18 the resurrected Jesus claims, "I was dead, and now look, I am alive for ever and ever! And *I hold the keys of death and Hades*" (NIV). As Bird explains, "Because Jesus descended and rose, the doors of death and the gates of Hades cannot prevail over the church."[22]

On the Third Day He Rose Again

The resurrection of Jesus is one of Christianity's most basic claims. Without the resurrection of Jesus, Christianity doesn't make sense. Paul even says, "If Christ hasn't been raised, then your faith is worthless" (1 Cor. 15:17). What makes the resurrection of Jesus so fundamental to Christian faith? We learn in

Paul's first letter to the Corinthians that Jesus's resurrection is the guarantee for Christians (1) that their sins are forgiven, (2) that they can have hope in their own bodies being raised, and (3) that Jesus was who he claimed to be (see appendix A for further details). Jesus's resurrection signals that sin and death have been defeated by love. The way of the cross proves itself to be the way of wisdom because it's the way of victory, of restoration, of newness and wholeness.

Perhaps it's easier to see this from the negative side. If Jesus was not raised from the dead, the cross seems to signal Jesus's defeat and Rome's victory. If Jesus was not raised from the dead, there's less reason for Christians to hope in their own resurrection. If Jesus was not raised from the dead, there's much less reason to embrace sacrificial love as the wisest way to live and affect meaningful change in the world. If Jesus was not raised from the dead, there's no reason to look to Jesus's sacrifice as a means of forgiveness: apart from the resurrection, the crucifixion of Christ would simply be the death of a mortal—and the death of one mortal would seem incapable of remedying the worldwide problem of sin. The Christian framework collapses without the resurrection of Jesus.

The resurrection is like God's guarantee to redeem creation, to bring the biblical story to its rightful conclusion. What God created was good, and though it's now broken, the resurrection shows that creation is going to be renewed. Even more, the resurrection points to a redemption that is more than restoration. After all, Jesus's body was not simply restored to its pre-death condition; instead, Jesus's resurrected body had a beyond-nature quality to it. There is continuity with Jesus's former, physical body (he could eat, be touched, and was recognizable in a peculiar sort of way), but there was also something new about his body (he could appear and disappear, and he could ascend into heaven). Jesus's resurrected body, then, is like a foreshadowing of an incredible new reality—of "new creation." The resurrection of Jesus is a sign that God will not simply restore creation back to its original state but will transform it beyond its original goodness. He will make it what it was always meant to be.

He Ascended into Heaven, and Is Seated at the Right Hand of the Father

The ascension of Jesus is probably the most underrated doctrine among Christians. Somehow, the weightiness and beauty of the ascension often go overlooked. Let's highlight four fascinating implications of this doctrine. First, to confess that Jesus "ascended into heaven" is to confess, among other things, that Jesus is vindicated. He is proven to be the true Messiah, the rightful king. Notice how the creed links Jesus's ascension with his being seated at the right hand of the Father. Obviously, this seating arrangement is a metaphorical description of Jesus being in a position of honor and power. This imagery comes from Psalm 110, a popular psalm in the early church that celebrates the triumphant and far-reaching reign of the king, who has conquered his enemies: "The Lord said to my lord: Sit at my right hand until I make your enemies a footstool for your feet. The Lord will extend your mighty scepter from Zion, saying, 'Rule in the midst of your enemies'" (vv. 1–2 NIV).[23]

Second, the ascension reveals Jesus to be the greatest possible priest. Returning to Psalm 110, the triumphant king is further described as a "priest forever" (v. 4 NIV). Jesus is not only high king but he's also high priest. The book of Hebrews uses Psalm 110 to teach that Jesus is the perfect mediator between God and humans (Heb. 2:17–18; 7:11–10:18).[24] We find a similar notion in Paul's writing when he connects the ascension with Jesus's "priestly" role of interceding for his people: "Christ Jesus, who died—more than that, who was raised to life—*is at the right hand of God and is also interceding for us*" (Rom. 8:34 NIV).

Third, the ascension attests that Jesus is not only king and priest but also Lord God. When the apostles witness Jesus's ascension, they apparently recognize Jesus's divine status, because they respond by worshiping Jesus (Luke 24:50–52).[25] Paul proclaims that God raised Jesus up and "gave him the name above all names"—a name at which "everyone . . . might bow and . . . confess that Jesus Christ is Lord" (Phil. 2:9–11). In this passage, Paul is describing Jesus with language elsewhere used for Israel's one God (Isa. 45:23–24). Thus the ascended Jesus proves himself to be Lord and God, the one who rightly receives the praise and honor due his status. As the Nicene Creed confesses, Jesus is "true God from true God"; his resurrection and ascension are confirmation of that claim.

Fourth, the ascension confirms something about God's plan for the material world. Jesus didn't ascend to heaven in a merely spiritual or immaterial way; he ascended in a body that had physical properties—he could eat and be touched. Jesus did not resurrect in the flesh only to later die (or to shed his flesh) before going off into heaven. So what happened to Jesus's resurrected body if it didn't die or get left behind? In some mysterious way, his resurrected body ascended to heaven. Exactly how this works is not clear. What is a bit more clear, though, is why it matters. If Jesus ascended in a physical body, it shows that it's possible for our own broken bodies to be transformed so that they are made fit to dwell in God's new creation, when heaven overlaps with earth. It reveals that it's possible for our broken world to one day be joined to the wholeness of heaven. Jesus's ascended body signals a new reality—one in which an earthly body can somehow abide in a heavenly world. As C. S. Lewis writes, "If the story [of Jesus's ascension] is true, then a wholly new mode of being has arisen in the universe."[26]

If that last line sounds confusing, keep in mind the New Testament vision of restoration. It's not a vision of an immaterial or ghostly existence. It's not us leaving earth to go to heaven. Instead, heaven will come to earth. Somehow, heaven and earth will overlap, as depicted in the vision of New Jerusalem coming down from heaven to rest on the earth. In our current state of brokenness, neither our bodies nor our world is fit for heaven on earth. But the ascension gives us a glimpse of how the created world will be united with heaven. Because of Jesus, "heaven on earth" will not simply be a saying; it will also be a reality. This new world will be good and whole, free of sickness and sin and death.

Excursus

Assessing the Ascension

Before moving on, it's important to clarify that when Christians claim that Jesus ascended, they are not claiming that he's gone. In some ways, the opposite is the case. For example, in Acts the account of Jesus's ascension is followed by his very active and real presence among Christians throughout the world.[27] As one reads the New Testament, the ascended Jesus is not characterized as some distant figure who's enjoying a hands-off retirement from his work on earth; instead, Jesus is actively indwelling the church—shaping believers' hearts and minds and empowering them to carry out their kingdom ministry of reconciliation and restoration.

To make sense of this, we might need to undo some mistaken notions of heaven as being "far off"—almost as if it were a distant physical realm. Heaven might be "far off" if we are speaking about the distance between its wholeness and our brokenness. But in Scripture, "heaven" is a way of trying to give a name to something indescribable—that is, "heaven" is a word for where God "dwells." But since God is not bound by space and time, we must recognize that our language is really limited here. We must avoid pressing any terms too far. So it's fine to speak of heaven as a place, because this is about the best we can do as humans attempting to speak intelligibly about "where" God is. We just have to remain aware that heaven's not a literal place bound by our notions of space and time. Once we remember that, we might fathom how heaven—even though we can't really comprehend it—is where God is most present. From Scripture we learn that God is near enough to hear our prayers, to comfort, and to intervene.[28] With this in mind, we can connect Jesus's ascension with his nearness to us. The ascended Jesus is able to be present wherever and whenever his people are gathered.

So if heaven isn't "up there," then why did Jesus's followers see him *ascend*?[29] I don't know. Perhaps his followers hadn't worked out the metaphysical details enough to realize that God isn't bound by space and time, and maybe they thought heaven was literally above them. And maybe Jesus decided that, rather than give them a lesson in metaphysics, he would simply demonstrate his reunion to the Father in a way they would grasp—by ascending. Although we may scoff at this, let's be clear: just because we take for granted that heaven isn't "up there," it's not like we have any real idea of "where" the heavenly realm is. Perhaps we'd prefer Jesus to have slowly faded out as though he were being "beamed up" (or maybe we'd prefer him to have stepped into a TARDIS). But whatever way he might have demonstrated to us that he was "going to heaven," he would still have had to accommodate it to our limited understanding. It's not as though, two thousand years later, we have so advanced that we are now capable of comprehending the actual mechanics or pathway for getting from earth to heaven.

He Will Come Again to Judge the Living and the Dead

It's hard for contemporary ears to hear language about judgment. We tend to automatically hear it as language of condemnation. That is, when we think of Jesus's coming judgment, we default into notions of guilt, condemnation, and punishment. That is precisely why we must understand this part of the Apostles' Creed ("he will come again to judge . . .") in light of everything else we've looked at so far. Our thoughts of Jesus's judgment must be informed by our understanding of Jesus's character and mission. We have seen Jesus's character—he's merciful, good, and concerned with justice. We have seen Jesus's mission—he goes about bringing restoration and reconciliation through acts of power, prophetic teaching, and sacrifice. With this is mind, we are better able to understand what it means to confess that Jesus "will come again to judge the living and the dead."

We know that his judgment will be trustworthy and good.[30] He will not be arbitrary or petty but will judge rightly. We know that his judgment will not be corrupted by that which corrupts any earthly judicial system—fear, greed, power, and callousness. We know that his judgment will not be harsh on trivial matters and soft on important matters. We know from the cross that he is merciful. And we also know from the cross that he doesn't look on sin as a trivial matter—he knows better than anyone its destructive force, because he not only bore the weight of sin but also took sin to its limits and overcame it. We know that the world was made through Jesus and that he sustains the world, which means that he alone knows the extent of the damage sin has done and continues to do in a world that was created good. And we know that, as God, Jesus will be judging not simply our actions but our motives as well, for he alone can see our hearts. As one New Testament author writes, "Nothing in all creation is hidden from God's sight. Everything is uncovered and laid bare before the eyes of him to whom we must give account" (Heb. 4:13 NIV).

So based on what we know of Jesus, his judgment will be characterized by justice, mercy, perfect insight, and appropriate standards. Further, we expect that his judgment will fit in with his mission to set the world right, to bring restoration. The claim that Jesus will "come again" calls to mind those Scriptures where Jesus's return signals resurrection and restoration. He will return as the uncontested and rightful king who will make his people and his creation whole. Not only will he make them whole but he also will make them something new—new creatures in a new creation. Their newness will allow for a heaven-on-earth existence, where there is wholeness and harmony—physically, socially, and spiritually. This wonderful reality is why, as Bird points out, the most common biblical metaphor for Jesus's return is a wedding feast—a vision of celebration and union.[31] For many early Christians, Jesus's return sounded like good news, not bad news.

When God sets the world right, part of his work will include righting wrongs. He is a God of justice, which means that he is a God who cannot merely overlook sin, evil, rebellion, oppression, and the like. As C. S. Lewis considers God's goodness and justice, he writes, "God is the only comfort, He is also the supreme terror: the thing we most need and the thing we most want to hide from."[32] Lewis's point is that the goodness of God is a comforting thing because it assures us that there really is such a thing as right and wrong, good and evil; it's also a scary thing, because—if we are honest with ourselves—we are aware that our hearts and actions have often been at odds with God's perfect goodness and justice. So as we consider the judgment to come, we may find it both comforting and scary. It's comforting because we are assured that evildoers will one day face judgment, that tyrants and sex traffickers and oppressors must stand before the judgment seat of Christ. It's comforting because we have hope that the oppressed and those denied justice will one day be vindicated. The bad guys don't win in the end, even if it sometimes feels that way now. It's scary, though, because we know that we're not always (or often) the good guys. We want those bad guys to face justice, but we may not want to face justice ourselves. After all, who of us feels capable to offer a defense for our own vices, our own pettiness, greed, apathy, pride, selfishness, and the like?

What will the judgment be based on? One thing—or possibly two. Most importantly, judgment will be based on whether one has been united with Christ.[33] By putting one's faith in Christ, one is united with Christ. Through Christ, one finds forgiveness and wholeness, deliverance from sin and death.[34] So the judgment is based (at least in part) on faith in Christ.

And what is the second thing that judgment might be based on? Well, here is where Scripture gets a little hard to pin down. In some places, it seems that we are saved by God's grace when we put our faith in Jesus, regardless of the future works we will or won't do. This seems to be the case in Paul's letter to the Ephesians: "For it is by grace you have been saved, through faith—and this not from yourselves, it is the gift of God—not by works" (2:8–9 NIV). However, we also find references in the New Testament where the coming judgment seems to be based on one's actions. For example, Jesus describes a judgment scene where one's fate is determined by how one treated "the least of these" (Matt. 25:31–46). And Paul tells the Corinthian church, "We must all appear before the judgment seat of Christ, so that each of us may receive what is due us *for the things done while in the body, whether good or bad*" (2 Cor. 5:10 NIV; see also Rev. 20:12).

So how do we reconcile these two potentially conflicting ideas? Is the coming judgment based on faith or on deeds? Ultimately, we trust that judgment will be based on our union with Jesus. Neither our faith nor our works make us righteous. Jesus does. The real question is how our faith and works play into our being united with Christ. Based on Scripture, I'm inclined to believe that we enter into union with Christ through our declaration of faith and not by works; however, this declaration of faith is simultaneously a declaration of commitment to faithful actions.[35] As one New Testament author puts it, "Faith by itself, if it is not accompanied by action, is dead" (James 2:17 NIV). Similarly, John writes, "The one who claims, 'I know [Jesus],' while not keeping his commandments, is a liar, and the truth is not in this person" (1 John 2:4). A faith that does not result in some degree of faithfulness is not Christian faith—such "faith" apparently doesn't entail lasting, saving union with Christ. I'm aware that this does not answer the question in a tidy way, but it does maintain the tension one finds in Scripture: Jesus saves by his grace; humans access this saving grace through a declaration of faith, which is also a declaration of loyalty.

Last, in the Bible it seems that one's actions might also be related to one's level of reward or punishment (Matt. 25:14–30; Luke 10:14). What exactly this means, I'm not sure. How can heaven on earth be any more heavenly? What could greater reward even entail within a holistically restored world? I don't know. Though, to be honest, I think it would feel only right if there were some way for the martyrs and Mother Teresas to be honored above me. And what about hell? Can hell be any more hellish? Well, actually, on this second question, there are some theories, which I tackle in appendix B.

So let's return to where the chapter began. Who is Jesus? What is Jesus? Where is Jesus? When is Jesus? Why is Jesus? Here's a brief recap:

- *Who?*—Jesus is the messianic king, God's only Son, Lord (God, Ruler, Master), high priest, savior, and a first-century Jew murdered under Pilate.
- *What?*—Jesus is truly God and truly human, eternal, unmade, resurrected with a renewed and glorious body.
- *Where?*—The Son was with the Father from all eternity, he was on the earth in the first century, he then ascended to heaven, and he is now present with the Father and with his people wherever they gather.
- *When?*—The Son is past, present, and future.
- *Why?*—Because of his self-giving love, the Son became human in order to redeem, restore, reconcile, renew, and bring reward and retribution to a broken and rebellious creation.

6

The Holy Spirit and the Church

We come now to the final section of the Apostles' Creed. After the lengthy confession about Jesus, this last bit of the creed feels like a rapid-fire list of six doctrines. If we slow down, take our time, and dig a little deeper into these doctrines, we can uncover their wisdom and their beauty. As we do so, we may find ourselves compelled by the vision of the good life that we discover embedded in these doctrines.

> I believe in the Holy Spirit, the holy catholic Church, the communion of saints, the forgiveness of sins, the resurrection of the body, and the life everlasting. Amen.

I Believe in the Holy Spirit

To say "I believe in the Holy Spirit" is not the same as saying "I totally understand the Holy Spirit." It's quite common for Christians to think of the Holy Spirit as more mysterious than the Father or the Son. So who or what is the Holy Spirit? We can start by noticing how the New Testament characterizes the Spirit with both personal and impersonal descriptors.[1] Like a *person*,[2] the Spirit bears witness, teaches, speaks, testifies, makes known, decides, and leads. Like something *impersonal*, the Spirit is referred to as firstfruits, a seal, and a pledge. Notice how this same combination of personal and impersonal shows up in Alister McGrath's description of the Spirit, where the

Spirit "brings life," "brings power," "convicts us of our sin," "is a pledge of our salvation," and "is our comforter."[3]

How can the Spirit appear both personal and impersonal? Once again we are reminded that our language is limited when describing a reality that is beyond our full comprehension. Part of the reason the Holy Spirit does not easily fit into our categories is that the Spirit is God. God's personhood is not limited in the ways human personhood is. More precisely, Christians think of the Holy Spirit as the Third Person of the Trinity. According to the doctrine of the Trinity, God is one being who is three persons (Father, Son, Spirit). We have already seen that Christians believe in one God who is both Father and Son. Now we complete the picture by learning about the Third Person of the Trinity: the Holy Spirit.

The distinct personhood and divinity of the Holy Spirit is attested to in both Scripture and church tradition. For instance, in statements where the Spirit is placed alongside the Father and Son, the New Testament implies that the Holy Spirit is God: Jesus instructs his followers to baptize people "in the name of the *Father* and of the *Son* and of the *Holy Spirit*" (Matt. 28:19); Paul blesses the church in "the grace of the *Lord Jesus Christ*, the love of *God*, and the fellowship of the *Holy Spirit*" (2 Cor. 13:13).[4] What is implicit in these Scriptures is later made explicit in church tradition. For example, the Nicene-Constantinopolitan Creed (AD 381) clearly claims that the Holy Spirit is God: "We believe in the Holy Spirit, the Lord, the giver of life. . . . With the Father and the Son he is worshiped and glorified."[5]

To summarize, the Holy Spirit (1) is part of the Trinity, (2) has personal and impersonal characteristics, and (3) works in the church—loving, uniting, guiding, empowering, convicting, comforting, creating, revealing, and saving. As we study the Holy Spirit, we get a picture of a God who is near. He's not the kind of God who merely speaks words of love while avoiding the messy business of close relationships. Nor is he the kind of God who tells folks how to live their lives and then leaves them to work it out by themselves. Instead, the Holy Spirit is the *loving*, *empowering*, *uniting* presence of God in the lives of his people.

- The Spirit is the *loving* presence of God. Paul's description of this is beautiful: "God's love has been poured out into our hearts through the Holy Spirit" (Rom. 5:5 NIV). "The Spirit himself testifies . . . that we are God's children!" (Rom. 8:16 NIV).[6]
- The Spirit is the *empowering* presence of God. This empowering work can take many forms, including the power to witness, to resist sin, to do miracles, and to be gifted to serve. As God dwells in believers through the Holy Spirit, his very real presence provides comfort and instruction (John 14:15–27).

- The Spirit is the *uniting* presence of God: "God sent the Spirit of his Son into our hearts," which allows us to call God "Abba, Father" (Gal. 4:6 NIV). The Spirit unites us with Christ, which frees us from the manipulative power of sin, enabling us to live a transformed life characterized by the "fruit of the Spirit"—a life of "love, joy, peace, patience, kindness, goodness, faithfulness, gentleness, and self-control" (Gal. 5:22–23).[7]

We could go on and on, but hopefully this suffices to show that the Holy Spirit plays a vital role in the Christian's life.

The doctrine of the Holy Spirit provides further reason to see that at the center of all reality is Love. God is three persons who, through all eternity, have been in loving community, united as one. It might be possible to think of the Holy Spirit as the Love that unites the Father and the Son. After all, this is consistent with the Spirit's work elsewhere, where the Spirit unites believers with God and pours God's love upon them. This would also help make sense of why Scripture refers to the Holy Spirit as both the Spirit of the Son (Gal. 4:6; Phil. 1:19) and of the Father (Rom. 8:11).[8] That is, the Spirit is both "of the Father" and "of the Son," because the Spirit acts as something like the loving bond that unites Father and Son. We are again reminded of how the Holy Spirit is "personal" in ways that are beautiful and unexpected. I like C. S. Lewis's description: "[This], by the way, is perhaps the most significant difference between Christianity and all other religions: that in Christianity God is not a static thing—not even a person—but a dynamic, pulsating activity, a life, almost a kind of drama. . . . The union between the Father and the Son is such a live concrete thing that this union itself is also a Person."[9]

Perhaps more than any other worldview, Christianity places loving relationship at the center of reality. A dynamic, unifying love characterizes the ultimate reality—the triune, three-persons-in-one God. This implies that Christians can fully bear the image of God only in community. If God exists in loving community, then reflecting the image of God requires us to be in loving community.[10] This is exactly the kind of thing we find in Scripture: the importance of a united, loving community—from Adam and Eve[11] to Israel to the church. How appropriate, then, that the next two lines in the creed focus on the Christian community.

I Believe in . . . the Holy Catholic Church

This statement is not a confession of allegiance to the Roman Catholic Church. The term "catholic" here is lowercase *c*; it means "universal." That is, the creed is claiming that the church is not limited to one location, race, or nationality. This confession naturally flows from the biblical teaching that believers are one in Christ, a unity that breaks through ethnic, social, national, and gender barriers.[12] For example, Paul can write, "You are all God's children through faith in Christ Jesus. All of you who were baptized into Christ have clothed yourselves with Christ. There is neither Jew nor Greek; there is neither slave nor free; nor is there male and female, for you are all one in Christ Jesus" (Gal. 3:26–28). Notice how Paul highlights three potential barriers to community: ethnicity (Jew/Gentile), social status (slave/free), and gender (male/female). Paul's point is not that Christians cease to be Jews or Gentiles, it's not that there are no more Christian slaves or free persons, and it's not that men and women stop being male and female. Paul's point is that these differences are no longer barriers to unity.[13]

This unity alongside diversity should be expected among a people who have pledged to follow the way of Christ, the way of humility and hospitality. After all, the inclusive nature of the church can trace its roots back to Jesus's practice of being in humble solidarity with marginalized people (lepers, prostitutes, tax collectors, Samaritans, centurions, blind people, lame people, widows, etc.). We can also see hospitality throughout the Old Testament, for example in the torah (Lev. 19:34; Deut. 10:18–19), in Abraham's example (Gen. 18), and in God's providing a home for humanity (Gen. 1–2). Similarly, Paul exhorts the church to embody the kind of Jesus-like humility and hospitality that is fitting for those who are united in Christ (Phil. 2:1–11).[14]

Not only is unity alongside diversity characteristic of Jesus's ministry, not only is it characteristic of the early church but it's also characteristic of new creation—of heaven on earth. The book of Revelation offers a glimpse of a time when people "from every tribe and language and people and nation" who have been made "a kingdom and priests to serve our God . . . will reign on the earth" (5:9–10 NIV). The vision is not of a single race or ethnicity but of the awesome beauty of unity alongside diversity. As God is three distinct persons who are united as one being, so will God's people bear God's image by being distinct persons who are united as one people in the kingdom of God.

A catholic/universal church should be marked by a value system that promotes unity alongside diversity. The church doesn't achieve this by adopting an "anything goes" ethic. Instead, the church does this by recognizing the shared dignity and calling of each person. Each person has dignity as one who is made in the image of God, one whom Jesus loved so much that he voluntarily became human, suffered, and died on his or her behalf. All people also have a calling to accept the love of Christ, to align their lives according to his kingdom, and to use their gifts and talents and resources for the good. Whereas the surrounding culture (both then and now) might prioritize ethnicity or social status (or wealth or beauty or whatever), the Christian is to prioritize Christ and his kingdom. (Here we might recall what we studied about Acts, where converting to Christianity entails a kind of cultural conversion.) A life dedicated to Christ and his kingdom is not an "anything goes" lifestyle but a lifestyle of love and holiness.

We have discussed the Christian concept of love already, but we haven't discussed holiness much. What exactly does the Apostles' Creed mean when it confesses belief in the *holy* catholic church? For help with this, we turn to the New Testament book of 1 Peter. In this work, Peter calls the church to "be holy, because [God is] holy" (1:15–16). The church's holiness is rooted in God's holiness; the church is holy because it is united with Christ. This means the church's holiness ought to correspond to God's holiness as revealed in Christ. When we think of "holy" today, we may think of people who are prudish or snobbish. That is not reflective of God's holiness, which is on display in his perfect justice, purifying love, and righteous purposes. If the church is to reflect God's holiness, it will do so by reflecting God's justice, love, and purposes.

The word "holy" can mean "set apart." To be "set apart" is not synonymous with being distant. Jesus was "set apart" in his holiness, yet he was present with the righteous and unrighteous. To be "set apart" is not about being *distant* but about being *distinct*—a distinction grounded in God's holiness. A holy church ought to be set apart by its distinct compassion, distinct goodness and justice, and distinct mission to bring reconciliation through lives of sacrificial love, abiding joy, and humble generosity. We see this theme of being set apart throughout the biblical plotline.

- At creation, humans were set apart to bear God's image, which included representing God in their caring rule over creation.
- Israel was set apart to represent God by being "a kingdom of priests and a *holy* nation" (Exod. 19:6 NIV), showing "wisdom and insight to the nations" (Deut. 4:6).
- The church is likewise set apart; it is "a chosen people, a royal priesthood, a *holy* nation, God's special possession" (1 Pet. 2:9–10 NIV).
- In fact, the Christian hope of heaven on earth pictures Christians continuing to reflect God's holiness as "a kingdom and priests . . . [who] will reign on the earth" (Rev. 5:10 NIV).[15]

A proper concern for holiness does not result in a stuffy religion. Instead, as we learn from James, "Religion that God our Father accepts as pure and faultless is this: to look after orphans and widows in their distress and to keep oneself from being polluted by the world" (James 1:27 NIV). Pure religion reflects God's love and holiness. If at the center of all reality is a God who is loving, impartial, and self-giving, then it makes complete sense that pure religion would reflect that through loving, impartial, and self-giving behaviors, such as caring for the most vulnerable in society (orphans and widows). And if at the center of all reality is a God who is good and just, then it makes sense that pure religion would reflect that by remaining "unpolluted" by the unjust and destructive power of sin. The church cannot be a holy people—a people set apart—if Christians practice an "anything goes" ethic. Instead, the church embraces its status as "holy" when Christians reflect God's holiness—his justice, love, and good purposes.

As Christians confess belief in "the holy catholic Church," we are often aware that many of our churches fail to embody proper holiness or catholicity. In this case, the creed acts as both a mirror and a compass. Like a mirror, it shows us who we are (sinners united in Christ, who are failing to live up to our holy calling); like a compass, it points us in the direction we are meant to go (a holy and loving community, working together as ministers of reconciliation).

One final note on the church that isn't mentioned in the Apostles' Creed: the Nicene Creed indicates that the church is "apostolic," which means that the church must be rooted in the teachings and witness of the apostles—those core leaders of the first generation of Christians who knew Jesus and his teachings in a special way. How might the church remain apostolic when it's been nearly two thousand years since the apostles died? The church's conviction is that the apostolic voice is found in the New Testament and in the rule of faith. The church remains apostolic, then, by submitting to the authority of Scripture and by honoring the wisdom of the rule of faith. This should be a warning that any church that becomes untethered from the Bible and the rule of faith is at risk of becoming something other than Christian.

I Believe in . . . the Communion of Saints

The language of the Apostles' Creed can once again be misleading here. "Communion" is not referring to the Eucharist, and "saints" is not referring to a group of super-holy dead people whom we've named cities after. "Saints" is a word that can be translated "holy ones." We just learned about how being "holy" is being "set apart," and what that entails. So when the creed mentions "saints," it includes every Christian, because all Christians are meant to be "set apart"—distinctly reflecting God's holiness.[16]

So if "saints" is a nickname for all Christians, what does "communion" mean? It means something like "fellowship," "partnership," or "solidarity." It's speaking of the bond that Christians should have with one another if indeed they have been united with Christ, if they are siblings in one family with God as their Father. This bond of communion among Christians resembles the bond within healthy families. Healthy families laugh together and cry together; they give their time and resources when another family member is in need; they desire each member of the family to thrive; and at their best, they work together by doing good in their communities.

We see such familial communion in the first biblical description of the brand-new church: "All the believers were together and had everything in common. They sold property and possessions to give to anyone who had need. . . . They broke bread in their homes and ate together with glad and sincere hearts" (Acts 2:44–46 NIV). We find a similar ethos in Paul's writings. As Paul is collecting funds for the struggling church in Jerusalem, he writes to the Corinthians: "It isn't that we want others to have financial ease and you financial difficulties, but it's a matter of equality. At the present moment, your surplus can fill their deficit so that in the future their surplus can fill your deficit" (2 Cor. 8:13–14).[17] Paul assumes that Christians in one location have a natural obligation to help out fellow Christians in another geographic, ethnic, or cultural location. Of course, for Christians this is all founded on God's gracious love: "This is how we know love: Jesus laid down his life for us, and we ought to lay down our lives for our brothers and sisters. But if a person has material possessions and sees a brother or sister in need but refuses to help—how can the love of God dwell in a person like that?" (1 John 3:16–17). This loving solidarity extends beyond financial care. For instance, we see that the church's family bond includes emotional solidarity as well. Paul tells the Roman church, "Rejoice with those who rejoice; mourn with those who mourn" (Rom. 12:15 NIV).

So to confess belief in the "communion of saints" is to confess that one belongs to the family of God, with the privileges and obligations that go along with that. This line in the creed makes me uncomfortable—in part because I don't want to share my time, resources, or emotions, and in part because I don't want to be taken advantage of by lazy or manipulative people. Sometimes our family members (whether it's our biological family or our church family) will take advantage of us, and that's a risk we must be willing to take as Christians. However, when a family member has a pattern of manipulation and deception, sometimes the most loving thing the family can do is to stop enabling these unhealthy patterns so as not to keep contributing to destructive behavior. We can see this in Paul's advice for dealing with those living undisciplined lives: "If anyone doesn't want to work, they shouldn't eat" (2 Thess. 3:10). Obviously, Paul is not referring to those unable to work because of age, infirmity, or unavoidable unemployment—he's referring to those who are able but not willing.

All this is to say that the church is called to be a gracious family, one where members love one another generously—but it's also to be a discerning family that won't enable patterns of destructive behavior. There's not a one-size-fits-all method for how to carry this out, but one should start by trying to embody this at the local level—practicing communion solidarity with members of one's church. We pursue the beautiful and messy work of loving those in our local church and then extend this love to others, Christian and non-Christian.

Excursus
Eucharist

Although the "communion" of saints is not referring to the Eucharist (also known as the Lord's Supper), it would be a shame not to mention this sacrament in a book that's covering the basics of Christianity. The observation of the Eucharist goes back to Jesus sharing the Passover meal with his disciples right before he was betrayed. Here's how the Gospel of Luke reports it:

> When the time came, Jesus took his place at the table, and the apostles joined him. He said to them, "I have earnestly desired to eat this Passover with you before I suffer. I tell you, I won't eat it until it is fulfilled in God's kingdom." After taking a cup and giving thanks, he said, "Take this and share it among yourselves. I tell you that from now on I won't drink from the fruit of the vine until God's kingdom has come." After taking the bread and giving thanks, he broke it and gave it to them, saying, "This is my body, which is given for you. Do this in remembrance of me." In the same way, he took the cup after the meal and said, "This cup is the new covenant by my blood, which is poured out for you." (22:14–20)

Over the years, the church has continued to honor this meal by coming together and breaking bread (Jesus's body) and drinking wine or juice (Jesus's blood). Here's how my colleague and friend John Mark Hicks summarizes this sacred event:

> *The Lord's supper is God's gracious presence among his people*. As a gospel event, God takes the initiative and graciously offers himself in communion with his people. The supper is God's gracious, reconciling and forgiving presence.

. . . Primarily the supper is a divine act rather than a human one. God graciously works hope, assurance and peace in our hearts at the table. . . .

The Lord's supper is our grateful response in covenantal commitment. While the supper is a divine act, it is nevertheless also a human one. It is a human affirmation of covenantal commitment and thanksgiving. When we eat and drink, we commit ourselves to the values of the gospel which the supper embodies. . . . When we sit at table with the Lord who humbled himself to give his life for others, we commit ourselves to the humble service of others. . . .

The Lord's supper is a fellowship of Divine Host with human guests. God comes to his people at the table. He is genuinely present through the living host, Jesus Christ. It is no mere symbolic fellowship, but an encounter with the Living God. That encounter . . . remembers the victory of God over the grave. . . . The present table is a foretaste of the eschatological table in the new heaven and new earth where God will fully dwell with his people.[18]

I Believe in . . . the Forgiveness of Sins

The claim "I believe in the forgiveness of sins" makes sense in a worldview where there truly is a right way and a wrong way to live. This confession carries an implicit acknowledgment that we sometimes (or often) choose the wrong way: we go wrong in our actions, our hearts, and our thoughts. We sin against God, ourselves, others, and even creation. To believe in forgiveness implies that our wrongs cannot simply be forgotten; they must be dealt with. Even more, it implies that we are incapable of fully righting our wrongs: we need mercy, not justice. We are confessing that if God doesn't have mercy, we are in trouble.

When we grasp this, we realize that forgiveness is not an inalienable right. We cannot presume that God has to either forgive or turn a blind eye. A holy and just God must right the wrong of sin. The scary question is "How will God deal with the damage and guilt of sin?" In perhaps the most beautiful event in the cosmos, God deals with sin by taking it on himself on the cross. "He was pierced for our transgressions . . . [and] the punishment that brought us peace was on him, and by his wounds we are healed" (Isa. 53:5 NIV). What a shame that the unique and shocking nature of this event has become so familiar! What a shame that its scandalous beauty goes underappreciated!

In the Christian worldview, God is not a kindly, grandfatherly figure who can easily forgive sin, as if sin weren't really that big of a deal. Instead, the cross shows precisely what a big deal sin is. Its presence is so corrosive, its damage is so far-reaching, its guilt is so damning that the only way to undo its effects is for God to become human, suffer, and die. In his life and death, Jesus exposes sin for what it is, defeats its power, bears its punishment, reverses its devastating effects, and displays his unimaginable love and mercy. The resurrection is proof that Jesus won and sin lost.

God has done for us what we could not do for ourselves. We must receive forgiveness as a gift that flows from God's grace and mercy. God doesn't force this grace on people but makes it freely available to them. In the New Testament, we read how people put themselves in a position to receive God's gift of forgiveness through the practices of confession, repentance, and baptism (1 John 1:9; Acts 2:38; 3:19).[19]

- Christian *confession* is threefold: (1) we confess that we have sinned and need mercy, (2) we confess our faith in Christ by trusting him to rescue us, and (3) we confess by pledging our faithfulness to Christ as our King and Lord.
- Christians practice *repentance* by striving to align ourselves—heart, soul, mind, and strength—with God's will. We don't do this alone but are aided by the Holy Spirit.
- In *baptism*, the initiate is immersed in or sprinkled with water. This sacred act marks the believer as being united with Christ's death and resurrection (Rom. 6:1–14). We "die" to our former life (characterized by the guilt and control of sin) and are "raised" to a new life (characterized by the grace and power of the Spirit).

Since we've received grace, mercy, and forgiveness, we are to be a people characterized by grace, mercy, and forgiveness. In the New Testament, forgiveness of sins can be described as forgiving guilt, forgiving debt, restoring relationship, being bought out of slavery, and rescue.[20] As a result, those who confess the creed should strive for lives that reflect this reality by engaging in acts of forgiveness, mercy, generosity, reconciliation, and restoration.

I Believe in . . . the Resurrection of the Body and the Life Everlasting

Since we've already discussed the resurrection and the life to come, I won't add much here. This part of the Apostles' Creed is simply making clear what is implied by Jesus's resurrection and ascension. That is, Jesus's resurrection and ascension don't only tell us something about Jesus but they also tell us something about the future. Just as Jesus's body rose from the dead and can now abide in heaven, so will the Christian's body rise from the dead and be able to abide in heaven on earth. As Paul tells the Philippians, "We eagerly await a Savior . . . , the Lord Jesus Christ, who, by the power that enables him to bring everything under his control, will transform our lowly bodies so that they will be like his glorious body" (3:20–21 NIV).

The creed specifies resurrection of the "body." Once again, we are reminded that Christians anticipate having physical bodies in the afterlife rather than being immaterial spirits. The ancient Greco-Roman world might have been okay with some notion of a *spiritual* life after death, but it scoffed at the Christian notion of a *bodily* life after death. That's because the ancient Greek world could be dualistic, assuming that the spiritual was superior (and possibly immortal) and the physical was inferior.[21] Christians, however, believe that God created the world "good," which includes our physical bodies. Christians also believe that Jesus was resurrected in a physical body that ascended to heaven. Therefore, Christians believe that God's work of restoration and renewal will restore and renew our physical bodies. Exactly how this will take place is a mystery, but I find Michael Bird's analogy really helpful: "Biochemists inform us that during a seven-year cycle the molecular composition of our bodies is completely changed. But in spite of the permanent state of mutation in which we exist, our personal identity is maintained, and we are the same personal and psychological entity that we have always been. The same is . . . true about our future resurrection bodies; they are remade, but we remain the same person."[22]

God will not limit his restoration to humanity but will in some way extend his renewal to the whole creation.[23] The one who created all things, sustains all things, and has reconciled all things will finish his masterwork (Col. 1:15–20). Heaven will overlap earth as God sets about making everything new (Rev. 21:1–5). The magnificent nature of this renewed reality is captured in the creed's language of "life everlasting." In this case, "everlasting" refers not only to how long it will last (forever) but also to its quality (infinitely good).[24]

Despite how otherworldly and possibly escapist this part of the creed sounds, it actually maps onto our this-world experience. Notice how the worldview we derive from this confession informs our everyday lives. When we look through these lenses, we see something that makes sense: (1) the world is in need of repair; (2) this broken world cannot be fixed by human effort alone—as history seems to prove again and again; (3) our current experience feels like limbo—we see hopeful signs of good to come, but we also grieve at the ongoing brokenness that surrounds us; and (4) we feel compelled to find ways to participate now in the work of restoration and reconciliation.

Amen

I'll conclude with Luke Timothy Johnson's apt comments on the word "Amen." His closing thoughts fit our recurring theme that the creed should inform one's life and one's worldview: "The Creed ends with the ancient Hebrew word 'Amen.' Amen usually concludes a prayer . . . and means: 'may it be in the manner you have spoken.' It declares our agreement and confirmation. . . . [By saying Amen, we mean] 'May we actually agree with these words we have said . . . and may our lives be ones that actually express these truths in a consistent and compelling way.'"[25]

PART 3

A CHRISTIAN POINT OF VIEW

7

The Distinctiveness of the Christian Faith

> Every [person] in the street must hold a metaphysical system, and hold it firmly. The possibility is that he [or she] may have held it so firmly and so long as to have forgotten all about its existence. This latter situation is certainly possible; in fact, it is the situation of the whole modern world. The modern world is filled with [people] who hold dogmas so strongly that they do not even know that they are dogmas.
>
> —G. K. Chesterton, *Heretics*

If you wear glasses or contacts for long enough, you sometimes get so used to them that you forget they're there. You stop paying attention to how the frames of your glasses outline your vision. You go numb to the discomfort of contacts. The same thing happens with our worldview "lenses." We may have looked through them so long that we've forgotten they're there. Or, even stranger, we may have gotten so used to our worldview lenses that we don't even realize that we're wearing such lenses—we think we're just looking at the world with no worldview, no metanarrative framework, nothing guiding our interpretations. This chapter will help us see that we all wear some sort of worldview lenses, even if we don't realize it. By comparing the Christian worldview with other worldviews, we become more aware of how we see the world and how others might see the world differently.

People sometimes think of Christianity as just another religion that is basically similar to every other religion, only with a few peculiar twists—like believing that Jesus was born of a virgin, crucified, and then came back to life. Such an attitude, however, reveals a gap in one's understanding of the Christian faith. In this chapter, I aim to show two things. First, I hope to give a clearer picture of how Christianity's distinctive worldview runs much deeper than a few odd beliefs and practices. Second, I want to demonstrate how some of Christianity's distinctive traits have become so integrated into contemporary Western thinking that we now take them for granted; that is, we are so familiar with these ideas that we forget they are Christian rather than the common wisdom of all cultures and ages. To help with this, I will survey a few recent books. The first, by Larry Hurtado, focuses on the way in which early Christians were peculiar in the ancient Greco-Roman world.[1] The second, by Alister McGrath, shows how early Christian orthodoxy differed from early Christian heresy in substantial ways.[2] The third, by Iain Provan, takes a wide-angle approach in order to capture how the Christian worldview differs in significant ways from other worldviews—both ancient and modern.[3]

Larry Hurtado's *Destroyer of the Gods*

In *Destroyer of the Gods*, Larry Hurtado, an expert in early Christian history, offers a balanced and fascinating account of early Christian distinctiveness and its impact. Hurtado is the kind of author who chooses his words carefully and deliberately, so let me quote him at length, and then I'll explain in more detail.

> Early Christianity of the first three centuries was a different, even distinctive, kind of religious movement in the cafeteria of religious options of the time. That is not simply my historical judgment; it is what people of the time thought as well. In fact, in the eyes of many in the Roman era, Christianity was very odd, even objectionably so. . . . When considered as a religion in that time, the most obvious oddity was Christianity's "atheism"—that is, the refusal to worship the traditional gods. . . . But Christianity was not simply odd; it was deemed dangerous to traditional notions of religion and, so it was feared, also for reasons of social stability. . . .
>
> [In addition to occasional martyrdom] there were other and much more frequent costs . . . for being a Christian in the first three centuries. For example, you might receive harassment and ostracism from family members, friends, and associates. Christian slaves of pagan masters might well have suffered corporal punishment, and wives of pagan husbands might well have received verbal and physical abuse. . . . [The] social costs of becoming a Christian in the first three centuries comprise another way in which early Christianity was distinctive. . . .

> From earliest years, however, what became Christianity went transethnic and translocal, addressing males and females of all social levels and generating circles of followers who were expected to commit to particular beliefs and behaviors from the point of initiation. . . .
>
> [One] of my purposes was to address, though only briefly, our cultural amnesia. The point is that each of the distinguishing features discussed in this book has become for us a commonplace assumption about religion. For example, whether we align ourselves with any religious faith or not, we likely think and speak in terms of a single deity, "God." . . . We also tend to think of ethnicity and religious affiliation as, in principle, distinguishable, with religious affiliation typically thought of as a voluntary choice. . . . [Early] Christianity actually introduced effectively the notion of a religious identity separate from one's national/ethnic identity. . . .
>
> The early Christian emphasis on, and teaching about, everyday behavior as central to Christian commitment is yet another distinctive feature that has had a profound subsequent impact. In the ancient Roman period and down through human history, what we call "religion" tended to focus more on honoring, appeasing, and seeking the goodwill of deities. . . . "Religion" did not typically have much to say about what we call "ethics." . . . [Our] unquestioned assumption that religions are all concerned with teaching about "ethical" behavior almost certainly derives from Christianity.[4]

Those are big claims, but Hurtado makes them using solid historical evidence and describes them with careful nuancing so as not to overstate his claims—bold as they may be. Let's consider these claims in more detail.

We begin with a few examples of how non-Christians regarded Christians as strange, often negatively so. This will help us see that Christianity was much more than just another run-of-the-mill religion but was instead something quite different. Examples of hostility toward early Christians are narrated throughout the New Testament book of Acts. This hostility shows up not only in the Jewish persecution of Christians but also in pagan persecution such as we find in the accounts where Paul is beaten and imprisoned. Outside the New Testament, we see other examples of disdain. For instance, Hurtado describes how one ancient Roman historian, Tacitus, characterizes Christians "as 'hated for their abominations' and as promoting 'a deadly/dangerous superstition.'" Tacitus goes on to say that under Nero's orders "an immense multitude" of Christians were arrested, convicted of "hatred of the human race," and then subjected to various forms of violent death.[5] Another ancient historian, Suetonius, refers to Christians as "a class of people given to a new and wicked superstition."[6] Still another ancient writer, Lucian of Samosata, labels Christians in the following way: "The poor wretches have convinced themselves, first and foremost, that they are going to be immortal and live for all time, in consequence of which they despise death. . . . Furthermore, their first lawgiver [Jesus] persuaded them that they are all brothers of one another after they have transgressed once for all by denying the Greek gods and by worshipping that crucified sophist himself and living under his laws."[7] More examples could be added (such as Celsus's concern that the Christians' refusal to honor the gods could lead to social unrest and retribution from the gods), but this should suffice to show something of how Christians were viewed. According to Hurtado, this kind of cultural disdain and hostility toward Christians "has no parallel" in the ancient Roman world. So what made Christianity so different, and how does that affect us today?

Perhaps what brought the most trouble on Christians was their insistence that God is one, that he alone is to be worshiped and revered, and therefore that worshiping any other god is both sinful and ignorant. Christians would have brought a lot less suffering on themselves if only they had honored other gods. Yet they did not, and their refusal to do so could hardly be kept secret. Devotion to the gods permeated daily life: from the daily prayers directed at one's household gods to the abundance of temples in the city centers to the ceremonial offerings of the businesspeople in trade guilds. Veneration of the gods was *everywhere*. (I got a sense of this while on a recent visit to Rome, walking through the ruins of the ancient Roman Forum, where there is temple after temple after temple, all to different gods.) Roman religious practice was not merely some compartmentalized slice of life, some internal and private set of beliefs. Instead, participation in the Roman religious life showed communal solidarity, support for the civic and Roman order, and common sense (given that you were appealing to gods who could offer protection and help for things both big and small).

We might be asking ourselves, "What about the Jews? Didn't they worship one God exclusively?" Yes, but here's the important difference: Romans put up with this Jewish oddity because it was seen as part of their unique ethnic peculiarity. In other words, they thought, "That's just the Jews being Jewish." But Christianity wasn't confined to a particular ethnicity. Instead, Christianity crossed all barriers—those of ethnicity, social class, gender, and location.[8] And it wasn't doing so at a gradual pace. There was an explosion of growth: the number of Christians increased from around ten thousand by AD 100 to two hundred thousand by AD 200 to around five million by AD 300.[9]

All of a sudden there were people from all walks of life who had formerly honored the gods and who now were unwilling to do so. Simply imagine how shocking, disrespectful, and brazen it must have looked when such people would no longer participate in the worship taking place in their own homes, city centers, and festivals. Now, we must try to wrap our heads around this: we take for granted that religion is a personal preference, which anyone from any ethnicity is free to take or leave—and yet, before Christianity's transethnic movement, the whole notion that religious choice could be separate from one's ethnicity was a rarity at best. This is not to say that there was absolutely no religious choice in the Roman world. Sometimes people would favor a particular deity or would join what is referred to as a "mystery cult." However, this was typically an *addition* to one's other religious obligations to honor one's household and ethnically determined deities, whereas Christians bid farewell to all other religious obligations.

But it's not just the exclusive devotion to one God that makes Christianity a bit peculiar. It's also the notion that this one God is both personal and loving. In today's climate, most people who believe in God assume that God is both personal and loving—and yet this notion was another distinct and influential feature of Christianity.[10] To be certain, some Romans might believe in something like a single divine being who is over everything, a being who is transcendent, matchless, and unfathomable. But for such folks, this divine being is neither personal nor loving (nor would this divinity prohibit honor being shown to lesser gods). In such an ancient mind-set, a perfect divine being must be changeless, which would disallow personal intervention or reciprocated love. On the one hand, Christianity shares belief in a transcendent, matchless, unfathomable being; on the other hand, Christianity is unique in considering this singular divine being to be personal, approachable, and loving. Once again, this Christian concept—a God who is simultaneously transcendent and loving—would have been bizarre in its day. Despite how odd this would have been in the ancient world, it's the taken-for-granted notion today. Pop-culture talk of God (by non-Christians who believe in God) assumes that God is omnipotent and omniscient while at the same time being accessible and loving. Is this religious plagiarism?

We've now looked at early Christianity's distinctive concept of God as well as early Christianity's distinctive transethnic and trans-local makeup. Now we'll consider early Christianity's distinctive ethics.[11] I'll limit myself to three examples of early Christianity's distinctive morality, all of which represent ethical stances that most people take for granted today but that made Christianity abnormal in its ancient context.

1. Christians would not participate in the practice of infant exposure—that is, abandoning unwanted babies to either die in the elements or be taken by those who would raise them to be sold as slaves or prostitutes. Many in the Roman world accepted infant exposure as common practice. We

see evidence of this attitude, for example, in the nonchalant way that a soldier writes to his wife about their unborn child: "If it is a boy, let it be, if it is a girl, cast it out."[12] In contrast, both Christianity and Judaism were exceptional in their condemnation of this practice.

2. Christians were distinctive in their teaching on marital fidelity. In the Roman world, it was typical for a husband to sleep not only with his wife but also with a mistress, prostitutes, and boys. In fact, some saw this as wise practice, a way to keep the husband from committing adultery. That's right! A husband could sleep around, and it wasn't a problem unless he slept with another man's wife or with a freeborn virgin.[13] In contrast, Christians believed that a husband must have sexual relations with only his wife; anything else was sinful. As for sleeping with young boys, Christians found this so repulsive that they appear to have coined a term for it. Whereas some Romans might refer to pederasts as "child lovers," Christians called them "child corrupters."
3. Christian morality was peculiar in that its morals were not confined to an elite few (which, in the ancient Greco-Roman world, would have often been the high-status males). Instead, Christian morality was expected of all Christians, whether male or female, high status or low status, recent convert or veteran believer. Implied by such ethical expectations is the belief in the inherent dignity and capability of all persons; everyone in the community was responsible to live a moral life. Further implied by such expectations is the countercultural concept that those in the upper echelons of society were not inherently superior to the low-status members of the Christian community; everyone had the same ethical standard. We might also include Christianity's distinctive concern for the poor within a culture wherein "Greco-Roman gods had no interest in the poor nor was organized charity a religious duty."[14]

We've seen how Christianity had something of a distinct ethic in the ancient Greco-Roman world through its condemnation of infant exposure, its marital and sexual mores, its concern for the poor, and its moral expectations of all believers—regardless of social status or gender. Hurtado is careful not to say that Christians were completely alone in these moral convictions. In fact, Christian ethics frequently overlapped with Jewish ethics. Nevertheless, such overlap seems to represent the exception rather than the rule of the ancient Roman world. The lasting ethical impact that is felt today seems to have been fueled by the largely unprecedented transethnic and transcultural spread of Christianity.

To summarize, the Roman world found Christianity "different, odd, and even objectionable."[15] This seems to have been a response to such characteristics as (1) Christianity's exclusive devotion to one God who is personal and loving; (2) Christianity's distribution across ethnicity, gender, status, and location; and (3) Christianity's abnormal ethical stances on such things as infant exposure, marital fidelity, and pederasty. And yet, despite Christianity's representing the minority opinion in its early years, its influence has stretched so far that many people today aren't even aware that there was ever any other opinion to be had on certain matters. Many simply take it for granted that, if there's a deity, this deity is likely one, transcendent, personal, and loving. Many simply take it for granted that ethnicity should not determine or limit one's religious choice. Many simply take it for granted that husbands should be sexually faithful to their wives and that pederasty is "child corruption" and not "child love." But here's the thing: these convictions that many now take for granted make sense within a Christian worldview, but not within every worldview, and perhaps not within many. After all, if such beliefs were simply obvious to all right-thinking people, then why weren't they obvious to the majority of the Roman world?

Excursus

Pliny to Trajan—a Surviving Example of Early Christian Distinctiveness

In an early letter (AD 112) written by Pliny the Younger to Emperor Trajan, the governor Pliny seeks advice about how to deal with Christians. I have italicized several lines in order to draw attention to the distinctive Christian traits we just read about, like Christianity's committed monotheism, distinct ethics (including sexual ethics), unusual diversity, rapid proliferation, and confession of Christ as God.

> It is my practice, my lord, to refer to you all matters concerning which I am in doubt. For who can better give guidance to my hesitation or inform my ignorance? I have never participated in trials of Christians. I therefore do not know what offenses it is the practice to punish or investigate, and to what extent. . . .
>
> Meanwhile, in the case of those who were denounced to me as Christians, I have observed the following procedure: I interrogated these as to whether they were Christians; those who confessed I interrogated a second and a third time, threatening them with punishment; those who persisted I ordered executed. For I had no doubt that, whatever the nature of their creed, stubbornness and inflexible obstinacy surely deserve to be punished. . . .

Soon accusations spread, as usually happens, because of the proceedings going on, and several incidents occurred. An anonymous document was published containing the names of many persons. Those who denied that they were or had been Christians, when they *invoked the gods in words dictated by me, offered prayer with incense and wine to your image*, which I had ordered to be brought for this purpose together with statues of the gods, and moreover cursed Christ—none of which those who are really Christians, it is said, can be forced to do—these I thought should be discharged. . . .

They asserted, however, that the sum and substance of their fault or error had been that they were accustomed to meet on a fixed day before dawn and sing responsively a hymn *to Christ as to a god*, and to bind themselves by oath, not to some crime, but *not to commit fraud, theft, or adultery, not falsify their trust, nor to refuse to return a trust when called upon to do so*. When this was over, it was their custom to depart and to assemble again to partake of food—but ordinary and innocent food. Even this, they affirmed, they had ceased to do after my edict by which, in accordance with your instructions, I had forbidden political associations. Accordingly, I judged it all the more necessary to find out what the truth was by torturing two female slaves who were called deaconesses. But I discovered nothing else but depraved, excessive superstition.

I therefore postponed the investigation and hastened to consult you. For the matter seemed to me to warrant consulting you, especially because of the number involved. For many *persons of every age, every rank, and also of both sexes* are and will be endangered. For the contagion of this superstition has *spread not only to the cities but also to the villages and farms*. But it seems possible to check and cure it. It is certainly quite clear that the *temples, which had been almost deserted*, have begun to be frequented, that the *established religious rites, long neglected*, are being resumed, and that from everywhere sacrificial animals are coming, for which until now very *few purchasers could be found*. Hence it is easy to imagine what a multitude of people can be reformed if an opportunity for repentance is afforded.[16]

Notice that Pliny describes Christians as distinctly monotheistic, identifiable by their refusal to worship other gods or offer prayers to Caesar's image and by their neglecting the pagan temple practices. They are distinctly committed to Christ as to a god, which is a commitment they honor by both their monotheism and their refusal to curse Christ. We also learn from Pliny that the Christian religion is coupled with an ethic of truth telling, fairness, and marital faithfulness. Moreover, Pliny describes these early Christians as notably diverse, made up of "persons of every age, every rank, and also of both sexes." And we can ascertain from his letter that Christianity seems to be proliferating, given that Pliny describes it as a "contagion [that] has spread not only to the cities but also to the villages and farms."

We also learn that these Christians resemble the early church we saw in Acts. Recall how Kavin Rowe described the church in Acts with the phrase "new culture, yes—coup, no."[17] Such a description fits the Christians that Pliny is encountering too. These Christians are not seeking to overthrow the political order, but they are causing a cultural disturbance in ways we might characterize as religious, political, economic, and social.

- They are causing *religious* disturbance by not worshiping gods and by leaving "established religious rites long neglected."
- They are causing *political* disturbance by placing Christ's authority above Caesar's.
- They are causing *economic* disturbance by deserting the temples and leaving "few purchasers" for animal sacrifices.
- And they are causing *social* disturbance by not maintaining the established social hierarchy; instead, they allow members of every age, rank, and sex. Plus, they even have deaconesses who are female slaves!

As is clear, the distinctiveness of Christianity was not always tolerated, which sometimes led to persecution and even death. Although Christians were not engaged in violent revolt, they nonetheless could pose a threat because their distinctive cultural impact could potentially undermine the religious, political, economic, and social foundation on which the empire was built. *We should not overlook the fact that their brand of cultural revolution—monotheistic, ethical, inclusive—which was deemed so deviant and dangerous, strikes us today as mild or even self-evident.*

Alister McGrath's *Heresy*

As we survey Christianity's distinctiveness, and as we keep in mind the disdain and persecution that dogged early Christians, we may start to become aware of an odd notion that many folks have uncritically bought into. There is a popular yet unhistorical idea that certain Christians wielded so much power and influence that they forced all other Christian groups to adopt their specific teaching and practice. In other words, right and wrong had nothing to do with truth and everything to do with the preferences of the powerful elite. Perhaps people get this mistaken notion by confusing early Christian history with later Christian history. Christianity certainly came into power in the fourth century, through Emperor Constantine, and there's an admittedly checkered history that follows the use (and abuse) of that power. Yet the situation facing the church in the first three centuries was quite different. As we've seen, early Christians faced persecution, sometimes on a large scale, sometimes on a smaller scale. They could be harassed for their refusal to honor the gods and for acting in ways that the culture deemed deviant or abhorrent. With that background in mind, we'll consider how early Christians navigated matters concerning orthodoxy and heresy. To get a better understanding, we'll turn to noted theologian Alister McGrath and his book *Heresy*. And to be clear on terms, by "orthodoxy" I am referring to teachings that the church regards as essential and central Christian beliefs; by "heresy" I am referring to teachings that are considered to break the bounds of orthodoxy.

McGrath hopes to correct the widespread but mistaken notion that orthodoxy "is nothing more than a heresy that happened to win out—and promptly tried to suppress its rivals and silence their voices." According to this inaccurate picture, "the distinction between heresy and orthodoxy is arbitrary, a matter of historical accident."[18] In other words, some people assume that what we now call "heretical" might be just as Christian as what we call "orthodox."

Somehow, this idea has gotten coupled with another unhistorical assumption—namely, that heresy was probably more revolutionary than orthodoxy. In this historical rewrite, the heroic heretics were challenging the stuffy, status-quo doctrine of the conservative orthodox believers. But, as McGrath persuasively argues, this set of ideas is simply untrue. In fact, the opposite was the case. As McGrath writes, "It needs to be made clear from the outset that it is historically indefensible to contrast a liberal, relaxed, gender-neutral, and generous heresy with a narrow, dogmatic, patriarchal, and rigid orthodoxy."[19] In fact, if anyone was revolutionary in the ancient Roman world, it was those Christians who confessed and practiced orthodox faith. To illustrate this, let's look at three examples of early heresies: Ebionitism, Arianism, and Docetism.

To help us compare orthodoxy and heresy, we may need a brief recap on orthodox doctrines about Jesus:

- Jesus is both truly God and truly human.
- Jesus is a distinct person from the Father.
- Jesus and the Father are one God.

If those three doctrines seem a little confusing to you, you're not alone. It's not easy to understand the nature of Jesus. It seems as though some heresies were attempts at making Christianity easier to comprehend within Jewish and Greco-Roman cultures.

Let's start with Ebionitism. This is essentially an attempt to make Christianity more compatible with the Jewish faith by claiming that Jesus wasn't divine. Instead, according to Ebionitism, Jesus was only a human who happened to be particularly gifted and empowered by God. Jesus is kind of like a super-prophet. Notice that Ebionitism is easier to fit into Jewish monotheism. Ebionitism gets around the problematic view that the one God is somehow more than one. Thus there doesn't seem to be anything particularly revolutionary about Ebionitism. Rather, this heresy seeks to align Christianity with the theological status quo.

Next we have Arianism. Proponents of Arianism claimed that Jesus was not equal with God but was created by God—that is, Jesus was a bit like a demigod who took on flesh and saved humanity. Unlike Ebionitism, Arianism had less to do with making Christianity compatible with Jewish faith and more to do with making Christianity compatible with certain philosophical notions. For Arians, Jesus couldn't be God, because they assumed that God, by definition, has to be both unchangeable and distinct from creation. For them, if God is distinct from creation and unchangeable, he could not take on flesh as a human. To become human would involve some measure of change, given both the obvious change resulting from taking on flesh and the inevitable changes that come with human life—growth, development, relationships, and so on. Plus, to become human would presumably make God less distinct from his creation. Once again, we see that heresy—in this case, Arianism—isn't particularly revolutionary but sticks closer to the theological status quo than orthodoxy does.[20] If anything is theologically revolutionary, it's orthodoxy.

Our third heresy is Docetism. Docetists didn't take issue with Jesus's divinity; they contested his humanity. For Docetists, Jesus was divine, but he only *appeared* to be human. In their minds, God could not have suffered and died on a cross—such an idea is too unconventional, too outside the box. Orthodox Christianity, in contrast, holds the revolutionary notion that God took on flesh, suffered, and died on behalf of his people.

Notice that, in these admittedly brief descriptions, all three heresies are being less than revolutionary in their thinking. Instead, they are trying to fit Christianity into already-present theological and/or philosophical categories. The church ultimately resisted these teachings, even though it would have probably made the church appear more respectable and sensible to accept them.

The church maintains a more controversial and revolutionary belief system, but not because it was imposed by the powers that be. Rather, orthodoxy better aligned with the early church's common convictions and practices. As McGrath explains, "The process of marginalization or neglect of these [early heresies] generally has more to do with an emerging consensus within the church that they are inadequate than with any attempt to impose an unpopular orthodoxy on an unwilling body of believers."[21] More specifically, the church recognizes two fundamental problems.

First, these heresies prove incapable of handling the weight of significant and firmly established Christian ideas. For example, when Athanasius (an early defender of orthodoxy) was arguing against Arianism, he reasoned that if Jesus was only a created being and not God (as was taught in Arianism), then Jesus couldn't save humanity, because only God can bring about humanity's salvation. Here we see Athanasius pointing to an already established Christian belief (that Jesus brought salvation) and then showing how orthodox teaching on the nature of Christ's divinity supported this Christian doctrine, whereas the heretical teaching could not. Or consider Docetism, which undermined the reality of God taking on flesh, dying, and resurrecting. As we've seen throughout our study, Christianity doesn't make sense apart from the doctrines of the incarnation, crucifixion, and resurrection.

To deny either Jesus's deity (as in Arianism) or his humanity (as in Docetism) is to create a domino effect that ends with a Christianity that has lost its rationale, beauty, and power. There are a few pivotal teachings on which the Christian system either stands or falls; the early defenders of orthodoxy were pointing this out, all the while grounding their arguments in Scripture and the apostolic tradition.

Second, these heresies were ultimately rejected because they also did not align with prevailing church practice. Denying Jesus's divinity (as in Ebionitism and Arianism) was clearly out of step with the church's prevailing practice of worshiping Jesus. If anything, the heresies of Arianism and Ebionitism were the real imposition on the Christian masses, who had been worshiping Jesus as divine from the beginning.

Orthodoxy didn't result from a powerful clergy imposing an unpopular belief system on the common folk; instead, orthodoxy was honoring the beliefs and practices that were already established and practiced by the people who made up the church.

Iain Provan's *Seriously Dangerous Religion*

In *Seriously Dangerous Religion*, Iain Provan considers how the Bible, especially the Old Testament, speaks to the kinds of questions we've been asking throughout this book. Specifically, he asks questions such as "What is the world?" "Who is God?" "Who are man and woman?" "Why do evil and suffering mark the world?" "How am I to relate to God?" "How am I to relate to my neighbor?" "What am I to hope for?" Provan considers how the biblical answers to these questions compare with the answers one might find in both the ancient and modern world. He certainly recognizes the overlap between the biblical worldview and the worldviews of other religions and philosophies. But he hopes, as do I, that the reader will see that there are also some crucial differences—and these differences are not just semantic: we say "heaven," you say "nirvana"; we say "church," you say "mosque." Instead, some differences lead to widely disparate conclusions about significant matters such as human dignity, hope, ethics, and purpose. Let's take a closer look.

Provan starts with the biblical concept of the world. As we've already seen, Scripture presents the world as (1) created, (2) distinct from the creator, and (3) good—not evil or inferior simply because it's physical. Such a perspective on creation was distinct in an ancient context and can be distinct in a contemporary context as well. Let's begin with the first two points noted above: the world is created and is distinct from the creator. As Provan explains, "In ancient Near Eastern thinking [and in many later philosophies and religions as well], the world as we know it emerges from a process through which the One becomes the Many. Separation occurs *within the One*, and singularity gives way to multiplicity in the emerging world. The gods of the various pantheons are themselves products of this process of separation and are thus part *of* the world, not separate *from* it."[22] You may need to read that twice—or three times! In short, many in the ancient world did not think of creator and creation as distinctly different (as Christians and Jews assume); instead, all things were understood to be part of the One.

Why does it matter whether the creator is distinct from the creation instead of all things being simply part of the One? It matters for a few reasons. For example, if the creator is not distinct from the creation, then everything is presumably bound by the rules of the cosmos, including the god(s). Any deity that arises from the One would be unable to interfere from the outside, since that deity would be a piece of the whole. Such a deity could not be relied on to set the cosmos right, since that deity is part of the broken cosmos. Further, if the creator is not distinct from creation, it becomes difficult to differentiate good from evil, since both good and evil would originate from the same source. Love and hate, selfishness and compassion, patience and rage: these would all be expressions of the One.

Is the biblical belief that the world is good really that distinctive? In fact, this notion clashes with certain philosophical and religious traditions (especially in the East). For some, the material world appears to be evil (as in Gnosticism or Manichaeism), inferior (as in Platonism), or an obstacle to greater reality (as seems to be the case in much of Hinduism and Buddhism). The way one's worldview makes sense of the material world will have profound implications for what it means to be persons. Are we spirits trapped in evil or inferior bodies? Are we nothing other than our material bodies? Are we embodied souls?

And it just gets messier. How one answers questions about personhood will inevitably be tied to issues of purpose and meaning and morality. If we are spirits trapped in bodies, then shouldn't our purpose be to escape the material world, either through withdrawal into meditation or through a rigorous asceticism designed to purge the spiritual from the material? In such a scenario, engaging in social justice and charity would seem to be low on the priority list. After all, why bail water from a ship that was never meant to float? Why stitch up a wound on a corpse?

Or we might consider the opposite perspective. What if we are nothing more than our material bodies? Doesn't this essentially commit us to believing that there's no ultimate meaning to life—that the concept of purpose is illusory? In this scenario, the wisest life goal would be to maximize pleasure and minimize pain. Social justice and charity would not seem valuable in themselves but only insofar as they enhance our personal lives.

In contrast to both of these anthropologies, Christianity regards humans as embodied souls. We treat the physical world, including our own bodies, with care, while recognizing that we are more than our bodies—having greater hope and greater purpose. The goal of life for Christians isn't to maximize pleasure and minimize pain but to be united with Christ, partnering with the Spirit to maximize goodness and minimize evil (even when this leads to decreased pleasure and increased pain). In Christian anthropology, the physical body isn't in conflict with the spirit; rather, our embodied souls are in conflict with sin. This Christian notion—where we are embodied souls—seems to offer the most viable framework on which to build a robust ethic, one in which physical acts of sacrifice, altruism, and compassion matter both in this age and in the age to come.

Provan continues by considering the nature of the divine and how this relates to other worldviews. The biblical God is *one*, *holy*, *loving*, and *personal*. Let's briefly consider these attributes in order.

1. God is *one*. Monotheism was a distinctive Jewish and Christian belief in the ancient world. True, some might trace all the gods back to the One, but even in such belief systems, there are multiple gods. In the

Bible, however, God alone is God. He creates everything, including those objects that other religions thought of as gods.[23]

2. God is *holy*. He is just and good. The gods of both the ancient Near East and the Greco-Roman world could be capricious and unjust, showing no greater virtue than the humans they ruled over.
3. God is *loving*. He is compassionate and concerned for the welfare of humans. The ancient Near Eastern gods and the Greco-Roman gods may have had moments of compassion and concern, but compassion was by no means their chief characteristic.
4. God is *personal*. He relates to his creation by communicating, guiding, intervening, and even becoming human and dwelling among them. This is different from certain philosophical and Eastern notions (e.g., Hinduism, Buddhism, and Platonism) where the ultimate Reality is an impersonal Being or Force.

Based on such a framework, the Christian worldview can make sense of the human instincts toward morality, love, and worship. The *oneness* of God, as we've seen earlier, can offer a basis for morality, especially when this God is understood to be *holy* and good. A *loving* God makes sense of the human instincts toward compassion and mercy and altruism. A God who is simultaneously holy and loving fits our instincts that both justice and mercy are good. The human impulse to worship or pray to God makes sense only if God is *personal*—that is, capable of hearing prayer and receiving worship. In contrast, those worldviews in which God is not one, holy, loving, and/or personal have greater difficulty holding together morality, altruism, and personal relationship with the divine.

Returning for a moment to the matter of humans, the biblical idea is that humans are created by God and declared "good." They are made for relationship with God and their fellow humans. They are tasked with "imaging" God as they caringly rule creation. And this dignified status is applied to both male and female: "in the image of God he created them; male and female he created them" (Gen. 1:27 NIV). We've already seen how other ancient Near Eastern creation accounts depict humans as slaves of the gods, tasked with doing the menial and arduous labor that the gods don't want to do. We can add to that how the Bible is distinctly democratic in viewing all humans, not just the king, as representing God, in contrast to some other ancient Near Eastern religions.[24] In the ancient Greco-Roman world, not all humans were considered to be created equal: slaves and women were deemed inherently inferior to free persons and men. The caste system of some Eastern faiths is also supported by notions about the greater and lesser worth of persons. Can we be certain that it is "self-evident that all men are created equal"? Many of us assume so, but certain ancient Near Eastern, Greco-Roman, and Eastern religions would apparently disagree. (And to be fair, plenty of Western democratic societies have not lived up to this ideal, as evidenced in their failure to treat women, minorities, and the poor as true equals.)

How might our notions about humanity play into ethics? For example, if someone's past karma has resulted in reincarnation within a lower caste, then it is conceivably wrong to alleviate the person's suffering and ostracism—as such actions may disrupt the karmic process. Or to treat a slave as an equal could be seen as working against the natural order, a foolish rejection of the proper way of things. If, however, we want to claim that all humans have inherent dignity and that all humans should be treated with the same standard of justice (regardless of ethnicity, gender, class, or caste), then we should have a basis for that. It's not clear whether some non-Christian worldviews can (or would) account for human dignity and equality. Does this point to a deficiency in those religious or philosophical systems?

We've thought about the nature of God, of creation, and of humans, so now let's ask the question "Why does the world seem messed up?" Almost every worldview recognizes that things don't seem quite right, but they don't all agree on the problem—or the solution. In the Christian system the world was created good, yet brokenness entered into the good world through misused free will and sin. Other worldview systems, however, see things differently.

- For the cosmic dualist, good and evil have always existed together in an eternal balance—there is a cosmic push and pull of right and wrong that seems destined to go on forever.
- For others, the problem stems from our spirits being caught in an evil or inferior material existence—if we could just escape or transcend the material, we would be better off.
- Or the problem is not about good versus evil or about spiritual versus material; rather, the problem is ignorance—if we only knew more about who we are and what the world is, we could align our lives properly.
- Or perhaps the problem is that we have become disconnected from the One—if we could just detach our notions of the individual self, we could achieve the proper state of being.

From this we can see a seismic clash of worldviews. Clearly, not all worldviews are saying the same thing. They sometimes hold mutually exclusive notions about central ideas—like the nature of humans, the problem with the world, and the way to make things right. In other words, to flippantly claim that every religion is the same is to fail to understand the basic claims that are being made; it dishonors and patronizes these faith systems by not taking their distinct claims seriously.

Perhaps we should say more about how the Christian system answers the question "Why does the world seem messed up?" According to the Christian metanarrative, the ultimate reality (God) is good, which means that evil is something distinct from and inferior to God.[25] Compare this view with that of the cosmic dualist, who believes that good and evil are two equal and eternal forces. Unlike the Christian, the dualist does not believe that ultimate reality is good; rather, ultimate reality is good and evil. Like the Christian framework, the dualistic framework can explain why the world seems a mix of good and evil. But, unlike the Christian, the dualist cannot claim that good is inherently superior to evil or will one day conquer evil.

We could also compare the Christian framework with the framework adopted by those who think that the problem is with the material world being evil or inferior. Like Christianity, this view recognizes that something is off in our world, and it shares the notion that humans are more than our finite, material bodies. However, unlike Christianity, it has trouble explaining our sense that the physical world has inherent beauty and goodness and value, including the dignity of our bodies. Further, it promotes an ethic of detachment or escapism that is at odds with the ethic of Christianity.

How might the Christian view compare with those systems that see ignorance as the main problem? For some, the problem is ignorance of perception: if we could simply see the truth about the world, we might find contentment in the way things are (maybe war isn't truly bad if we see it in the right light). Like Christianity, this view acknowledges the value of wisdom, of seeing through fog and perceiving truth. Unlike Christianity, this system makes perception the only problem, which means there's nothing truly evil. To make perception the main issue would seem to make light of much human experience. Some experiences of brokenness cannot easily be categorized as a matter of perspective. Tragedy and injustice are more than merely a way of looking at things. There seems to be a deeper brokenness at work, which Christians name evil or sin.

For others, the problem of ignorance is a problem of knowledge—we just need more information and better thinking. Like Christianity, this view recognizes that how we think matters. Unlike Christianity, this system considers knowledge sufficient to fix the problem. For Christians, the issue is bigger than knowledge—sin distorts not only our ability to know what's true but also our ability to live according to what's true. As Roger Olson writes, "'To know the good is to do the good' is *not* the biblical perspective; it is the Greek and generic philosophical perspective that underlies the modern idea that education is the solution to everything. According to the biblical story of humanity, behavior is controlled by the heart more than by the mind or reason."[26] For the Christian, knowledge is good, but knowledge doesn't defeat all evils.

Last, how might the Christian view compare with those traditions that consider the problem to be dissociation from the One, where the solution is to give up one's clinging to the self in hopes of being reabsorbed into the One? Like Christianity, this view holds an important place for connectivity—being connected both with something transcendent and with one another. Unlike Christianity, this view doesn't seem to allow for lasting personhood and individuality. In the end, it ironically seems to undermine our desires for connection and relationship. Instead of being in relationship as individuals, we would all be absorbed into a uniform oneness—with nothing left to relate to. Such a "togetherness" ultimately seems to result in being alone. In contrast, Christianity anticipates union-with-individuality. In Christianity, selfhood is not abandoned but is retained and brought into a perfect union of loving relationship. The triune God provides a glimpse of this reality: three persons united as one. This Christian concept seems to better capture our instincts that each of us matters as a distinct person. It fits our intuition that every person is to be valued as a unique individual. Plus, if everything is part of the One, then the One is partly the problem; whereas in Christianity, creation has a separateness, which means that God is not part of the problem—God is the only solution, the only being with the power and purity to restore what's broken.

Perhaps one of the more controversial and distinct Christian ideas is the notion that humans cannot fix the world (or themselves) on their own. Christians are to strive for the good but not expect to achieve utopia, because evil and brokenness run too deep in human hearts and institutions. God's help is needed. The ultimate solution cannot be limited to gaining more knowledge, trying harder, adopting new insights, or pursuing detachment. Part of being a Christian is this humbling move where one admits that humans cannot right all their wrongs, nor can they heal the brokenness around them through their efforts alone. The Christian hope is that God will one day make all things right, repairing and renewing the broken world, freeing it from sin and evil. In the meantime—in the already/not-yet—Christians partner with God as ministers of reconciliation.

We might conclude by noting that not every worldview contains hope. Those worldview systems that hold onto hope typically have very different convictions about the realization of that hope. Is hope for a future state that will be material or immaterial or both; for restoration or evacuation; for absorption-without-personhood or union-with-individuality? Whether the hope is heaven or nirvana or Brahman, these can mean very different things given that they are wedded to very different cosmologies, anthropologies, theologies, and ethics.

Precisely because other traditions and religions have different views on humanity, divinity, the world, and what's wrong with the world, these worldview systems will sometimes clash. Some Christian beliefs and practices simply cannot fit within other worldview systems. Similarly, some beliefs and practices of other worldviews simply cannot fit within the Christian system. Hopefully at this point it's a bit clearer how pieces of the Christian metanarrative fit together. Hopefully it's also clear why many of these pieces are vital—indeed, nonnegotiable. That is, without some of these basic worldview beliefs, the Christian system begins to collapse. By way of review,

- God is one, holy, loving, and personal. God is the sovereign, transcendent creator of everything.
- Creation was made good but has been damaged by sin and evil.
- Humans are made in God's image, with special dignity, distinction, and worth—but they too are sin-damaged, incapable of achieving wholeness for themselves or the world.
- The ultimate hope rests with a compassionate and just God putting the world back to rights, bringing heaven on earth wherein humans live in a unifying love with God and one another.
- This hope rests on Jesus being truly God and truly human, living a life of perfect faithfulness, being crucified then raised to life, and ascending into heaven to be with the Father.
- When Christians pledge themselves to Christ, they are entering into the new covenant Jesus inaugurated—a covenant that entails certain ethical expectations.

Hurtado's book *Destroyer of the Gods* helps us see that Christianity was distinct in its ancient context. Christians were misfits in the ancient world because their metanarrative clashed with the dominant metanarrative—religiously, ethically, socially, and politically. When we fail to see Christianity's distinct metanarrative today, it may be a case of cultural amnesia. It may also be a case of worldview plagiarism wherein other worldviews are borrowing

Christian concepts—even when those worldviews lack their own metanarrative framework to adequately support those concepts.

In *Heresy*, McGrath shows us that orthodoxy was not a power play of the elites who were trying to squelch the revolutionary heretical teachings. Instead, orthodoxy was often a countercultural position, more outside-the-box than heresy. However, Christians deemed it necessary to take the more revolutionary path of orthodoxy, in part because they discerned that the Christian system required it. Some doctrines are essential, in the sense that Christianity ceases to be Christian without them.

Last, in *Seriously Dangerous Religion*, Provan shines a light on Christianity's distinctiveness by asking some penetrating questions that expose how worldviews sometimes clash on fundamental matters that have far-reaching impact. It really matters how one understands divinity, humanity, the world, the problem, and hope.

As we consider this, we may recall the assertion of G. K. Chesterton that the most practical and important thing about a person may indeed be his or her view of the universe.

8

Christianity and Life's Big Questions

At the beginning of this book, we saw Alex Rosenberg's proposal for how a thoughtful atheist would answer life's big questions:

> *Is there a God?* No.
> *What is the nature of reality?* What physics says it is.
> *What is the purpose of the universe?* There is none.
> *What is the meaning of life?* Ditto.
> *Why am I here?* Just dumb luck.
> *Is there a soul? Is it immortal?* Are you kidding?
> *Is there free will?* Not a chance!
> *What happens when we die?* Everything pretty much goes on as before, except us.
> *What is the difference between right and wrong, good and bad?* There is no moral difference between them.
> *Why should I be moral?* Because it makes you feel better than being immoral.
> *Is abortion, euthanasia, suicide, paying taxes, foreign aid—or anything else you don't like—forbidden, permissible, or sometimes obligatory?* Anything goes.[1]

So how might a Christian who understands the Bible and the Apostles' Creed answer these same questions? Here's my attempt:

Is there a God? Yes, the one God who is Father, Son, and Holy Spirit.

What is the nature of reality? Ultimate reality is a triune God who creates out of love. This God, who is transcendent and immanent, created a good world that he sustains yet is distinct from. Reality is not dualistic, pantheistic, or merely physical.

What is the purpose of the universe? God presumably created out of the overflow of his love and joy and goodness so that creation might share in and reflect that love and joy and goodness.

What is the meaning of life? To be loved and to love.

Why am I here? To bear the image of God, to be a minister of reconciliation, to care for and rule creation as a kingdom and priests.

Is there a soul? Is it immortal? Humans are embodied souls. Only God is immortal, but God will gift his people with resurrected bodies that will neither decay nor die.

Is there free will? Yes, though we're not 100 percent free, because of spiritual, physical, social, and environmental factors.

What happens when we die? Our bodies return to dust, though at some future point all will face God's judgment: for some, this will mean destruction; for others, restoration—physically, socially, and spiritually.

What is the difference between right and wrong, good and bad? In short, right is based on God's holiness, love, and will; wrong is that which rejects, hinders, or opposes God's holiness, love, and will.

Why should I be moral? Because we were created to love, because it's the proper response to the God-given gifts of life and redemption, and because God will judge all people justly.

Is abortion, euthanasia, suicide, paying taxes, foreign aid—or anything else you don't like—forbidden, permissible, or sometimes obligatory? Our ethical choices are truly important—to God, to ourselves, to others—which means that some actions are forbidden, some are permissible, and some are obligatory.

Let's explore these answers one by one with a bit more detail and explanation.[2]

Is There a God?

Yes, the one God who is Father, Son, and Holy Spirit.

I like that Rosenberg begins with the question about God's existence. It's the right question to begin with, because the answer has a dramatic impact on every other question. For Rosenberg, answering this question with a "no" means that all of life is reducible to physics. This belief, then, compels

Rosenberg to deny that life has real meaning, that morality is objective, that the soul exists, that something happens to us after death, and that we have real freedom of choice. In contrast, responding "yes" allows for a whole different set of answers about meaning, morality, the soul, the afterlife, and free will. For Rosenberg, atheism isn't just denying the existence of God; atheism is also denying the very foundation for purpose, objective morality, the afterlife, and free will. In other words, according to Rosenberg, you can't say, "I *do not* believe in God, but I *do* believe that the universe has a purpose, that my life has real meaning, that some things are really evil, and that I have the freedom to make decisions." Instead, one must say, "I *do not* believe in God; *therefore*, life is ultimately meaningless, good and evil are social constructs that aid human survival, there is no hope of life after death or of things being set right, and it doesn't really matter what I think because I was predetermined to hold this view anyway."

To be clear, belief in God doesn't guarantee meaning, morality, afterlife, or free will. It all depends on what this God is like. A God who creates on a whim or out of boredom is not a God who gives our universe and our lives purpose. A God who creates beings to enslave might provide us with purpose, but not the kind of purpose we'd want.

Belief in God also doesn't guarantee a basis for morality. Perhaps God has no real morals. Or perhaps, as some religions teach, there are two equal powers: one characterized by mercy, love, joy, and fairness, and the other characterized by selfishness, hate, fear, and cruelty. In such a scenario, there is no ultimate morality, because both powers are equal and therefore have an equal claim to what is "right" and "wrong." In this cosmic dualism, morality is apparently at a stalemate. Humans may prefer one power over another, but that preference is not the same as objective morality. For morality to be more than a preference, it needs to be based on an unrivaled standard—not two or more rival standards. For Christians, this unrivaled standard is the one God who created all things and who is holy and good. If God has created all things, then nothing else can rival his standard for what is right and wrong. If there are multiple, uncreated gods, then there may be no ultimate standard for morality. But if there is one God, and if everything can trace its existence back to God, then this allows for objective morality.

Belief in God also doesn't guarantee the existence of the soul or the hope of an afterlife. God might create beings that have no souls, that have no ability to exist after death. Lots of people who believe in the soul don't believe that all creatures (like insects) have souls. In the Christian system, when God created humans, he created beings that could be natural and supranatural at the same time: we have bodies, yet we are not merely our material bodies.

Belief in God also doesn't guarantee free will. God may have created a universe that is preprogrammed down to the smallest detail. Believing in free will requires more than belief in God; it requires belief in a God who is capable of creating something with real choice.

Belief in God gets us only so far when it comes to our worldview and answering life's big questions. Practically speaking, some deists and atheists could answer life's big questions pretty similarly. Some deists believe in a God who created the world and then left it alone, never to be tinkered with again. Although the deist believes in God, his God can be so distant and disengaged that there is little reason for the deist to believe in any real meaning in life, any real morality, any soul, any afterlife, or any free will. For all practical purposes, a deist's worldview might be identical to an atheist's—just with the addition of an absentee God.

In sum, not only does it matter that one believes in God but it also matters what kind of God one believes in. The Christian believes in the one God revealed as Father, Son, and Holy Spirit. What I hope to show in the rest of this chapter is how the Christian's view of God will provide distinctive answers to life's big questions. In the previous chapters, we've looked at who the Christian God is; now we're going to think about how this shapes our worldview—how it teaches us to answer life's pressing questions.

What Is the Nature of Reality?

Ultimate reality is a triune God who creates out of love. This God, who is transcendent and immanent, created a good world that he sustains yet is distinct from. Reality is not dualistic, pantheistic, or merely physical.[3]

In the Christian worldview, God has created everything—everything traces its origin back to God. God is the ultimate reality, and everything else stems from this reality. So to answer the question "What is the nature of reality?" we must start with the nature of God. According to the Bible, God is a God of love. When he creates the world, he doesn't create out of need, because he doesn't need anything. Instead, it appears that he creates as an expression of his love. Christians believe that while God is one being, he is three persons: Father, Son, Holy Spirit. Although this is impossible to fully understand, it does help explain how God is love and how creation is an expression of God's love. If God were one being and one person, it would be difficult to understand how God is, by nature, a being of love.[4]

But if God has always existed in a loving union, we can see how God is by nature a being of love.

This is a bit theoretical, so it's helpful to remember how God expresses his love in concrete ways. I'll highlight three examples of God's love, one associated with each person of the Trinity. First, God the Father created humans, giving them the dignity of bearing his image and inviting them to share in a loving relationship with him and other humans. Second, God the Son became human and suffered and died on our behalf. This was not a move that was out of character for God. Instead, God did this precisely *because* this is his character, his true nature. He is a God of love—and not just a shallow or emotional kind of love but a sacrificial, humble, serving, costly love. Third, God the Spirit dwells within his broken and imperfect people, pouring his love into them, filling them with mercy, peace, and strength so that they might become new people, restored and redeemed.

The triune creator God is both *transcendent* and *immanent*—God is both *distinct from* and *present to* creation. Creation comes from God, but it is not God. How exactly this works is a bit of a mystery. But Scripture is clear: there is a distinction between God and his creation. As Roger Olson writes, "The world belongs to God, but the world also has a relative autonomy."[5] This is not pantheism, where everything is part of God (*pan*—"all"; *theism*—"God"). At first, pantheism seems sensible because it avoids having to wrestle with how God created something that is not God. On closer inspection, however, pantheism is problematic because it requires that brokenness and evil are part of the divine. Pantheism must assume that disease and death are part of the divine nature and that child molesters and tyrants are expressing the divine nature through their actions. The pantheists' God is not merely a god of love, justice, and morality. The pantheists' God is a mosaic of beauty and horror that provides little hope, little moral foundation, and little reason to regard love as central to reality.

In contrast, the Christian can claim that some of creation reflects God (for he created it) and some of creation does not reflect God (for he is distinct from his creation and has given it some autonomy). God's creation doesn't always reflect God's character or nature. Somehow, what God creates is not only distinct from God but also has some degree of freedom to resist and rebel against God.

God is not a physical being but is spirit. God does not appear to be bound by space and time the way his physical creation is (though he can operate within the bounds of space and time when he interacts with his creation). Olson helpfully explains that God is both supernatural ("beyond nature, not bound to nature and nature's laws, free over nature, not controlled by nature") and personal ("having intelligence, thought, intentions, actions, and some degree of self-determination").[6] Unlike God, humans are embodied souls, which makes us something like physical-spiritual beings. The awkward phrase "physical-spiritual" captures the Christian notion of the mysterious bond between body and spirit. Whereas dualists tend to emphasize the separation of physical and spiritual, the Christian recognizes their intimate connection. The dualist often assumes that the spiritual side of humans is superior and largely disconnected from the physical side of humans. In the ancient world, the Gnostics were dualistic, so they devalued the physical body and hoped for a future existence that was purely spiritual. Similarly, Buddhism is largely dualistic; the Buddhist longs to escape from the suffering of this world and reach the nirvana of a purely spiritual world.

The Christian, in contrast, assumes that the physical and spiritual are distinct but are nonetheless deeply intertwined—perhaps inseparable—in humans.[7] We are something like embodied souls. Hence, the Christian hope is not to escape from the physical world but for it to be restored. Within the Christian metanarrative, the physical creation was originally good, it has been corrupted by sin, and it will one day be made whole and new—free from corruption and decay. We look forward to resurrected bodies that are free from the spiritual corruption of sin, having been made whole through the renewal of God's Holy Spirit.

Because humans are hybrids—embodied souls—our restoration is brought about in a physical-spiritual way. Jesus, the one who is both truly God (who is spirit) and truly human, takes on physical brokenness (especially in his crucifixion and death) and spiritual brokenness (by taking on sin). Jesus resurrects in a physical body that is renewed by the Spirit: a physical-Spiritual body. This is the basis of Christian hope, of new creation—a restoration of our broken and corrupted physical-spiritual existence.

In the meantime, we are in limbo in the already/not-yet. God's Spirit is *already* transforming us in those intertwined physical-spiritual ways. The Spirit shapes our hearts (what we love), our minds (how we think), our bodies (how we act), and our communities (how we organize society). But new creation is *not yet* fully arrived. No human is fully transformed in this life. We continue to sin (though hopefully less and less) and our bodies continue to deteriorate (because our present bodies cannot fully escape the current corruption of sin and death).

Before moving on, we must make a final observation about how the world reflects God's nature. Ultimate reality is individual-communal. From all eternity there has been a community of three persons existing in loving unity. Fittingly, human existence is most in tune with reality when individuals belong to a loving community. We've seen how the Bible teaches that humans were created to be in loving relationship with God and with one another. From the first chapters of Genesis, God declares that "it is not good for the man to be alone" (Gen. 2:18 NIV). And throughout the Bible, God works to form loving, just communities (e.g., Israel and the church). Therefore, Christianity cannot simply be an individualistic religion, where it's all about *me* and *my* healing and *my* purpose. Since the triune God is communal, it makes sense that we reflect God's image in loving community.

Yet there is a balance, for Christianity is not so focused on the communal that the individual person becomes sidelined or forgotten. The Trinity is three distinct persons in one being. There is *both* individuality *and* community. The Bible and the Apostles' Creed demonstrate this by speaking of each person of the Trinity separately, honoring the unique beauty and majesty of Father, Son, and Holy Spirit. In a similar way, each and every human matters as a one-of-a-kind person, as a soul to be cherished and loved and celebrated for his or her unique makeup—personality, talents, interests, physical characteristics, gifts, and more. The Christian hope of restoration is, therefore, a hope for a restoration that is both individual and communal. Each of us is restored, and we live together in a union of perfect love. Unlike Hinduism, Christianity does not look forward to a nirvana where souls merge into a oneness wherein individual distinction is lost. Instead, Christians anticipate a union-with-individuality where the oneness of loving community does not result in the loss of our individuality. In fact, we expect that only by remaining distinctly individuals can we truly express loving unity. By remaining distinct individuals, we are loving and cherishing something different from ourselves. (After all, if we are no longer distinct persons but a single entity, the whole concept of love seems to be forfeited; in order to love, there needs to be another person to love.)

To summarize, Christianity is not pantheistic (where everything is God), nor is it dualistic (where the human body and spirit are independent), nor is it naturalistic (where the physical reality is the only reality). Instead, Christians believe in a physical-spiritual creation that is in some way distinct from its creator. Furthermore, Christianity is neither hyper-individualistic (where the individual person can fully thrive apart from community) nor hyper-communal (where the individual person loses his or her distinctiveness). Instead, Christians believe that humans are made to exist as individuals in community, a union-with-individuality that reflects the loving unity of a three-persons-in-one God.

What Is the Purpose of the Universe?

God presumably created out of the overflow of his love and joy and goodness so that creation might share in and reflect that love and joy and goodness.

I'll be brief here since my answer to this question is explained in more detail in the answer right before this question and in my answer to the next two questions below. I will, however, point out one thing here that I don't cover elsewhere: the purpose of *nonhuman* creation. That is, why did God create stars and planets, mountains and rivers, animals and plants? The short answer is that we don't fully know. From studying Scripture and theology, we gather that God created such things because he delights in goodness for goodness' sake. A God who is beautiful and good creates something that is beautiful and good because it's a natural expression of his nature and character. The purpose of nonhuman creation is, at least in part, to be beautiful and good. It is declared "good" in Genesis 1, and it will be renewed one day when God reconciles all things to himself (Col. 1:20). All creation is exhorted to praise God:

> Praise him, sun and moon;
> praise him, all you shining stars. . . .
> Praise the Lord from the earth,
> you great sea creatures and all ocean depths,
> lightning and hail, snow and clouds, . . .
> you mountains and all hills,
> fruit trees and all cedars,
> wild animals and all cattle,
> small creatures and flying birds. (Ps. 148:3, 7–8, 9–10 NIV)

Biblical scholar Richard Middleton rightly asks, "[How] do mountains and stars worship God?" He answers, "Certainly not verbally or with emotions. Rather, mountains worship God simply by being mountains, covered with lush vegetation or with steep crags or glaciers. . . . And stars worship by being stars, burning with nuclear energy."[8] Thus the purpose of the natural world is to be good and beautiful and magnificent, worshiping God by reflecting God's goodness and beauty and magnificence—simply by being the very thing it was created to be.

Recall that humans were meant to care for creation and to lovingly rule it. This suggests that nature has an additional purpose: being a source of joy and delight and growth for humans. Nature fulfills its role as humans delight in it and as it provides humans with opportunities to grow in knowledge, wonder, and caretaking.

What Is the Meaning of Life?

To be loved and to love.

If the heart of all reality is a God of love who creates out of love, then the meaning of life is *to be loved and to love*. We immediately go wrong if we get these two out of order. We don't first give love and *then* receive love. Instead, we *first* receive love and then give love. We start out loved. There is no need to earn this love, because we are created out of love. Ideally, we will recognize God's love as a gift, an unearned grace. And as we recognize this unearned love, we respond by loving God, loving ourselves, and loving others. Unfortunately, it never works quite so smoothly. Perhaps we do not recognize that we are loved because those who were to be God's agents of love (parents, societies, governments) have failed in their tasks, making us unaware of the truth of our loveliness. Perhaps we do recognize that we are loved, but we waste that love in selfish ways, not sharing love with others. Ideally, we are given love and give love; in actuality, we don't know love or we don't appreciate love, so we struggle to share love.

For the Christian, God's love isn't expressed merely in creating objects of love and worth; God's love is further expressed in Jesus's becoming human, suffering, and dying on humanity's behalf. Crucifixion is a vivid display of God's love. For those who wonder whether they are lovable, the cross answers with a resounding "Yes!" Once again, notice the direction love moves. Jesus initiates a loving rescue, we accept this love, and then we share it with others. It's not the other way around—we do not love others in order to earn Jesus's cruciform rescue. God is aware of our weaknesses, our brokenness, and the corruption of the world that we're born into. God comes to us and loves us in dramatic fashion: while we are sinners living in a sinful world, he takes on flesh and dies the death of a slave. For Christians, the ultimate meaning of our lives starts here.

Accepting God's love requires us to acknowledge that we are simultaneously lovable and broken. We are lovable—Jesus's life and death have made that crystal clear. We are broken, but not so broken as to be unlovable. In fact, as is typical of God, his light shines even brighter in our darkness. It is a love that is overwhelming to comprehend—a love that will take on suffering and humiliation and death itself, all to rescue a people who so often squander that love in apathy and ingratitude.

Jesus's love does not simply rescue the believer. Jesus's loving Spirit indwells and empowers the believer. Jesus's love goes further than providing a clean slate and a fresh start. His love gives us a new heart and a new hope. If we let it, Jesus's love will make us the people we were always meant to be—people characterized by Jesus's love, joy, peace, and goodness. What is the meaning of life? It is to accept the gift of God's love—in the very midst of our brokenness—and to allow that same love to flow out of us as we love God's good, beautiful, and broken creation.

Why Am I Here?

To bear the image of God, to be a minister of reconciliation, to care for and rule creation as a kingdom and priests.

For some Christians, the standard reply to the question "Why am I here?" is the answer "To worship God." Although such an answer is not wrong, it can be misleading. It sounds like humans are to spend all their time singing worship songs. Plus, it makes the afterlife sound like an eternal church service. Once again, Middleton is quite helpful here: "If mountains worship God by being mountains and stars worship God by being stars, how do humans worship God? By being human, in the full glory of what that means."[9]

On the basis of what we've looked at, humans are fulfilling their calling when they bear the image of God, when they work at the ministry of reconciliation, when they live as a kingdom and priests. If we don't know the biblical story, then these descriptors are confusing. Walking up to people and telling them that they are to be ministers of reconciliation would be quite strange, conjuring up images of clergy dressed in religious garb and engaged in rituals that seem largely disconnected from "the real world." Or telling people that their purpose is found in being a kingdom and priests might bring to mind repellent images of religious crusaders, expanding a kingdom at the point of a sword, propelled by a misguided sense of divine right and approval.

But those who know the biblical story have a better sense of what these words mean. For Christians, to bear the image of God should mean that the primary model for our lives is the true image of God—Jesus Christ. Jesus shows us who God is, and he is the standard for how to bear God's image as a human. Of course, this doesn't mean that we all strive to be first-century carpenters who are crucified in our thirties. Instead, it means that we seek to model our lives according to Jesus's character and mission. As we look to Jesus's character, we see a man who is faithful, courageous, compassionate, humble, honest, and good. And as we look to his mission, we see him working to bring restoration—physically, socially, and spiritually. Therefore, if we want to live out our purpose as those who bear the image of God, we strive to be a people whose character and mission is modeled after Christ's: a people characterized by faithfulness, courage, compassion, humility, honesty, and goodness; a people who work diligently to bring restoration in all aspects of life. Once again, we do this because we are loved—because we trust the one who made us in love, who rescued us by his cruciform love, and who indwells us with his love.

If we understand what "image of God" means, then phrases like "ministers of reconciliation" and "kingdom and priests" make better sense. The word for "minister" in the Bible is the same word for "servant." And "reconciliation" means "repairing what's broken." Thus the true "ministers of reconciliation" will embody the servant-heartedness and humility of Jesus as they work to repair what's broken in the world. As for "a kingdom and priests," there are a couple of things to keep in mind. First, the kingdom is ultimately God's kingdom and therefore should reflect God's love and justice. In the first chapters of the Bible, humans are told to "rule" the earth; in the last chapters of the Bible, there is a vision of God's people "reigning" over the earth. This rule must not be tyrannical and selfish, because it should reflect God's self-giving character and good purposes. Second, priests function as God's representatives on earth, those who mediate God's presence to his creation. To be a kingdom and priests is not about joining a group that dresses in formal regalia and performs sacred rituals; instead, to be priest-like is to embrace our holy calling to represent God to the world—lovingly and justly sharing God's presence in whatever way is fitting to the situation in which we find ourselves: rejoicing with those who rejoice, mourning with those who mourn, righting wrongs where possible, mending what's broken as appropriate, speaking the truth in love, shining hope into dark places, and performing countless other acts of mediating God's goodness to the world. This hallowed vocation is for all Christians: young and old, single and married, male and female, rich and poor, minority and majority, educated and uneducated, charming and awkward.

Is There a Soul? Is It Immortal?

Humans are embodied souls. Only God is immortal, but God will gift his people with resurrected bodies that will neither decay nor die.

We find that the question about the soul presses on us because it gets at human identity. Who, or what, are we? Are we simply these bodies, a combination of muscles, bone, skin, and organs? Are we nothing more than our biology? Or are we something else, something more? We have such complex thoughts, such deep feelings, such bonds of love. We can hardly help but wonder if we humans are simply accidents—nothing more than our physical bodies—with no soul or spirit or life force that exists after our inevitable deaths. We have such a strong sense of self. When we say "I," we can hardly help but think of ourselves in all our mental, emotional, and physical intricacy. How might the Christian concept of the soul speak to this experience?

In the Bible, we find references to something that we might think of as a soul, but it's not entirely clear how to understand these biblical passages. For example, in the Old Testament one occasionally reads about Sheol, a kind of shadowy place of the dead. On a couple of occasions, spirits of the deceased seem to arise from Sheol and momentarily speak to the living. This might lead Christians to conclude that after death one's soul or spirit lives on in a kind of shadowy existence. But the biblical details about Sheol are vague, and I don't think there's much to build on, so I think we should be hesitant to speculate. Whatever one makes of these references to Sheol in the Old Testament, it is pretty clear that Sheol is not heaven or nirvana or bliss. It's more like a place of nothingness—no true life, besides maybe the merest hints of ongoing existence.[10] The Old Testament is not dualistic in the sense that the physical body is bad and the immaterial spirit is good. Instead, the Old Testament is deeply holistic in the sense that our physical bodies are necessary for our flourishing; if our souls survive without our bodies, then it's an incomplete or unsatisfying existence. Sheol seems to represent just such an incomplete existence. In fact, Sheol comes across as something closer to a state of nonexistence than existence.

In the New Testament, there are also hints that the dead may have some kind of nonphysical existence after death, as bodiless souls or spirits. Here are just a few examples: Jesus tells a parable where two men die and are taken to some kind of waiting place of the dead (Luke 16:19–31); as Jesus nears death, he promises the man crucified beside him, "Today you will be with me in paradise" (Luke 23:43); Paul describes his death as to "be with Christ" (Phil. 1:23); and Revelation envisions the martyrs as calling out to God after their deaths (Rev. 6:9–11). None of these examples is clear about what happens after death. For some Christians these texts don't prove anything, because they are too vague, raising too many questions.[11] For others they suggest a kind of disembodied existence after death—something like a bodiless soul or spirit. Regardless, the New Testament is clear that, whatever exactly happens to a person at death, that person's existence is incomplete if he or she is apart from the body. This is why time and again the New Testament emphasizes the physical, bodily nature of the resurrection. While other ancient worldviews were okay with the afterlife of one's spirit, most in the ancient world found the Christian idea of a physical resurrection odd or off-putting.

So are we humans more than our bodies? Yes. Does this mean that our "true self" is our soul or spirit? Not exactly. It's more accurate to realize that our true self is our soul united with our body. This is what it means to be human: we are embodied souls. This makes Christians distinct from dualists, who tend to prioritize the spiritual and undervalue the material world. And it makes Christians distinct from pure naturalists, who reject the spiritual realm and think that the material world, including our material bodies, is all that there is—a world with no transcendent value or inherent goodness, merely a happy (or unhappy) accident, a place with no real hope on an inevitable path toward a cold and dark nothingness.

Is the "soul" part of us immortal? I don't think so, for two reasons. First, Christians believe that only God is truly immortal—the only being who has existed from all eternity and who cannot be destroyed. Everything else (whether spiritual or physical) was created by God and can be destroyed by God. Second, when God created all things, he created something distinct from himself. In other words, what God creates is not God, which implies that creation doesn't share in God's unique being. Part of God's unique being presumably includes his immortality. If creation doesn't share in God's unique being, then the human soul is unlikely to be immortal. At this point, Christianity differs from some other religions and worldviews that believe creation shares God's unique essence—so that all creation is in some ways a part of God. But if we recall our discussion earlier on pantheism, this idea gets messy quickly because it forces one to believe that death, disease, and evil are also part of God.

If souls are not inherently immortal, how can Christians believe in eternal life? Eternal life is possible only if God gives it as a gift. God is the source of life, which means that God can sustain our lives forever and ever. (And if God chooses not to sustain a life, it will cease to exist—the human soul cannot sustain its existence independent of God.) What's more, God doesn't sustain our lives in some sort of immaterial, ghostlike state. He gives us life in our fully human condition, as resurrected bodies.

In sum, (1) humans are embodied souls, (2) human souls are not inherently immortal because only God is immortal, (3) humans are not fully alive or complete unless their bodies and souls are united, and (4) God can choose to gift our resurrected bodies with eternal life. Christianity offers a distinct perspective on human nature: humans are special creatures who are more than their physical bodies (unlike what atheists and naturalists believe); yet Christians also think that the physical body is good, beautiful, and necessary for being fully human (unlike what some dualists believe). Because God is distinct from his creation, Christians do not assume that the human soul is immortal (unlike what some pantheists and dualists believe); however, because God is distinct from his creation, Christians have reason to hope that God is wholly good and that he will fix our broken world (unlike what some pantheists believe).

Is There Free Will?

Yes, though we're not 100 percent free, because of spiritual, physical, social, and environmental factors.

Are we masters of our own destiny or helpless hostages of fate? Are we free to be whoever we want? Can we do whatever we want? Are our choices limited by our physical, social, or spiritual makeup? Why does it feel as if sometimes we are in control of our thoughts and choices but at other times our thoughts and choices are almost beyond our control?

The answers depend both on whom we ask and on our big picture. For Rosenberg there is no free will, because the universe is a closed system where the physical facts fully determine all reality. Physical particles have no mind, no intentionality, and essentially no free will. Because our brains are physical, they must obey the laws of physics, regardless of how physically complex brains are. Therefore, our brains cannot escape the reality of physics, which is that everything must obey the blind, purposeless, will-less physical laws. Our brains are simply being swept along in the inescapable current of physical laws. Everything we think and do is the unavoidable result of physical processes that came before us, that will continue long after us, and that we have no control over. Thus all our thoughts, choices, and actions are fully determined for us because they are fixed by the unbending laws of physics—and there is no outside force (like a soul or God) that can alter these physical facts. The result? No free will. We have only the illusion of free will because it helps us survive.

How does the Christian metanarrative speak to the issue of free will? The best way to answer this is to look at recurring themes and ideas in Scripture. The Bible doesn't give a single, explicit teaching about free will, but it does imply that God grants humans some degree of free will.[12] This assumption is particularly apparent when we reflect on how (1) God desires to be in a relationship of reciprocal love with us, (2) God gives commands that can be disobeyed, and (3) God holds humans responsible for their sin and injustice. Let's briefly consider these one at a time. First, a relationship of reciprocal love implies that humans have the freedom to love God or not love God. If they are merely preprogrammed or forced to love, it would be a lower form of love and not the robust, deep kind of love that is characteristic of God. Second, the fact that God gives his people commands that can be disobeyed implies a freedom of will to either obey or disobey. If there is no freedom, it's hard not to see God as unwise (giving us commands that we are helpless to obey or disobey), cruel (torturing us with rules that we have no power to keep or break), or deceptive (pretending that we have choice and knowing that we will fail, all so he can show his superior goodness and mercy—though if it's all a charade, then it would seem to call into question his goodness and mercy). Third, if God holds humans culpable for their actions, this implies that they have some measure of responsibility for their actions. Otherwise God would seem unjust, punishing people for something they cannot help—like punishing someone for obeying the law of gravity or a robot for carrying out its preprogrammed operations.

So the Bible implies that, even though God is all-powerful and all-knowing, he has given humans real (and not imaginary) freedom of choice. In Scripture, humans don't have *complete* freedom but *partial* freedom. After all, God remains in control: God can still raise up rulers and bring down nations, he can bless and punish, he can call a people to be his special representative in the world, and so on. What this suggests is that God is so powerful that he is capable of granting free will while still maintaining control. In other words, God can be all-powerful without being a cosmic puppet master—God is that amazing. How is this possible? My guess is that God is so powerful and intelligent that he can allow us to have trillions of decisions but can weave these decisions into his grand will or overarching plan. Our choices are real, our choices matter, but they cannot derail or jeopardize God's plan. As C. S. Lewis so cleverly wrote, "You will certainly carry out God's purpose, however you act, but it makes a difference to you whether you serve like Judas or like John."[13] So my speculation is that God gives us real freedom of choice but that this choice is limited to some degree as God weaves our choices into his larger purposes.[14]

Let's look at this from another angle by considering the question of free will in light of the biblical view of humans. We start with the idea that humans are physical, spiritual, and social beings. We are embodied souls who are made to be in relationship with others. How might this perspective on human nature help us think about free will?

From Alex Rosenberg's perspective, a completely closed physical system seems to rule out the possibility of free will. Rosenberg may be right to think this way, though there are some detractors.[15] Regardless, Christianity is not based on a completely closed physical system. By identifying us as embodied souls, Christianity offers us a reason to believe that humans are not trapped in lives that are predetermined by the physical universe. Because we are embodied souls, there's good reason to expect humans to have some degree of personal autonomy and responsibility—our soulishness presumably offers some independence from a closed, predetermined physical world. At the same time, because we are embodied souls, humans are affected by the interplay of the physical realm (our bodies, brains, and surrounding culture) and the spiritual realm (sin or the Holy Spirit).

Certain limitations are imposed on us by the physical world. There are the obvious limitations of our physical bodies: we aren't free to walk through walls, breathe underwater, fly with our arms, or escape death. Perhaps more to the point, we aren't free to choose our ethnicity, our natural talents, our genetic dispositions to disease, or whether we're born into an environment filled with support and opportunity or with neglect and scarcity. These factors, which are out of our control, limit our freedom.

The spiritual realm is also a factor in our freedom (or lack thereof). Humans can be manipulated or controlled by sin, or they can be freed and empowered by God's Spirit. Either way, the spiritual reality is shaping the human will. Scripture implies a kind of partnership at play between the human and these spiritual influences. That is, in some ways sin manipulates humans, but in other ways humans willingly give themselves to sin. (Recall how humans can be seen as "slaves to sin" while being simultaneously responsible for their actions.) Similarly, God's Spirit can empower humans, but humans must be willing to give themselves over to the Spirit's influence. (Recall our study of Philippians: "Work out your salvation . . . , for it is God who works in you both to will and to act" [2:12–13 NIV].) God doesn't force his grace or his Spirit on a person; rather, he offers some measure of choice for whether the person will accept or reject this gift.

If we add the social and environmental dimensions to this picture, we find further factors that shape our free will. As we've seen, humans are made to be in relationship; we are incomplete when isolated from community. This means, though, that these relationships will inevitably influence who we are, how we think, the choices we make, and the actions we take. We are social beings, which means we are shaped by our social environments. Our families, friends, enemies, and cultures will all have some effect on our lives. For example, even at a most basic level our births determine for us the family and culture into which we are born, which means that we have no control over what our first language will be, what values will first be instilled in us, what education we will first receive, or what religion/worldview/philosophy will first be introduced to us. We may grow up to embrace our family and culture of origin, or we may come to reject it; either way, our upbringing will have had an impact on our lives even though we did not choose to start our lives in that social environment.

To summarize: (1) The Bible implies that humans have real freedom of will. (2) Our freedom is to some degree limited by God's sovereign, overarching will. (3) Humans are embodied souls: physical-spiritual-social beings. This means that (a) some of our freedom is limited by our physical bodies, (b) some of our freedom is limited by spiritual forces that can manipulate or empower us, and (c) some of our freedom is limited by the social and cultural environments in which we find ourselves. (4) Because we are more than our physical bodies—because we are embodied souls—there is reason to believe that we have some degree of free will—the freedom necessary, for example, to engage in relationships of reciprocal love.

What Happens When We Die?

Our bodies return to dust, though at some future point all will face God's judgment: for some, this will mean destruction; for others, restoration—physically, socially, and spiritually.

What happens when we die? This is a question we both like and don't like to think about. It's too important and mysterious not to think about. But it can also be unsettling to contemplate our deaths—it can make us feel small, vulnerable, and unimportant. Yet if we don't face the question about death, we may lack a sufficient answer to the question about how to live wisely.

What we find when we wrestle with the question of death is how closely this question is tied to matters of hope and accountability. Notice how Alex Rosenberg answers the question about what happens when we die: everything pretty much goes on as before, except us. If Rosenberg is right, then death is the end of our personal existence—and death is the ultimate fate of the whole universe. And if he's right, then death wins in the end: we have no reason to hope that things will really change, to hope that the world will cease to be plagued by oppression, hate, greed, corruption, suffering, and so forth. Yes, there are still bright spots of love and happiness, art and beauty, and these are to be cherished. Nonetheless, there is no hope that wrongs will be righted, no hope of reunion with loved ones who have died, no hope of anything beyond our few decades of existence. This is particularly tragic for those whose fleeting lives have been filled with pain and sadness. We die, and the universe marches forward without us, on its way to its own inevitable end.

For some, there may be a certain freedom to this view: freedom from nagging guilt, freedom from having to fear the justice of God, and freedom from any real duties or expectations. But this freedom comes at a cost: freedom from the hope that things will be set right one day, freedom from our lives having ultimate purpose and meaning, freedom from love being anything other than an illusion, and freedom from the conviction that morals really matter and that oppressors will face justice. If God and the afterlife are illusions, then hope is also an illusion. We can check the math: no God + no afterlife = no hope that all will turn out right.

God will make things right through restoration and just judgment. God's work of restoration and renewal will be more beautiful and satisfying than anything we can imagine. It will be a holistic restoration, as God brings physical, social, and spiritual renewal. God will gift his people with resurrected bodies that are uncorrupted and incorruptible. God will honor his people with the joyous task of caring for the renewed creation, and he will gather his people together to dwell in peace and love, reconciled to God and to one another. And all of this is possible because of Jesus—his life, death, resurrection, and ascension.

The other side of God's restoration project will be his just judgment. Those who are united to Christ need not fear God's judgment because they are united to the holy and righteous one whose death and life have atoned for sin. For others, God will judge their lives justly and deal with their sins appropriately. The precise nature of the judgment is open to debate (see appendix B). What does not seem open to debate, though, is that God's holiness and justice compel him to do what is right with regard to sin and injustice. The biblical images of such judgment are not cozy; rather, they can be scary. No people who stand before God on their own merits will stand before God with confidence, because they will stand before a perfect and holy being who has seen all their actions (public or private) and who also knows all that resides in their hearts. In whatever way deemed fit, the righteous judge will make it so that all wrongs are righted, all debts paid, and all punishments meted out.

What Is the Difference between Right and Wrong, Good and Bad?

In short, right is based on God's holiness, love, and will; wrong is that which rejects, hinders, or opposes God's holiness, love, and will.

Questions about right and wrong are closely tied to the other questions we've asked. After all, "right and wrong" make sense only if you have some idea about ultimate reality and purpose. If, as Rosenberg believes, ultimate reality is an indifferent, impersonal, accidental universe, then "right and wrong" don't really exist. How could they? There's no basis for ultimate right and wrong in a universe that has no purpose and no intention. This is why Rosenberg answers this question about right and wrong by saying, "There is no moral difference between them." In case there's any confusion, he continues: "Is abortion, euthanasia, suicide, paying taxes, foreign aid—or anything else you don't like—forbidden, permissible, or sometimes obligatory? Anything goes." To be clear, he still thinks that humans should follow certain moral intuitions, because it makes life better. But moral instincts are not based in ultimate truth or objective reality; they are just evolutionary survival instincts. He cleverly calls this "nice nihilism"—for the most part, being nice makes life better—but, at the end of the day, anything goes because nothing is truly right or wrong.[16]

For Christians, ultimate reality is a God of love and goodness who wills for his creatures to share in his love and goodness. Therefore, the measuring stick of "right and wrong" is the love and goodness and will of God.

- God's love is active, sacrificial, and merciful.
- God's goodness is just and true.
- God's will is to share his love, and for humans to respond by loving God with all their heart, soul, mind, and strength, and loving others as themselves.

Consequently, "right" is characterized by a love that is active, sacrificial, and merciful; by a pursuit of that which is truly good and just; and by a conformity to God's will for loving relationship.

As we might expect, Christians should think that "wrong" is that which rejects, hinders, or opposes God's love, goodness, and will. If "right" is active, sacrificial, merciful, loving, just, and true, then "wrong" is apathetic, selfish, merciless, hateful, unjust, and false. That which is "right" promotes God's will that humans be loved and give love; that which is "wrong" inhibits God's love from being experienced and paid forward to others. For Christians, right and wrong are real because God is real, because love is real, because goodness is real, and because God's will is real. While Rosenberg can claim that "anything goes," the Christian ought to believe that our ethical choices are truly important—to God, to ourselves, to others, which means that some actions are forbidden, some are permissible, and some are obligatory.

Why Should I Be Moral?

Because we were created to love, because it's the proper response to the God-given gifts of life and redemption, and because God will judge all people justly.

My answer to this question is pretty self-explanatory: I offer three basic reasons to be moral. First, we act morally because this is how we were made to act. To ask, "Why should I be moral?" is like an eagle asking, "Why should I soar?" or a fish asking, "Why should I swim?" or an artist asking, "Why should I create?" or a scientist asking, "Why should I discover?" or a parent asking, "Why should I care for my child?" This is how we thrive and flourish, because this is how we were created to thrive and flourish. To some, this might sound too restrictive: "What if I don't want to live this way? What if I don't want someone to tell me how to live my life?" This is where Christian faith comes into play, specifically faith in the character of God. Christians believe that God has revealed himself to be a God of love and goodness, a God who does what is best for us. This is pivotal: Will we trust God to lead us on the best path for our lives, or will we trust ourselves to forge our own path? This question takes us back to where we started this journey. Will we put our faith in God's good will for our lives, or will we pridefully choose our own path by plucking the fruit from the tree of knowledge of good and evil?[17]

Second, we should conduct ourselves morally because life is a gift, and the proper response to this gift is gratefulness. Gratefulness is our way of showing that we understand both the nature of the gift and its cost. If a child's parents worked overtime to save up money to buy their child a car on her sixteenth birthday, the proper response of the child would be gratefulness—a gratefulness that understands the nature of the gift (for instance, by recognizing that a car needs proper fuel, regular oil changes, etc.) and the cost of the gift (for instance, by driving the car with appropriate caution and care, understanding her parents' sacrifice). Each of our lives is a gift of God, something that we could not earn or create for ourselves. The proper response to this gift is gratefulness—a gratefulness that understands the nature of the gift (for instance, by recognizing that our lives are meant for love and goodness) and the cost of the gift (for instance, by expressing gratitude and paying forward mercy).

At first glance it might seem that our lives were not that costly to God. Perhaps had sin never entered the picture that might be the case. But Christians believe that God has gifted us not only with our initial life but also with new life, made possible by Jesus's life, death, and resurrection. This was a gift more costly than we can fathom—an immortal, all-powerful being who sets aside his power and immortality to become a poor human, serving his creatures, and even dying on their behalf. The cost is incalculable. Through this sacrifice, he gave us back our lives—free from sin and corruption, capable of life eternal. The proper response to a gift so incredible and so costly is gratefulness, reflected in a life that values the nature and cost of the gift. Such a life will inevitably mirror that of the gift giver: a life of mercy, humility, service, compassion, and sacrifice.

Third, we are to live moral lives because we will one day face a just judgment before a good and holy God. Because there is a good God, there is a moral standard. And because he's a holy God, he will do what is right as he judges according to this moral standard. He will judge rightly and completely as he gives an inside-out examination of a person's life—taking into account one's heart, thoughts, and actions (and, I imagine, taking into account one's social and cultural environment, so as to judge fairly). If judgment is inescapable, and if judgment is based on God's moral standard, then it is foolish to live immorally.

So when it comes to life's big questions, which system is right: Christianity, atheism, pantheism, or dualism (or something else)? There's no simple answer to this. There are no clear tests that can definitively prove one system's superiority over another. So what do we do? One option is to step back and look at the big picture to see if one system makes better sense than the others. For example, does Rosenberg's atheism make sense? Yes and no. There is a kind of logic to his responses, although it leads one to a place that ends up being hopelessly circular. One major problem for Rosenberg is that human thinking may end up being delusional. Here's the situation as Rosenberg sees it:

- There's no God, but through the evolutionary process humans developed this illusion about God because it was better for survival.
- There's no purpose or meaning in life, but through the evolutionary process humans developed this illusion about meaning because it was better for survival.
- There's no free will, but through the evolutionary process humans developed this illusion about free will because it was better for survival.
- There's no morality, but through the evolutionary process humans developed this illusion about morality because it was better for survival.
- There's no mental realm of thought (only the physical processes of our brains), but through the evolutionary process humans developed this illusion about thought because it was better for survival.

Notice the problem at the end? If atheism is true, how would anyone ever know (since human thinking is merely physical, in which case our thoughts are part of the predetermined physical world)? Our thoughts are controlled by fate, by chance, by survival—neither by reason nor by truth.[18] Plus, how can we trust our thinking when so many of our natural thoughts (about God, purpose, morality, and free will) end up being inaccurate according to

Rosenberg? To those who complain that one cannot test Christianity because one cannot test the supernatural, guess what? Atheism cannot be tested either, because there may be no escape from the delusion and preprogramming of human thought. We may not be able to trust our own thinking.

We humans either have to toss our hands in the air and give up, or we have to believe that human thinking can be trusted, that it's not ultimately delusional. The problem, of course, is that such an assumption could force us beyond atheistic naturalism. It may force us to admit that we're not reducible to our physical selves. At the very least, it would force us to put faith in speculative ideas about how free will and reliable thinking can emerge in a closed, physical system. It pushes one to take at least a modest leap of faith. We have no definitive reason to trust that our thinking can be freely and accurately aimed at truth and reason. "But," someone may protest, "I still have good reasons to trust my thinking, even if those reasons cannot be proved with certainty," to which I'd say, "You sound a bit like a thoughtful Christian." Christians cannot prove our faith beyond a doubt, but we have some pretty good reasons for our faith. And we will be turning to those very reasons in the next chapters.

But before we do, let's consider for a moment that our thoughts can lead to truth. Let's assume that our thinking has some degree of reliability. Which strikes us as more likely: that our deepest intuitions about life, morality, and the soul are illusions, or that our deepest intuitions contain truth that points us to a greater reality—one where life is truly precious and meaningful, where good and evil are real categories and not just opinions, where humans are more than their physical bodies, where love is real, and where death doesn't have to be the end of the story?

9

Challenges to the Christian System

There are many good reasons to find Christianity compelling, but before we get to those we first need to address four reasons people commonly give for rejecting Christianity:

1. How can anyone believe in a good and powerful God when there is so much suffering?
2. How can anyone believe the Bible in a scientific age?
3. Can Christians really believe that their belief system is right and everyone else's is wrong?
4. If Christians are right, then why is the church's history so full of hypocrisy and evil?[1]

In what follows I am not trying to give the final answers to these questions, nor am I even trying to suggest that these questions have fully satisfying answers. Instead, I want to show that, despite the real challenges that some of these questions pose, there are thoughtful ways to respond that don't require Christians to abandon central faith claims, deny science, or be irrational. I'm also hoping that the reader will keep in mind that no worldview can escape difficult questions. For example, the atheist doesn't have to face difficult questions about God's nature and character, but she must face questions like these: "Is there really no ultimate meaning or morality, and maybe no free will? At the end of the day, are humans simply highly evolved animals with no ultimate purpose, and no hope for anything beyond this life? Can it be true that love isn't objectively good, and evil isn't objectively bad?" Every worldview has serious questions to face, but I hope to show that the Christian system can handle its difficult questions in a way that is far more satisfying (at an intellectual level and an instinctive level) than is the case with other worldviews.

How Can Anyone Believe in a Good and Powerful God When There Is So Much Suffering?[2]

If God is so good and loving, why does he allow so much pain and cruelty and needless suffering? If God really has power over sickness and death, why doesn't he use the tiniest fraction of that power to eradicate cancer, AIDS, or Parkinson's disease? If God is so merciful, why doesn't he show a little mercy to the starving and destitute? If God is so just, why does he allow sex trafficking and slavery? To be honest, when I allow myself to face the horrors of the world, there are times when I can't help but think, *Maybe life is simply meaningless. Maybe there really is no hope, no healing, no loving and powerful being who cares for us. Maybe all the pain and injustice and suffering in the world are just meaningless features of a meaningless universe.*

I've been feeling this more personally as my wife and I have started fostering infants.[3] We recently brought a two-week-old girl home from the hospital. She couldn't come home from the hospital right away because her mother was a drug addict, which meant the baby had to stay longer to have morphine to help her go through withdrawal. We took this sweet child home and watched her fight a battle that shouldn't have been hers to fight. It was heartbreaking, because this little girl didn't choose this life, didn't choose this mother, didn't choose to enter the world addicted. And this kind of thing is happening all across my city, my state, my country, and the world. Innocent humans enter life with the odds stacked against them. Being so close to such brokenness forces me to pray, "God, why would you let this happen? How could you sit by? What chance do these babies have in life?" And yes, I do at times wonder if I'm praying to no one, if there's just too much misery in this world to maintain belief in a good, loving, all-powerful God.

Most of my suffering is secondhand, so I don't want to overreach in this chapter, as though I can fully empathize with the full weight of this problem. Perhaps it would be better to turn to Christians whose suffering is more personal. For example, when C. S. Lewis lost his wife, he journaled about his grief in raw and honest language:

> Where is God? . . . [Go] to him when your need is desperate, when all other help is vain, and what do you find? A door slammed in your face, and a sound of bolting and double bolting on the inside. After that, silence. You may as well turn away. The longer you wait, the more emphatic the silence will become. There are no lights in the windows. It might be an empty house. Was it ever inhabited? It seemed so once. And that seeming was as strong as this. What can this mean? Why is he so present a commander in our time of prosperity and so very absent a help in time of trouble? . . .
>
> Not that I am (I think) in much danger of ceasing to believe in God. The real danger is of coming to believe such dreadful things about him. The conclusion I dread is not "So there is no God after all," but "So this is what God is really like. Deceive yourself no longer." . . .
>
> Talk to me about the truth of religion and I'll listen gladly. Talk to me about the duty of religion and I'll listen submissively. But don't come talking to me about the consolation of religion or I shall suspect that you don't understand. . . .
>
> Sooner or later I must face the question in plain language. What reason have we, except our own desperate wishes, to believe that God is, by any standard we can conceive, "good"? Doesn't all the *prima facie* evidence suggest exactly the opposite? . . .
>
> What chokes every prayer and every hope is the memory of all the prayers [we] offered and all the false hopes we had. Not hopes raised merely by our own wishful thinking; hopes encouraged, even forced upon us, by false diagnoses, by X-ray photographs, by strange remissions, by one temporary recovery that might have ranked as a miracle. Step by step we were "led up the garden path." Time after time, when he seemed most gracious he was really preparing the next torture.[4]

I hesitate to add anything beyond this, as if I could somehow provide a satisfying answer to the question at hand. No, I can't provide a satisfying answer. The most I can do is to show how I try to make sense of the problem of suffering at both an instinctive level and an intellectual level.

Instinct

Instinctively, in our guts, we find that so much suffering seems wrong. It's not simply *meaningless*, it's *wrong*, a sign of brokenness or evil. That is, the atheist may have an even more difficult problem than the Christian when it comes to the problem of suffering. The atheist essentially has to say, "There is no problem. It's a meaningless event in a meaningless universe. What you're experiencing is sad and painful, but it's not categorically wrong or evil or contrary to the way things should be. It's just the way things are." Surely that cannot be accurate. Surely we cannot accept that starvation, suffering, and child abuse are not ultimately wrong or bad, that they're not a sign of evil and brokenness in the world. When I held that drug-withdrawing newborn and wondered whether God was real, I knew that the flip side was even worse—to believe that there was no good God, to believe that this sweet child's life was ultimately meaningless, and to believe that her suffering was not actually wrong.

To say that some suffering is wrong or evil or broken is to suggest that there is such a thing as right or good or whole. Try to explain how something is wrong without a concept of rightness; try to explain how something is broken without a concept of wholeness. As we've already seen, if there's no God, then there's no ultimate rightness or goodness or wholeness, which means that suffering isn't ultimately wrong or evil or broken. If at a gut level we recognize that some suffering is truly wrong, we are recognizing that there must be something that is truly right and whole, which is only truly possible if God exists.

Let's consider three ways that the Christian metanarrative might help make sense of our instincts about suffering and evil. First, according to Scripture, a good God created a good world. Although this sounds simple, it provides a foundation for believing that there is a way things ought to be. That is, Christians can recognize that some things are wrong or evil or broken, because they have a standard for what is right and good and whole. Our instinctive sense that some things are deeply wrong corresponds to a deeper reality that a right standard exists, a standard for how things really ought to be. Our instincts are not based on illusion; instead, something really has gone wrong in the world, something truly is broken, something desperately needs to be restored.

Second, Scripture speaks to our frustration with God's way of handling suffering and evil. That is, sometimes we feel that God's response is inadequate and insufficient. The Bible names this. Throughout Scripture we read of people who are voicing their anger, sadness, and frustration to God—expressing their deep distress that things are not how they should be and that God is not responding how they'd want him to.[5] The Bible doesn't pretend that there are no problems, no difficulties, no unanswered questions. This isn't stoicism, where wrong and evil are simply a matter of perspective. This isn't cosmic dualism, where wrong and evil depend on which team one is on. From a biblical perspective, suffering and injustice are very real, ongoing problems.

Third, when God deals with the world's brokenness through Jesus, he does so in a way that speaks to the human heart. God doesn't deal with suffering from afar; he doesn't stay clear of the messiness. He enters into our world, he experiences our pain, and he takes our brokenness on himself, bearing the weight of it on the cross. He was "a man of suffering, and familiar with pain" (Isa. 53:3 NIV). The Bible doesn't answer all our questions about suffering and evil. It does, however, tell how God gives of himself, joining us in our pain and sorrow. Jesus even joins us in our sense of abandonment, voicing his own agony to God from the cross: "My God, my God, why have you left me?" (Mark 15:34; cf. Ps. 22:1). Jesus's willingness to join us in our pain speaks to our souls. As much as we want someone to fix our pain, we also want someone to empathize with us and to be near us. This is the beautiful and distinct Christian response: in Jesus's incarnation and death, God has joined us in our pain and suffering; in so doing, Jesus has made it possible for us to become fully healed; because of Jesus, we have reason to hope that one day all will be made well and new and whole. At some future point, Jesus will return to finish the work he began, and he will set all things right. Perhaps, just as God redeemed Jesus's suffering by transforming it into something beautiful, God will similarly redeem all our sorrows and sufferings and transform them into something meaningful and beautiful.[6]

As Lewis grieved the loss of his wife, he eventually came to see glimpses of God's love in the midst of his sorrow. Specifically, this came about as Lewis reflected on his wish that he could have taken his wife's suffering into his own body so that she might be spared. As Lewis reflected on his desire to trade places with her, he realized that this is what God did for us. God took our suffering in himself.[7] This didn't answer all Lewis's questions, but it did help.

I still have questions about how to make sense of all of this. Nonetheless, the answers that I find in Christianity are more satisfying than the answers I find in other worldviews. The Christian answers resonate with my instincts that something is truly wrong in our world, that suffering isn't the way things are supposed to be, and that the best response to suffering will include both empathy and healing.

Intellectual Insights

We've considered the problem of suffering at an instinctive level; now let us consider it from more of an intellectual level. Doesn't suffering prove that God either doesn't exist or that he isn't all-good or all-powerful? After all, if God were all-good and all-powerful then he would prevent all suffering and evil—right? Let's look at a few ways one might tackle this problem.

First, one could take the atheistic route: since there is no God, suffering is simply a meaningless event in a meaningless world. But as I've explained above, this view is not without its own problems. Second, one could take the dualistic route: there is not one all-good and all-powerful God but two powers that are in conflict—one good, one evil. This view makes some sense of how life is a mixture of good and evil, but as we've seen earlier, this view also has its own problems. (For example, good and evil become a matter of perspective; plus, there's no hope of things being set right.) Third, one could take the free-will, monotheist route: an all-good and all-powerful God gives his creatures some measure of free will. God does so even though free will can lead to suffering, because free will is also the best (or only) way for God to achieve the greatest good. Here's how C. S. Lewis explains it:

> God created things which had free will. That means creatures which can go either wrong or right. Some people think they can imagine a creature which was free but had no possibility of going wrong; I cannot. If a thing is free to be good it is also free to be bad. And free will is what has made evil possible. Why, then, did God give them free will? Because free will, though it makes evil possible, is also the only thing that makes possible any love or goodness or joy worth having. . . . The happiness which God designs for his higher creatures is the happiness of being freely, voluntarily united to him and to each other in an ecstasy of love and delight compared with which the most rapturous love between a man and a woman on this earth is mere milk and water. And for that they must be free.
>
> Of course, God knew what would happen if they used their freedom the wrong way: apparently he thought it worth the risk. Perhaps we feel inclined to disagree with him. . . . If God thinks this state of war in the universe a price worth paying for free will—that is, for making a live world in which creatures can do real good or harm and something of real importance can happen, instead of a toy world which only moves when he pulls the strings—then we may take it [that] it is worth paying.
>
> When we have understood about free will, we shall see how silly it is to ask, as somebody once asked me: "Why did God make a creature of such rotten stuff that it went wrong?" The better stuff a creature is made of—the cleverer and stronger and freer it is—then the better it will be if it goes right, but also the worse it will be if it goes wrong. A cow cannot be very good or very bad; a dog can be both better and worse; a child better and worse still; an ordinary man, still more so; a man of genius, still more so.[8]

William Lane Craig explains suffering in a way similar to this, but he adds a few comments that might help clarify what Lewis seems to be saying. First, Craig explains that just because God is all-powerful doesn't mean that God can do the logically impossible or absurd. In this case, we might assume that God cannot create free creatures who are not truly free to obey or rebel. Further, we might assume that God cannot create a world where one can experience deep and mutual love if one is not free to accept or reject or return that love.[9] Such scenarios seem logically impossible—freedom without free will, mutual love without choice. For God to create truly free creatures who are truly free to love, it seems that even an all-powerful God can do that only by making creatures who are truly free to reject love and reject the good.

Second, Craig draws our attention to the limits of human knowledge. As he does so, he is representing a philosophical perspective known as skeptical theism. This view is widely recognized by both atheist and theist philosophers as offering a sufficiently rational explanation for how an all-good and all-powerful God can exist alongside suffering. Here's the simple version from Craig:

> For all we know, it's possible that in any world of free persons with as much good as this world, there would also be as much suffering. . . . For God could have overriding reasons for allowing suffering in the world. . . . It may well be the case that a world with suffering is, on balance, better overall than a world with no suffering. In any case, it is at least *possible*, and that is sufficient to defeat the [claim that an all-loving God prefers a world without suffering]. . . . Giving the dizzying complexities of life, we are simply in no position to judge that God has no good reason for permitting some instance of suffering. . . . Only an all-knowing God could grasp the complexities of directing a world of free people toward his envisioned goals.[10]

The basic argument is that an all-good and all-powerful God *could* have reasons for allowing suffering, even if those reasons are not clear to us because of our limited grasp of the larger situation. Perhaps our world must have the potential to get this messy if it is also to allow humans the potential for deep love, real choice, significant purpose, and/or some other goods. To restate Lewis: "If God thinks this state of war in the universe a price worth paying for free will—that is, for making a live world in which creatures can do real good or harm and something of real importance can happen, instead of a toy world which only moves when he pulls the strings—then we may take it [that] it is worth paying." It's logically defensible to believe that there are satisfying answers to the question at hand, even if those answers are too complex for humans to fully grasp. It's a rational answer, though it may feel less than satisfying. What makes this answer a bit more satisfying for Christians is that God has proved his trustworthiness and compassion by taking on our flesh and our suffering in order to restore us. We have solid reason to trust that God is doing what is best, even if we cannot fully grasp God's reasons. Such a position is neither illogical nor unfounded.

How Can Anyone Believe the Bible in a Scientific Age?

It's certainly possible to read the Bible as teaching that the earth is flat, that God lives in a distant sky above the earth, that the universe is only a few thousand years old, and that diverse biological life was created in a matter of days. The scientific evidence to the contrary makes it difficult (and sometimes absurd) to believe these things anymore. And yet there are countless people, including numerous scientists, who go on believing in God and trusting the Bible. How can they do this? Are they simply too stubborn to give up their faith? Are they not willing to honestly face the difficult questions that would certainly destroy their religion? I suspect that some are sticking their heads in the sand. But not all are. In fact, there are many brilliant scientists who think that Christianity and science are not rivals but friends.

Indeed, there is a long and beautiful tradition of Christians who have regarded science as a friend of the faith, because they believed that "the heavens declare the glory of God; the skies proclaim the work of his hand. Day after day they pour forth speech; night after night they reveal knowledge" (Ps. 19:1–2 NIV). Some of the most prominent Christian scientists today include Francis Collins (leader of the Human Genome Project and director of the National Institutes of Health), Alister McGrath (priest, scientist, and professor of theology at Oxford), and John Polkinghorne (priest and professor of mathematical physics at Cambridge).

If we look further back, it may surprise the reader to know that both Isaac Newton and Charles Darwin were buried in a church—Westminster Abbey. Whatever their beliefs, the church held these scientists in esteem. Here's an interesting description of Darwin's memorial service:

> Although an agnostic, Darwin was greatly respected by his contemporaries and the Bishop of Carlisle, Harvey Goodwin, in a memorial sermon preached in the Abbey on the Sunday following the funeral, said "I think that the interment of the remains of Mr Darwin in Westminster Abbey is in accordance with the judgment of the wisest of his countrymen. . . . It would have been unfortunate if anything had occurred to give weight and currency to the foolish notion which some have diligently propagated, but for which Mr Darwin was not responsible, that there is a necessary conflict between a knowledge of Nature and a belief in God."[11]

Similarly, we shouldn't forget that the big bang was initially proposed by a Catholic priest, Georges Lemaître. Early on, some critics rejected Lemaître's proposal, in part because they thought the big bang sounded too much like it pointed to a creator![12] At the time, many thought the universe was eternal, so that an idea of a beginning "bang" might suggest the idea of a cosmic beginner—God. Somehow, history has allowed us to forget that the big bang theory initially seemed to some folks (including the pope at that time) like evidence *for* God rather than evidence *against* God, as it is now oddly misunderstood.

So how might scientifically minded Christians reconcile their faith with modern scientific findings? What are we to do when the Bible seems to assume that the earth is flat and only a few thousand years old? The answer is that we take the Bible *more* seriously, not *less* seriously. We give serious consideration to the nature of the Bible: what the Bible is, what it's trying to communicate, and how it's trying to communicate. In short, we take seriously that the Bible is a special revelation from God, in which God communicates to people using their language and style in order to reveal who God is, who we are, and who we're called to be.

It's especially important to realize that the Bible was written in certain languages, at certain times, and within certain cultures. This is a vital point: God communicates through the Bible while working with the limitations that come with language and culture. So for most readers of the Bible, some translation is required. And here's another vital point: *we need not only the language translated but we need the culture translated as well.* Sometimes once the ancient biblical languages are translated into our modern language, we wrongly assume that no more explanation or clarification is needed. In particular, we sometimes fail to recognize that the Bible is written not only in a foreign language but also in a foreign culture and with the use of "foreign" genres—genres like law, Hebrew poetry, ancient historiography, and wisdom literature. If we don't understand the ancient genres, we are likely to make some mistakes in interpretation. We already apply this rule with nonbiblical literature. For example, we know not to force poetry into the straightjacket of literalism, lest we risk ruining metaphors and similes. When it comes to Scripture, though, we are less familiar with ancient genres so we need additional help.

Thus, studying the Bible sometimes requires us to translate not only the ancient language but also the ancient genre and ancient culture. This isn't to say that one needs a PhD to understand the central truths of Scripture; it's simply to say that scholars can help us understand certain parts of Scripture that require extra "translation." Many scholars would say that the biblical creation accounts are one of those places where some extra "translation" can be really helpful.[13] As we saw in chapter 4, there are good reasons to believe that Genesis 1–2 is not portraying a strictly scientific or modern historical description of the cosmos.

As God communicated with his people, he was willing to meet them where they were, without them needing to have complex knowledge of the cosmos. Sometimes this meant that God didn't correct their cosmic map, because it wasn't vital to his message whether they happened to believe that the earth was flat or that the sun moved across the dome of the sky. God wasn't deceiving them but was instead interested in teaching a more significant truth. And let's be honest: almost no one reading this book really understands the physics of the big bang, and every scientific explanation we've been given has been accommodated to our limited understanding of quantum physics—and yet we don't therefore assume that scientists are deceiving us because they have to accommodate their theories to make them accessible to us.

Perhaps another example would be helpful. My wife and I just had an early version of "the talk" with our young daughter. She had been asking us about babies, and we had been advised that it would be wise to give her some age-appropriate answers. So we talked about how mommies have "eggs" and daddies have "seeds," which led to a conversation about God's gift of marriage, about why her body is special, and about why people should respect one another's private parts. We communicated truth to her in a way that she could grasp and that spoke to the matters that were most pertinent. However, we were not concerned if she currently has in her mind the unscientific idea that daddies' seeds are like watermelon seeds and mommies' eggs are like chicken eggs! When she gets to the point where she has a more scientific view of "seeds" and "eggs," she hopefully won't think we lied to her; instead, she'll understand we were communicating truths in a way she could grasp at that time. Similarly, when God communicated to an ancient audience, he accommodated his teaching so that his truths would make sense within a less-scientific culture. As science advances it doesn't reveal that God lied, only that God in his grace humbly communicated in a way that ancient peoples could understand. God's truth doesn't change, even when we "grow up" in our scientific understandings. The Bible is still authoritative special revelation from God, even though God was communicating truths to an ancient people in an ancient language within an ancient genre in order to teach them about who he is, who they are, and who they're called to be.

It's not just the Bible and parents who teach truths with models that aren't technically accurate. This happens in science as well. For example, numerous scientific models and diagrams are used to capture an idea or theory, even though such models are technically inaccurate. I was just speaking to a colleague about our models of the solar system, which teach truths about the planets orbiting the sun even though the typical solar-system model is astronomically (pun intended) off scale. Similarly, Alister McGrath notes how the popular model that depicts the atom as a "miniature solar system" isn't technically accurate either. The model is, however, a helpful way to depict an atom and to communicate certain truths about atoms that are otherwise hard to comprehend.[14] The model communicates truth, but it's not intended to have a perfect correspondence to the reality it depicts. The model of the atom becomes deceptive only when someone mistakenly claims that the model is in exact correspondence with the reality it depicts. Perhaps we can make an analogy: the biblical model of creation (a flat earth made in six days by God dividing the waters and placing a dome in the sky) is communicating timeless truths (the sovereignty of God and the goodness and orderliness of creation); the creation model becomes deceptive only when someone mistakes the model for an exact correspondence with the reality it depicts (e.g., by arguing that the earth is flat and that the sun revolves around it).

But how does one tell the difference between the model and the truth being communicated? When is the Bible making a truth claim, and when is it simply accommodating ancient concepts? To be honest, it's not always clear. At this point, it's wise to proceed with humility and ask questions such as the following:

- *What genre is this communicated in?* For example, does the genre indicate that its details are to be understood figuratively, straightforwardly, or somewhere in between? We don't interpret poetry the way we interpret history, or the way we interpret law, or the way we interpret parables, or the way we interpret wisdom literature, and on it goes. Genre matters.
- *What else does the Bible say on this matter?* For example, sometimes the Bible shows flexibility about details regarding the time line and mechanics of creation. This flexibility might be a clue that such details are not the important truth being communicated but are signs of accommodation.
- *What have Christians throughout the ages thought about this?* Christians have been fairly uniform in their belief that God is the creator of everything, but they have not been uniform in how they interpret the creation account in Genesis 1–2; instead, many realized early on that Genesis 1–2 is probably not meant to be taken as a scientific account of creation. (It may even be surprising to learn that more recent heroes of the faith, like C. S. Lewis and Billy Graham, were okay with evolution.) In contrast, the church has strongly affirmed that the crucifixion and resurrection of Jesus must be understood as historical events, not metaphors.

- *What's the scientific evidence related to this issue?* On this question, the assumption is that God's revelation in Scripture and God's revelation in nature can go hand in hand. Therefore, when solid scientific evidence seems to be at odds with Scripture, it's an invitation to double-check our interpretation of Scripture to make sure we have not misunderstood Scripture. In other words, *it may not be science and Scripture that are at odds but science and our mistaken interpretation of Scripture.*

I think that some folks fear that bringing science and the Bible into dialogue will result in whittling away Scripture to the point where there's almost nothing of substance left. They seem scared that science will reign supreme and Scripture will be reduced to an ancient and mostly outdated self-help book. That idea is wrong: although science can help us describe and understand the natural world, by its very definition it cannot tell us whether there is a reality beyond the natural world and how that greater reality affects our present lives. Ironically, most people who claim that science is the only way to discover truth are making a faith claim, not a scientific claim. Science cannot tell us that science is the only way to truth. How could it? Notice how little sense this claim makes when it's spelled out: since science, by definition, cannot tell us about something beyond the natural world, then nothing beyond the natural world exists. That's simply bad reasoning.[15]

Can Christians Really Believe That Their Belief System Is Right and Everyone Else's Is Wrong?

I don't understand why some people object to the notion that one's own worldview might be right and others' might be wrong. If we are going to believe that something is true, then we typically have to believe that its opposite is not true. If I believe that God exists, then I have to believe atheism is wrong. If I believe atheism is true, then I have to believe theism is false. If I believe that this natural world is all there is, then I have to believe that every religion is wrong about a central issue.[16] If I believe that humans have inherent dignity, then I have to believe that oppressing humans is wrong. This all seems fairly straightforward. There seems to be no rational way around this. We could try hiding behind the maxim "there are no truths." But this proves itself to be useless in this discussion for at least two reasons. First, the claim "there are no truths" is itself a truth claim. Whoops! Second, the logic is unsustainable: if "there are no truths" then it cannot be a truth that "there are no truths"; therefore, there *are* truths. It's a self-defeating notion.

Because of this, I cannot help but think that the question "Can you believe you're right and others are wrong?" is a bit immature. It strikes me that the more mature question is something like this: "Do you have good reasons for believing you're right and others are wrong?" or perhaps "Are your beliefs strong enough to honestly engage with and be challenged by the available evidence—from reason, science, experience, and intuition?" When it comes to Christianity, I think the answer is a solid "yes"—as I hope to show in this chapter and the next.

I've been addressing this issue from a logical perspective. My guess, though, is that those who ask this question are actually showing the virtue of intellectual humility. They look at how big the world is and are overwhelmed by how many different and contradictory ideas there are. All the while, they are trying to be honest about their limited resources for properly evaluating the tremendous amount of information available. It is a daunting experience to honestly and humbly search for truth.

I don't have a foolproof formula to offer, no religious arithmetic: intuition + reason + science + experience = worldview certainty. I do, however, believe that Christianity is compelling in a way that other worldview systems are not, because of its unparalleled ability to make sense of the evidence from science, experience, intuition, and reason. Christianity does leave some questions unanswered or insufficiently answered. But so does every other worldview system. I also remain convinced that Christianity's nagging questions are easier to bear than those of other worldview systems.[17]

If Christians Are Right, Then Why Is the Church's History So Full of Hypocrisy and Evil?

The reality of the church's failings is one that every Christian would do well to consider. The weightiness of this reality can be felt at a historical level (as we think about the many evils that have been connected to the church), at a communal level (because many of us have probably experienced the hypocrisy or immorality of Christians inside and outside church settings), and at a personal level (as some of us Christians are all too aware of how meager our own moral growth can be). Obviously I cannot address all these issues, but I hope to offer some insight about how one might make some sense of this. In what follows, I will be leaning heavily on Alister McGrath's excellent essay "Does Religion Poison Everything?"[18]

In this essay, McGrath responds to the notion that religion does such great harm that humans would be better off without it. I have read several of

McGrath's works, and I don't recall another essay where I sensed him being so frustrated. He tends to be gentle and charitable toward those with whom he disagrees. In this essay, though, his critique carries a bit more sting. While I can't say for sure, I think he's irritated because he's arguing against writers (such as Christopher Hitchens) who are confidently heaping contempt on religion even though they lack the solid evidence to be so confident in their claims. In McGrath's own words:

> This simplistic [notion that religion poisons everything] can only be sustained by doing violence to the facts of history, the norms of evidence-based argument and the realities of contemporary experience. Hitchens achieves this feat largely by ignoring any evidence to the contrary and papering over the many cracks in his argument with aggressive bullying rhetoric that intimidates those who wish to challenge him on rational or historical grounds. . . . [It is assumed], without any serious argumentation or appeal to evidence, that the naturalistic [i.e., atheistic] worldview proposed as a replacement for religion will generate more happiness, compassion or peace than religion can.[19]

Let's look a bit closer at the evidence. As I mentioned, Christianity has been connected with a number of evils on both a large scale and a small scale. But is that the whole story? Not exactly. Is there strong evidence indicating that things would be better without Christianity (or any other religion, for that matter)? No.

Let's start with the claim that humans would be better off without religion. When we look closely, we will discover a hidden logical flaw in this idea. The basic notion is that there is no God, religion is a human invention, and religion turned out to be a bad invention. But wait! If religion is a human invention, then religion isn't the real problem; humans are—they came up with it, after all. Getting rid of religion won't necessarily fix the problem, for the only viable alternative would seem to be reliance on "that same [human] rationality and morality [that] gave rise to religious ideas and values" in the first place.[20] In other words, this atheistic critique of religion winds up being a critique of humans.

If humans are the problem, what's the solution? For the atheist, it would seem to be placing one's hope in humans—but we've just pointed out humanity's unpromising track record. Perhaps the atheist can appeal to "progress." But what does "progress" even mean when it comes to morality or the concept of human flourishing? If there are no ultimate standards of morality or purpose, then "flourishing" and "progress" are meaningless terms. Flourishing and progress are in the eyes of the beholder. In other words, each person defines "progress" and "flourishing" as he or she sees fit. Of greater import is how flourishing and progress get defined by those with the power to enforce their ideas. Was it not the case that Vladimir Lenin and Adolf Hitler convinced or coerced people into accepting their own perverse concepts of progress and human flourishing? It makes little sense to put one's hope in progress when the concept of progress is meaningless, an idea that gets defined by whoever happens to be in power. To anyone under the impression that "progress" and "the good" are concepts that everyone agrees on, I'd recommend reading Friedrich Nietzsche's *Antichrist*. Here are a few snippets:

> What is good?—Whatever augments the feeling of power, the will to power, power itself, in man. What is evil?—Whatever springs from weakness. . . . The weak and the botched shall perish: first principle of *our* charity. And one should help them to it. What is more harmful than any vice?—Practical sympathy for the botched and weak—Christianity. The problem that I set here is not what shall replace mankind . . . but what type of man must be *bred*, must be *willed* as being the most valuable, the most worthy of life, the most secure guarantee of the future. . . . Pity thwarts the whole law of evolution, which is the law of natural selection. It preserves whatever is ripe for destruction; it fights on the side of the disinherited and condemned by life. . . . What, then, is the meaning of *integrity* in things intellectual? It means that a man must be severe with his own heart, that he must scorn "beautiful feelings."[21]

For Nietzsche, progress looks like the "strong" putting the "weak" in their proper place, and doing it with a cold, callous disregard for compassion or pity—which thwarts progress.

This brings us back to something we've seen throughout our study—the ultimate problem is not humans or religion, the problem is sin. From a biblical perspective, humans are created in the image of God, yet they have been corrupted by sin. Jesus overcame sin through his faithful life, his willing crucifixion, and his miraculous resurrection. Through the Holy Spirit, Jesus's power is made available to the church. This power enables people to resist temptation, to break free from the controlling influence of sin, to stop loving what they shouldn't love, and to start loving what they should love.

That sounds great in theory, but it doesn't always match experience. Why is that? If Christians are free from sin, why don't their lives reflect that? To answer this, we need to think about how God brings about change in his people. God tends to bring about change in people gradually rather than immediately. God acts like a parent who is teaching a child to ride a bike, instead of like a computer programmer uploading new data into a system. God seems to prefer working alongside his human subjects, giving them help without overpowering them, strengthening them without taking complete control. Like the parent who runs alongside the child learning to ride a bike, God is there to provide balance and strength. But, to stick with the analogy, God doesn't stick the child in the basket, pedal the bike himself, and then pretend that the child can ride a bike; nor does God typically skip the learning process and simply implant bike-riding skills into the child. This is not to say there are no exceptions—sometimes God has reasons to work in more dramatic ways. God's tendency, however, is to patiently partner with humans in their slow and stumbling growth.

I think part of the reason God works this way is that he desires genuine relationship with his people, and working alongside them is more relational than doing all the work for them. I think God prefers this approach because it doesn't override free will; in fact, it better allows for it. Free from the controlling power of sin, Christians can choose whether to partner with God. However, the habits of sin are so ingrained in a person's heart, body, and mind that if God were to perform an immediate and complete transformation of a person, it might require God to overcome the person's free will. But through the slow and gradual process of daily submission to God, a Christian is transformed into a person who, at the center of her being, is someone who has, step by step, freely aligned herself with God's will. Yes, she needs help, but if the help comes gradually, she is capable of partnering with God along the way, slowly surrendering her will to God as she becomes the kind of person God seeks—one who freely chooses him. As C. S. Lewis writes, "[God wants] creatures whose life, on a miniature scale, will be qualitatively like his own, not because He has absorbed them but because their wills freely conform to His."[22]

How does all of this help explain why the church can seem plagued by hypocrisy and evil? First, it is a reminder that Christians are always works in progress. Christians have done, and continue to do, evil because they are not fully aligned with God's will. They may be forgiven, but they are not yet perfected. Sometimes the symptoms of sickness linger long after the right medicine is taken.

Second, and relatedly, because God doesn't typically overwhelm someone's will, the church contains many people who claim to be Christians even though they resist God's transformative work. To return to our medical analogy, some people start treatment but never follow through to the end, which means they never get fully cured, or they get sicker, or they spread their infection to others. To switch metaphors, such so-called Christians are like adults who never mature out of toddlerhood because of foolishness or fear. They make for poor representatives of Christianity's transformative power. Further, such consistent refusal to partner with God can become so habitual that these so-called Christians can basically become their habit: they become those who, at the core of their being, resist and reject God (even while claiming otherwise). Such so-called Christians are like good eggs that have turned bad—at one time they had all the potential to hatch into birds that could soar; instead, they have gone rotten and turned into foul things to everyone around them.[23]

Third, because God partners with people by meeting them where they are, it can be a bit misleading to try to compare the morality of any one Christian with that of any one non-Christian. Even from a Christian point of view it should be *expected* that some non-Christians seem to be more principled than some Christians. When God begins his slow and steady work on a converted scoundrel, the scoundrel will certainly appear to lag behind a non-Christian who through life or luck has been gifted with a better moral disposition. But when God's work is completed in the scoundrel (in this life or the next), and his heart is like Christ's, then he will be far advanced beyond the non-Christian who never allowed God to transform him.[24]

We have been looking at this question from a more individualistic perspective, so it may help to zoom out to a broader perspective. Just as the individual Christian is a work in progress, so is the collective Christian community. Even the earliest churches in the New Testament made the mistake of blending their Christian faith with some of the brokenness of their culture. For example, the Corinthian church was dishonoring the poor in their midst (1 Cor. 11:22), and the Jerusalem church was apparently struggling with ethnic discrimination (Acts 6:1). Christians believe that when the church exhibits evil and corruption (which it has throughout its history), it is the result of the church's collective resistance to God's will. When the church is being faithful, it is embodying the humble, sacrificial, reconciling, justice-seeking, merciful love of God to the world. Too often, however, the church resists its calling and embraces a corrupted set of ideals or goals—replacing humility with pride, sacrifice with greed, reconciliation with division, justice with injustice, mercy with scorn.

The problem, then, is not Christianity *itself* but the Christian *hybrid*—that is, Christianity blended with corrupt ideals, goals, morals, and so on. The so-called Christians who supported Hitler had abandoned the central ideals of their namesake (Christ) and replaced them with a racist social-Darwinist worldview.[25] The same could be said for the corruption that has always been present in the church. Some may want to respond that Christianity is the problem. They assume there would be less war and violence without religion. McGrath, however, offers a few counterexamples to this idea, including Lenin's violent oppression of religion in the Soviet Union.[26] One doesn't need religion to explain large-scale atrocities. Humans do that all on their own.

Furthermore, there are numerous examples of Christians bettering society. McGrath even quotes Michael Shermer, president of the Skeptics Society, as saying, "For every one of these grand tragedies there are ten thousand acts of personal kindness and social good that go unreported. . . . Religion, like all social institutions of such historical depth and cultural impact, cannot be reduced to an unambiguous good or evil."[27] One need think only of the immeasurable good done by institutions that have their roots in the Christian faith—from universities to hospitals to orphanages to relief agencies—not to mention masterpieces in art, literature, and music.[28] And at a local level, one usually doesn't need to look hard to find Christians sponsoring charities, volunteering to help the suffering, and practicing other forms of no-strings-attached kindness. One particularly fascinating example was uncovered by sociologist Robert Woodberry in his award-winning research project, conducted out of the University of Texas. He concluded, "Areas where [nineteenth-century] Protestant missionaries [who were not commissioned by the state] had a significant presence in the past are on average more economically developed today, with comparatively better health, lower infant mortality, lower corruption, greater literacy, higher educational attainment (especially for women), and more robust membership in nongovernmental associations."[29]

In sum, religion doesn't poison everything; sin does. Sin works through individuals and institutions and cultures in order to corrupt peoples and systems and societies. Sin can poison Christians, who can then poison the church—leading to the evils committed by Christians on large and small scales. When a person becomes a Christian, the Holy Spirit empowers that person to break free from sin. The Holy Spirit seems to partner with believers to transform their lives at a slow and gradual pace, allowing them to freely align their lives with God's will. Thus many Christians will continue to struggle with sinful behaviors, as it can take a long time to change the habits of heart, mind, and body. Sadly, other Christians will give up on this slow transformation process, which means that their lives will be unlikely to reflect the Holy Spirit. Therefore, it is true that some Christians do not live more ethically than some non-Christians—either because they are still works in progress or because they have ceased to progress. However, it's also the case that many Christians live morally upright lives and that the Christian faith is responsible for a great deal of (often overlooked or ignored) good. Furthermore, Christians trust that when God completes his transformative work in believers, their lives will be markedly distinct.

10

Not Blind Faith

In this chapter, I'm not aiming to prove that Christianity is true but to show why it's both reasonable and compelling. Although much could be said on this topic, I will limit myself to three areas:

1. The intuitive, explanatory power of the Christian metanarrative
2. The historical evidence for the resurrection of Jesus
3. The cosmic evidence of a creator

These three areas cover three complementary angles: we might think of the first as internal evidence, the second as historical evidence, and the third as a kind of hybrid of scientific and philosophical evidence. What makes Christianity particularly compelling is its ability to make sense on numerous levels: intellectually, instinctively, experientially, and scientifically.

The Intuitive, Explanatory Power of the Christian Metanarrative

If you've ever read or listened to Alister McGrath, chances are you've learned his favorite C. S. Lewis quote: "I believe in Christianity as I believe that the sun has risen—not just because I see it, but because by it, I see everything else."[1] Lewis's point is that one can tell the sun has risen by looking directly at it, or one can tell it has risen by looking at what it shines its light on. The same can be true of Christianity. One can look at Christianity itself (the Bible, the creeds, the historical evidence), or one can look at the "light" that

Christianity shines on our world. That's what we're going to do in this section. Instead of looking directly at the sun, we will see how the sun illuminates our world. That is, instead of looking directly at Christianity, we will see how the Christian worldview illuminates our lives and our world. For both Lewis and McGrath, one of the most compelling reasons to believe in Christianity is its ability to make sense of our lives—its explanatory power.

Based on what we've looked at so far in the book, how might the Christian "sun" help us to see the world around us? For starters, we learn that there is a God who is beyond nature, is three in one, and created the world in love. What "light" might this shine? As we've discussed, belief in the one creator God makes possible objective morality: real right and real wrong, ultimate purpose and meaning for our lives, free will that isn't simply an illusion, and the hope of lasting personhood and restoration.

Plus, the distinctly Christian belief in a three-in-one God provides a basis for how capital *L* Love is not only real but also at the heart of ultimate reality. Further, the Christian belief that God lovingly created a good world makes sense of our experience of the world as a place of beauty and goodness. The awe that grips us when we look at the ocean or the night sky is an appropriate response, a proper recognition of beauty—not merely an accidental by-product of evolution. We'll discuss at the end of this chapter how belief in a creator also makes sense of where everything came from (as opposed to the unlikely alternatives that the universe either came into existence on its own or is eternal). And if there is a God, it explains why there is evidence that, in general, humans are prone to be religious, regardless of the culture we find ourselves in.[2]

The Christian metanarrative tells how God created humans in his own image, how God gave humans freedom to either partner with him or go their own way, and how humans used that freedom unwisely, thereby spreading brokenness throughout the world—physically, socially, and spiritually. What light might these Christian plot points shine on our world? The belief that all humans are created in the image of God makes sense of our intuition that all humans have worth and purpose and dignity—a belief that is harder to justify in some other worldviews. The Christian doctrine of free will corresponds with our experience of choice and autonomy. Our deepest instincts tell us that life is not fully determined by the blind fate of physics. The Christian notion of sin's corruptive power makes sense of our experience of the world as a place that is simultaneously beautiful and broken: the world was made good (this corresponds with our sense of the wonder and worth of the world); yet, the world has been corrupted by sin (this corresponds with our sense that something is not right in the world physically, socially, and spiritually).

According to a Christian metanarrative, evil and brokenness are not simply illusions or matters of personal preference; rather, some things are truly good and other things are truly evil. Furthermore, good and evil are not equal (as in some dualistic frameworks); rather, good is superior and original, whereas evil is the perversion of the good.

We learn from the Christian metanarrative that God took on the physicality and brokenness of his creatures in order to rescue and renew his creation. This distinctly Christian belief portrays God as deeply loving, humble, sacrificial, merciful, and dedicated to his creation. "This is how the love of God is revealed to us: God has sent his only Son into the world so that we can live through him. This is love: it is not that we loved God but that he loved us and sent his Son as the sacrifice that deals with our sins" (1 John 4:9–10). This unique doctrine is compelling not only because it strikes us as instinctively beautiful and right but also because it's so unexpected—it's not the kind of thing that someone would make up. Other worldviews might claim that God is love, but without the Trinity and the crucifixion, can this claim make as much sense? Is this a case of trying to borrow Christian ideas without the foundation that supports the ideas?

Jesus's incarnation and crucifixion draw our attention to another aspect of the Christian metanarrative that rings true—namely, we humans cannot fix ourselves. We need something more than better laws, better education, better economies. We need a power greater than we are, a power capable of transforming us into the kind of people we truly desire to be—as individuals and as societies.

Within the Christian metanarrative, we find God calling people to partner with him in bringing renewal. Such a partnership is broadly characterized by loving God wholeheartedly and by loving one's neighbor sacrificially and empathetically. More specifically, it looks like people who embody compassion, joy, peace, patience, kindness, goodness, faithfulness, gentleness, self-control, humility, and courage. Instinctively, many of us recognize the true goodness of these virtues. And yet if such virtues are truly good, we require a worldview wherein that makes sense. It makes sense in the Christian framework because of Jesus, who reveals in his life and death how God's nature corresponds with these virtues. The same may not be the case for other metanarrative frameworks.

Last, the Christian framework carries within it the hope that one day God will set all things right—physically, socially, and spiritually. We will dwell in the renewed creation, heaven on earth, with resurrected bodies that are no longer plagued by sin, sickness, and death. No other system offers hope of holistic restoration in the way Christianity does. In atheism, there is no ultimate purpose or goal, which means that hope is more like wishful thinking than confident expectation.[3] In certain dualistic systems, the powers of good and evil are balanced, which seems to nullify any reasonable hope that good will ultimately overcome evil. In polytheistic systems, there is no supremely good and powerful god that is expected to set all things right. In Eastern religions, hope seems to be primarily about escape and absorption, not restoration and renewal. Among monotheistic religions—including Judaism and Islam—Christianity has arguably the most compelling basis for hope: the resurrection of Jesus and the transformative presence of God's Holy Spirit in our lives.

In sum, the Christian worldview provides a compelling framework that helps us make sense of our intuition and experience. It fits our instinctive beliefs that

- morality is real—good and evil are not illusions;
- our lives can have meaning;
- every human has inherent dignity and worth;
- we have some free will (our thoughts and actions are not entirely predetermined);
- personhood is not an illusion—we humans are more than our material bodies;
- death is not the end of our individual stories;
- love is central to reality;
- the best lives are those characterized by peace and mercy and sacrificial love;
- the natural world is full of wonder and beauty and goodness;
- something has gone wrong in our own lives and in our world;
- we humans cannot fix everything on our own; and
- there is reason to expectantly hope for restoration—physical, social, and spiritual.

Several of these ideas might fit within other worldview frameworks, but only Christians can rationally claim that all these ideas fit well within their belief system. To reject Christianity in favor of another belief system is to say that at least one (and probably several) of these instinctive ideas must be false. If someone were to reread this list closely, he or she may find it quite difficult to consider rejecting any of the deeply intuitive ideas that are all contained within the framework of Christianity. Such breadth of explanatory power is part of what makes Christianity so compelling.

The Historical Evidence for the Resurrection of Jesus

We saw in chapter 5 that the crucifixion of Jesus is a fairly well-established historical event. However, the fact that the crucifixion is historical doesn't tell us much about the reasonableness of Christian faith; it simply confirms that its founder, Jesus, died. People throughout the ancient world believed in Jesus's crucifixion without feeling any compulsion to embrace Christian faith. Believing in the resurrection, however, will almost certainly lead all but the most stubborn to Christian faith.

N. T. Wright, one of the world's leading New Testament scholars, wrote a seven-hundred-plus-page book on the resurrection—not including the thirty-five pages of bibliography.[4] How does someone write this much about one topic? Well, Wright painstakingly researched how the idea of "resurrection" was understood in the ancient Greco-Roman world, in the Old Testament, in the New Testament, and in the Christian writings of the first couple of centuries after Christ. Based on his extensive and impressive historical research, here's his conclusion: "Historical argument alone cannot force anyone to believe that Jesus was raised from the dead; but historical argument is remarkably good at clearing away the undergrowth behind which skepticisms of various sorts have been hiding. The proposal that Jesus was bodily raised from the dead possesses unrivaled power to explain the historical data at the heart of early Christianity."[5]

Can historical research prove the resurrection of Jesus? According to Wright, no. But it can reveal that a handful of historical events, such as the empty tomb, likely happened. It can show that followers of Jesus came to hold unprecedented beliefs about the Messiah and the resurrection. And it can bear witness to how these beliefs were clung to even in the face of pain, shame, and death. I will try to summarize Wright's argument in four points. Though the first two points are a bit tedious, there's a significant payoff.

1. When people in the ancient world used the term "resurrection," they were talking about rising from death in a bodily or physical form.

This is how the larger Greco-Roman world understood "resurrection." The larger Greco-Roman world also happened to think that resurrection was nonsense. Some folks may have believed that there was life after death for one's *spirit*, but they didn't believe in life after death for one's *body*. In the ancient world, it was basically only Jews who believed in the "resurrection"—that God would raise the righteous dead and restore their bodies.[6] But even among the Jews this belief wasn't universal: some Jews (such as the Pharisees) believed in a future resurrection, but other Jews (such as the Sadducees) did not. Those Jews who believed in the resurrection expected God to raise all the righteous dead together at the last day. No one was thinking that God would start the process early by resurrecting the Messiah before the resurrection of everyone else. Finally, when ancient Jews spoke of the resurrection, they often connected it to ideas such as the restoration of Israel. To summarize, in the ancient world no one believed in bodily resurrection except for some groups of Jews who believed the righteous would all be resurrected together at the end of time and that their resurrection would be accompanied by the restoration of Israel. This naturally leads into our second point.

2. The Christian concept of resurrection was unique and unprecedented in the ancient world.

The Christian doctrine of the resurrection was already distinct in the larger Greco-Roman world, because the larger Greco-Roman world didn't believe in bodily resurrection. Furthermore, it was distinct from Jewish notions of resurrection in three important ways:

a. Christian resurrection entailed a dying and rising Messiah.
b. Christians claimed that God resurrected an *individual* before resurrecting *all* the righteous.
c. Christian resurrection was reframed beyond the focus of the restoration of Israel.

On points a and b, I'll quote Wright: "Nobody imagined that any individuals had already been raised, or would be raised in advance of the great last day. . . . There are no traditions about a Messiah being raised to life: most Jews of this period hoped for resurrection, many Jews of this period hoped for a Messiah, *but nobody put those two hopes together until the early Christians did so*."[7] As for point c, Christians expanded the idea of resurrection beyond the restoration of Israel, connecting resurrection with "the moral restoration of human beings . . . [and] the Gentile mission in which all would be equal on the basis of faith."[8]

Christians further stood out by making the resurrection foundational to their belief system. Even more, the New Testament authors and other early Christian writers held these doctrinally distinctive views with shocking consistency.[9] Whereas Jews held a range of beliefs about the resurrection, Christians of the first two centuries maintained a surprisingly consistent belief that Jesus rose from the dead in an imperishable body.

3. If early Christians were going to fabricate a story (or hallucinate about Jesus's resurrection), it's highly unlikely that they would have made up *this* story (or that they would have all hallucinated so similarly).

Sometimes the truth *is* stranger than fiction. Following are some reasons why the unusual details surrounding Jesus's resurrection work to support its authenticity.

a. The first reported witnesses to Jesus's resurrection were women, even though the testimony of women was often disregarded in the first-century world. (In other words, if one were going to invent witnesses in the first century, one wouldn't invent female witnesses; however, precisely because the female witnesses are mentioned, this suggests the account is not fabricated.)[10]
b. The Gospels report that those who encountered Jesus often didn't recognize him immediately (which is not the kind of story one would make up in order to strengthen eyewitness testimony).[11]
c. The Gospel writers rarely tie Jesus's resurrection to specific biblical proof texts (which one might expect if the disciples wanted to bolster their claims among fellow Jews).
d. Jesus's resurrected body didn't shine like a star, as one finds in Daniel's vision of the resurrected righteous (Dan. 12:2–3). Again, we'd expect a fabricated story to more explicitly parallel biblical descriptions.
e. No one was expecting the Messiah to be crucified and rise from the dead, much less to rise before the great resurrection at the last day. Other self-proclaimed Messiahs around this time were also killed by Rome, and none of their disciples claimed that these "Messiahs" had been resurrected.
f. As we'll see shortly, the disciples' story would make sense only if they managed to pull off both an empty tomb and eyewitness testimony about seeing the resurrected Jesus. That is to say, the disciples would have been particularly foolish to make up a story that required so much risk and work to verify.
g. The disciples would have had to do all this while knowing that these claims would lead to their being persecuted and ostracized. They had little to gain and much to lose by spreading news about Jesus's resurrection. Yet they held firm, even though it cost some of them their lives.

To put this concisely, if the disciples were going to make up a story, one would expect them to make up a story that had more-credible ancient witnesses, that recounted how the resurrected Jesus was immediately and unquestionably recognizable, that better fit biblical parallels, that was an all-around closer fit to Jewish expectations, and that wouldn't make them a target of persecution.

If we consider that nobody was anticipating an individual resurrection before the great resurrection at the end of time and that nobody was anticipating a dying and rising Messiah, then wouldn't the disciples have been much more likely to fabricate a story (or hallucinate) about encounters with Jesus's spirit rather than his resurrected body?

- This would better match both Jewish and Greco-Roman expectations.
- It would be much easier to lie (or hallucinate) about.
- It would fit more closely with Old Testament stories (like Samuel's spirit appearing from Sheol to reprimand Saul in 1 Samuel 28).
- And it would not require the risk of stealing and hiding Jesus's body.

As Wright says, "If you were a follower of a dead Jesus, in the middle of the first century, wanting to explain why you still thought he was important, . . . you would not have told stories like this. You would have done a better job."[12] It might make sense to us today to think that the disciples would concoct a scheme about a resurrected Messiah, but it wouldn't have made sense to first-century Jews in Jerusalem.[13] So why did the disciples tell the resurrection story the way they did?

4. The disciples truly believed that Jesus actually was resurrected from the dead, because (a) the tomb was empty and (b) they encountered the resurrected Jesus.

Let's start with the empty tomb. If Jesus's dead body had still been in the tomb, then the disciples' claims could have been pretty quickly falsified. If someone could have produced Jesus's dead body, this would have proved that Jesus was not resurrected and that any encounters with him had only been spiritual encounters—not physical. But the empty tomb seems like a historical fact. After all, it's unlikely that Jesus's followers would have stolen and hidden the body (both because of the risk and because it wouldn't have made sense to fabricate an individual resurrection of a crucified Messiah in the first century). Further, it's unlikely that the Roman or Jewish officials would have concealed Jesus's body, since revealing the body would have provided solid evidence that the Christians' claims were false. Additionally, belief in the resurrection thrived right in Jerusalem, where Jesus was killed, which should have made it that much easier for Christians' opponents to prove them wrong, since his entombed corpse would theoretically have been nearby.[14] But Jesus's body was never produced, which suggests that the tomb was empty.

An empty tomb, however, doesn't prove the resurrection; it may just point to grave robbers. However, the empty tomb is not the only evidence; there are also numerous claims that people encountered the resurrected Jesus. These encounters neither fit the mold of Jewish expectations nor sound like something Jews at that point in time would have fabricated if they were wanting to strengthen their claims. On top of all of this, Jesus's resurrection appearances are strange. For example, Jesus is both recognizable and unrecognizable; Jesus can eat and be touched like a person with a physical body, yet he can appear and disappear as though he's a spirit. Despite the strangeness of the resurrection encounters, they have a kind of consistency across the Gospels and other New Testament writings. And Paul even tells us that there are more than five hundred eyewitnesses to this unprecedented reality, some of whom are still around to be questioned—a bold claim if he's bluffing (1 Cor. 15:3–8). How would Paul have gotten this many people to lie (and thereby face persecution)? Or how would he have gotten this many people to believe such an unprecedented and unexpected hoax? Or how would anyone have pulled off such a large-scale shared hallucination? I've just asked "how"; the equally difficult question is "why?" If Paul is lying, he has little to gain and a lot to lose.

In summary, if we understand that "resurrection" meant a bodily resurrection, and if we understand that nobody except certain Jews believed in the resurrection, and if we understand that those Jews expected only a one-time resurrection of all the righteous, and if we understand that nobody was looking for a dying and rising Messiah, then we begin to see how incredibly unlikely it is that anyone would have made this story up in the first-century world. And we could add to this that the Gospel writers were making claims that, if not true, were pathetic attempts at fabrication, because they had less-credible witnesses who didn't always recognize Jesus at first, and when they did recognize Jesus, he didn't tightly fit the mold set by the Old Testament or by Jewish expectation. Again, it seems quite unlikely that anybody would make up (or hallucinate) this story. On top of all of this, we add the likelihood that the tomb was truly empty and that hundreds of people made claims that they encountered a resurrected Jesus—not a ghostly or spiritual Jesus (for we are keeping in mind that the early church was fairly uniform in its description of Jesus's unprecedented and unexpected bodily resurrection). When we put all of this together, we see that there is good reason to view

Jesus's resurrection as the best explanation for the disciples' unprecedented beliefs, the empty tomb, and the eyewitness testimony.

So the resurrection starts to look like a plausible way to explain the disciples' claims of Jesus's resurrection—claims they held so strongly that many of them died for it. What about other possible explanations for the disciples' claims about Jesus's resurrection?

- Could the disciples have simply made the whole thing up? Maybe, but that would conceivably have required them to somehow get access to Jesus's body and hide it, then convince hundreds of people to see something unprecedented (or lie about seeing it), all so they could become the targets of persecution. This scenario doesn't seem likely.
- Could the disciples have simply hallucinated? Maybe, but that wouldn't explain the empty tomb, nor how they got so many people to have the same hallucination, nor how they all happened to hallucinate about something that wouldn't have even been on anyone's mind in the first century.
- Could it be that Jesus didn't really die but survived or was resuscitated? Maybe, but that would require us to imagine that crucifixion was not really that brutal (which goes against the historical evidence) and would once again make no sense of the disciples' willingness to become the targets of persecution simply because they encountered a battered Jesus who would surely have been in a broken and miserable condition—hardly the kind of encounter to inspire confidence in Jesus's victory over sin and death.[15]

It may not be possible to prove that Jesus rose from the dead, but that's the explanation that arguably makes the most sense of the empty tomb, the hundreds of eyewitnesses, and the disciples' steadfast and historically unanticipated belief in the Messiah's resurrection.[16]

Many are familiar with C. S. Lewis's idea that Jesus is best understood as a liar, a lunatic, or Lord. That is, if Jesus really made the claims that we encounter in the Gospels, then he could be a liar (he makes outlandish claims that he knows are false) or a lunatic (he makes outlandish claims that he actually believes are true because he's crazy) or the Lord (he makes outlandish claims that are true because he is God incarnate).[17] We can apply a similar idea to the early Christian claims about the resurrection: they could be lies (knowingly false claims about Jesus's resurrection), lunacy (delusions that the disciples mistake for truth), or legitimate accounts (honest claims about a real historical event). Since we've already established why the early Christian claims are unlikely to be either fabrications or hallucinations, I'd suggest we open ourselves to seeing them as historical.

The Cosmic Evidence of a Creator

I put the least weight on this final argument.[18] This is not to say that I believe the argument is weak. It's just that I don't have the expertise to sufficiently evaluate it one way or the other. Even so, it strikes me that a scientific and philosophical investigation into our universe makes it seem more likely there is a God than there isn't. I will try to avoid making any detailed scientific arguments here. Instead, I will try to give a general description of the predominant scientific conclusion about the beginning of our universe. Then I'll suggest how, if that scientific conclusion is indeed correct, there is good reason to suspect that the universe was created by God.

Our universe appears to have begun around fourteen billion years ago in what is commonly referred to as the big bang. What happened in the moments right before the big bang is a mystery (and may always be). The "blast" from the big bang set the universe in motion. Nothingness gave way to space that expanded and even now continues to expand. The conditions of the big bang seem to have been just right to make it possible for there to be stars and planets, as well as the conditions necessary for organic life. There is some debate about just how fine-tuned the early universe needed to be and just how unlikely it was that the early universe had the conditions it had. Nonetheless, the prevailing view is that our universe appears to have won the lottery. Or, rather, we humans won the lottery, because a universe that was only slightly different would not have allowed for anything like life as we know it. Stephen Hawking writes, "The laws of science, as we know them at present, contain many fundamental numbers. . . . The remarkable fact is that the values of these numbers seem to have been very finely adjusted to make possible the development of life. . . . [It] seems clear that there are relatively few ranges of values for the numbers that would allow the development of any form of intelligent life. Most sets of values would give rise to universes that, although they might be very beautiful, would contain no one able to wonder at that beauty."[19] To be clear, Hawking thinks that such observations have a natural explanation, not that they point to a creator.

McGrath offers some specific examples of our oddly hospitable universe: "If the strong coupling constant were slightly smaller, hydrogen would be the only element in the universe. . . . If the weak fine constant were slightly smaller, no hydrogen would have formed during the early history of the universe. Consequently, no stars would have been formed. . . . If the gravitational fine structure were slightly smaller, stars and planets would not have been able to form. . . . If stronger, the stars thus formed would have burned out too quickly."[20] The consensus is that the chances of our universe producing life seem almost incomprehensibly unlikely.

How might we account for our finely tuned universe? One option is that our universe is simply lucky. The big bang had a one-in-a-bajillion chance of producing a hospitable cosmos, and shockingly it worked out. If the skeptic has a hard time believing in the resurrection, then she probably has a similarly hard time believing in a universe that was so unfathomably lucky. A more respectable option is to offer sophisticated speculations about the early universe, which might explain how a seemingly unlikely set of conditions wouldn't seem so unlikely if we knew more about the early universe. One author, describing the mysterious moments immediately following the big bang, comments, "When energy levels are that high, quantum effects are extremely significant, physics is entirely speculative, and just about everything is up for grabs."[21] Such speculative physics about the early universe is what we find in Hawking's *A Brief History of Time*, where he offers a tentative explanation for why the hospitality of our universe may have arisen from purely natural phenomena—an explanation that combines an inflationary model, quantum mechanics, and the curvature of space-time.

The speculative idea that is currently gaining the most traction is the concept of the multiverse, which is like a conglomeration or generator of an astronomical number of universes. While our own universe seems infinitely unlikely, it becomes a bit more likely if there are an immense number of universes being contained within (or generated by) the multiverse. The multiverse is a speculative idea that is difficult (or maybe impossible) to prove, though it may fit with some ideas in string theory and inflation.[22]

For the multiverse to work as an explanation for our finely tuned world, it would seem to require a few important conditions.

- First, and most obviously, it requires that there is such a thing as a multiverse, and there is currently no scientific consensus on the matter. The scientific jury is out on this highly speculative idea.
- Second, it requires that the multiverse contains (or generates) not simply lots of universes, even billions of universes, but an unfathomable number of universes. The fine-tuning of our universe appears so precise that unless the multiverse has generated an astronomical number of universes, our finely tuned universe would still be extremely unlikely.

- Third, these many universes all need to be different from one another. On this point, consider how we might write out the fraction ⅓ as a decimal. It would be .33333—and those threes would go on infinitely, but they would always be threes. Even if the multiverse were generating an infinite number of universes, if it generated the same kind of universe each time, then we would still have a problem, because the multiverse would just be producing an incredible number of the same nonfunctioning universes. A multiverse that creates an infinite number of universes is likely to create a one-in-a-bajillion universe like ours only if it is creating a bajillion universes of a bajillion different types.

By some happy accident, we need a multiverse that happens to contain (or generate) universes, and by some happier accident, this multiverse must be insanely large or productive, and by the happiest accident of all, this multiverse must contain (or generate) universes that are different from one another. If the fortuitous precision of our own universe is hard to explain, it would seem that the fortuitous makeup of the multiverse is similarly hard to explain. String theory and inflation may indeed lend some credibility to the notion of a multiverse, but that only pushes the issue back: How did there come to be a world filled with (or generating) worlds that are all different from one another?

So what conclusions can we draw based on the unlikely hospitality of our universe? I'm hesitant to make any grand claims about this being proof of a creator God. Such "God of the gaps" arguments don't have the strongest track record. Just because there is something currently unexplained by science does not mean that God must be the answer. As a Christian, I wouldn't lose sleep if the multiverse were proved true. If God can create through the big bang, he can create through the multiverse. And yet the conditions of the big bang and the seeming fine-tuning of our universe are not easy to ignore. It's hard not to see the handiwork of a creator, one who crafts a universe where life is possible.

The rub for me when thinking about a cosmos that has no creator God is that this forces our concept of the cosmos into a framework where (1) there is no purpose behind anything and (2) stuff is eternal or self-creating. Let's start with the second point. If there is no God, it would seem that the universe must have brought itself into existence out of absolute nothingness. Absolute nothingness—no space, time, gravity, matter, laws, particles, anything—then, from nowhere and for no reason, the universe![23] If the multiverse is the source of our universe, this seems only to push the problem back: Did the multiverse create itself out of absolute nothingness? Or maybe the multiverse finds its origin in an even greater multiverse, but did that multiverse create itself? Is it turtles all the way down? It strikes me as far-fetched to imagine that anything—especially the cosmos—pops into existence out of absolute nothingness.

If the cosmos doesn't create itself, another option is that either the universe or the multiverse is eternal: somehow, an eternal past lies behind the big bang. There are some potential problems with this notion. For instance, one has to assume that the law of entropy didn't apply to the pre-big-bang conditions; otherwise, sometime in the universe's eternal past disorder would have overtaken everything before it arrived at the present. Think about it: if the universe has an eternal past, then entropy has had an eternity to bring disorder before now. Relatedly, one has to deal with philosophical problems related to eternity. For instance, how does something with an eternal past ever arrive at the present? (That's a fun head-scratcher.)

Maybe the best explanation for the origin of the cosmos is not found in speculations about the multiverse, an eternal universe, or a self-creating cosmos. Maybe it makes more sense to consider that the universe was created by a being that is not bound by the cosmos's laws of space and time. Maybe a transcendent God makes the most sense of where the universe came from.

Where does all this leave us? Perhaps we look for the presence of purpose and order. If, on the one hand, God created the universe, then one would expect to find evidence of purpose and orderliness in the universe—because God presumably created with intentionality and design. If, on the other hand, the universe came into existence on its own or has always existed, then one would expect to find randomness and disorder—because the universe obviously has no will, purpose, or intentionality.

What do we find: order or disorder? It depends on whom one asks and where one looks. For theoretical physicist Sean Carroll, the evidence for a creator is underwhelming. If God's purpose was to create life, then why the strict parameters of fine-tuning, why are there so many galaxies that seem unrelated to life, and why are there particles that seem inconsequential to the existence of life?[24] These are points worth considering, even if they seem easy to explain. One merely has to imagine that God had more than one purpose when creating. For example, maybe God purposed to create life *and* beauty. Distant galaxies may have little relevance for our lives, but we still find them beautiful and fascinating—perhaps because they were made to be beautiful and fascinating. Suppose I were to deny the beauty of the stars and distant galaxies, claiming that they are just massive accidents of space that we find beautiful only because our neurological wiring evolved to like bright objects for some completely unrelated reason. My guess is that most people would scoff, arguing that stars and galaxies are truly beautiful, something that we are right to marvel at. Of course, such a knee-jerk response would make the most sense if stars and galaxies were created to be beautiful rather than if they (and we) were simply random accidents.

We also take it for granted that our universe is orderly. Shouldn't a world that has no purpose, that was one colossal accident, lack order? Instead, we find the opposite. There is structure, law, predictability. There's no avoiding the orderliness of our world. It doesn't seem as though we're simply imposing orderly categories on a disorderly world; rather, we are discovering and describing order that is already there.[25] We'd expect it to be impossible to impose order on a non-ordered world; plus, what would be the point? Furthermore, from an evolutionary perspective the human ability to discern order is quite odd unless there really is order to be discerned. But we don't just discern order in those simplistic ways that aid survival—hunting, gathering, reproducing. We also discern complex mathematical order at the microscopic and macroscopic levels, which has little direct bearing on our survival.[26] It's hard to avoid the conclusion that the orderliness of our universe is real and not an imposition or illusion. It's also hard to avoid the conclusion that we humans have a strange knack for discerning order, a knack that isn't self-evidently explained by evolutionary development. According to Alister McGrath, Albert Einstein claimed that "the most incomprehensible thing about the universe is that it is comprehensible."[27] The question for us is whether this orderliness (in our world and in our thinking) is more likely to be the result of purposeful creation or chance and accident.

If the universe shows evidence of purpose, and if the universe had a beginning, what does that point to? It points to something (or someone) that created both space and time. The most likely candidate seems to be something (or someone) that is not bound by space or time: an eternal, supernatural being—a God. But what kind of God? A God who brings something out of nothing, who creates beauty and order, who patiently waits for creation to unfold, and who seems to partner with his creation in bringing forth life—a God who resembles the Christian God.

I'm well aware that I cannot *prove* that Christianity is true. I hope, however, to have shown that there are compelling reasons to *believe* that Christianity is true. I hope that you might even share my perspective that Christianity offers the best way to make sense of our experience, intuition, reasoning, hopes, and longings. I also hope that you come away with a new level of respect for the historical evidence for the resurrection of Jesus. Finally, I hope you recognize that science and philosophy are not the enemies of Christian faith; instead, science, philosophy, and Christianity can play nice together.

Appendix A

More about Paul's Theology

Why spend more time on Paul? Two reasons. First, there's some great stuff we can learn from Paul that I didn't cover in chapter 3 because the chapter was getting too long. Second, in my experience, many people operate with a distorted view of Christianity because they have misunderstood Paul. This appendix offers a chance to dig a bit deeper into Paul, clarifying some issues that trip people up and cautioning against reading Paul in ways that skew the Christian metanarrative.

1 Corinthians

Paul writes to the Corinthian church a fairly long letter that is packed full of theological insight and practical advice. I'll limit myself to four important takeaways from this letter.

1. *Jesus, and his sacrificial death, represent true wisdom (1 Cor. 1:18–30).* For Paul, "God's wisdom" is revealed in the cross of Christ; or, as he says a few verses later, Christ Jesus "became wisdom from God for us" (v. 30). Here we are reminded that one's concept of wisdom is bound up in one's worldview. Paul is aware that the cross appears foolish to both the Jewish and the Greco-Roman worlds.

- It seems foolish to claim one's King and Lord took on flesh, only to be crucified, suffering the humiliating punishment of slaves.
- It seems foolish to believe that life is found in sacrifice, by taking up one's cross and following Jesus. Only a fool would forfeit status, security, and comfort as a strategy for living life to the full.

Nevertheless, the Christian sees the world differently. If Jesus is Lord and Christ, then true wisdom recognizes that God is compassionate beyond our expectations, that God loves in extraordinary and self-giving ways, that the world is broken, and that working to put the world right might require embracing a way of life that seems distorted and counterintuitive (see also James 3:17). Perhaps it should come as no surprise that a sin-corrupted world views the cross as foolishness, that a world going the wrong direction would mistake the way forward as going backward.

2. *The cross brings unity by breaking down arbitrary barriers of social status (1 Cor. 11:17–34).* The early church gathered for meals as part of its fellowship. In the first century, meals could be times to showcase status divisions: a host could honor or dishonor people based on what he served them and where he seated them. The Corinthian church was perpetuating some of these social and economic divisions at its communal meals. In particular, these meal practices were "humiliating those who have nothing" (v. 22 NIV). To remedy this, Paul calls attention to Jesus's final meal with his disciples, in which Jesus speaks of the bread and wine as his broken body and spilled blood. Paul reminds these Christians that when they gather as a church and share bread and wine, they are to honor Jesus's sacrifice. Paul is essentially saying, "How can you proclaim the sacrificial death of your Lord while simultaneously shaming the poor?" To humiliate the poor is to show that one hasn't truly embraced a worldview in which Christ is the wisdom from God. That is, the value system of Christ (humility, compassion, sacrifice, and the inherent worth of each individual) is fundamentally at odds with the value system of the Corinthian church's surrounding culture (a value system based on status, achievement, and power). By embodying sacrificial love, Christ turned that broken value system on its head, thereby breaking down barriers to unity that were based on arbitrary matters like social and economic status. We don't judge Christ based on these arbitrary standards, so we shouldn't judge others based on them either.
3. *What we do with our bodies matters (1 Cor. 6:12–20).* Some Christians in Corinth had very lax sexual morals, because—and here's the important

part—they thought that what they did with their bodies didn't matter; it was only their spirits that were important. These Corinthians were holding on to an unchristian, dualistic mind-set in which the body and spirit are independent and/or disconnected. In ancient culture, it was not uncommon to regard one's physical body as bad, inessential, or less significant, whereas the spirit was the good, essential, or more significant part of the human. Some Christians in Corinth had not given up this misguided notion; it seeped into their ethics—they figured that what they did with their bodies didn't really matter, since only their spirits mattered, so they continued to visit the temple prostitutes. Paul, in contrast, believes the body and spirit are intertwined, perhaps inseparable. As we've seen, humans are something like embodied souls. For Paul, what one does in one's body, one does in one's spirit. Paul's high view of the body also better fits into the Christian hope, where our resurrected bodies will inhabit a renewed creation.

4. *The resurrection is of utmost importance for the Christian faith (1 Cor. 15).* I borrow heavily here from Richard Hays, one of the leading scholars on Paul, as I attend to five points from Paul's teaching on resurrection.[1] First, Paul presents resurrection as a matter of "first importance" (v. 3 NIV). It's of first importance because Christianity depends on the resurrection; otherwise, the logic of the Christian worldview quickly unravels into inconsistency and incoherency, as I've explained earlier.

   Second, Paul teaches that if there is no resurrection, then "our preaching is useless and your faith is useless" because claims about Christ and his teaching would be shown to be false (v. 14). This would also mean that Christians "are still in [their] sins" (v. 17) because the sacrifice of Christ would be revealed to be simply the death of a mortal—and the death of a mortal is incapable of remedying the problem of sin (v. 17).

   Third, Christ's resurrection gives believers confidence that they too will be resurrected. Jesus is the "firstfruits" of the resurrection (v. 20 NIV).

   Fourth, "If the dead are not raised, hope, suffering, and faithfulness are pointless."[2] Once again, this leads us to think about the need for consistency within a worldview. The resurrection is the source of hope—the expectation that things will all be set right one day. This hope, therefore, can sustain people through difficulties like suffering, scorn, and sacrifice that arise when they faithfully follow Jesus in a corrupt world. Without this hope of restoration, sacrificial love may not be worth it. Paul understands what hangs in the balance when he writes, "If the dead aren't raised, let's eat and drink because tomorrow we'll die" (v. 32). Or again, "If we have a hope in Christ only in this life, then we deserve to be pitied more than anyone else" (v. 19). If one's worldview lacks hope of things ever being set right, then the wisest thing to do is to maximize pleasure and minimize pain. Sacrificial love may be nonsensical if, at the end of the day, wrongs will not be righted, crookedness won't be made straight, and injustices won't be rectified.

Fifth, as I discussed in greater detail elsewhere, "resurrection means transformation of the body."[3] Our current bodies are subject to death, decay, and corruption; the transformed, resurrected bodies will not be. Instead, through the Holy Spirit they will be like Christ's resurrected body. Don't be mistaken: the new body will not be immaterial or ghostly. It will be a physical body, but one healed of its corruption and brokenness so that it is free of sickness, sin, and death.

Galatians

Not everyone agrees on how to read Paul's letter to the Galatians. It's even possible to read Galatians as saying almost the opposite of what I've claimed elsewhere in this book. That is, some people think Galatians is teaching (1) that the Old Testament law is bad, (2) that our actions are ultimately unimportant, and (3) that all that really matters is that we believe in our minds that Jesus died and was raised. I don't know if any scholars would put it quite so simplistically, but these basic ideas are not hard to find among many confessing Christians. Others, including myself, think there's a more accurate way to read Galatians that better fits the biblical metanarrative (and that better fits a close analysis of the details of Galatians itself).

Let's start by examining a couple of key verses:

> [We] know that a person is not justified by the *works of law*, but by *faith [of/] in Jesus Christ*. So we, too, have put our faith in Christ Jesus that we may be justified by *faith [of/]in Christ* and not by the *works of law*, because by the *works of law* no one will be justified. (2:16 NIV)

> It is for *freedom* that Christ has set us *free*. (5:1 NIV)

If you're confused by the quotation above from Galatians 2:16, you're not alone. There is some question about exactly what Paul is saying here, particularly with his references to "works of the law" and "faith of/in Christ." Galatians 5:1 raises questions about the precise nature of the freedom we have in Christ. So we have three interpretive head-scratchers: (1) "works of the law," (2) "faith of/in Christ," and (3) "freedom."

What are we to make of these three ideas in Galatians? Here's a popular but off-base way of interpreting what Paul is saying:

- works of the law = good deeds
- faith in Christ = a belief that I hold only in my mind
- freedom = no ultimate accountability for my actions

According to this line of interpretation, we cannot be justified by our actions (works of the law) but only by what we believe (faith in Christ). When we hold the right belief we are granted freedom (from having to act morally upright), though, of course, it's ideal for someone to be good out of thankfulness to God. It should be clear how this line of interpretation clashes with what we've studied elsewhere in this book. So how else might we interpret all of this?

Let me offer an interpretation that better matches what Paul was actually trying to communicate.[4] It's not that the interpretation above is completely wrong, but it's not completely right either. A close analysis of Paul's language and logic reveals the following:

- works of the law = torah observance, especially circumcision (the sign of the old covenant)
- faith of/in Christ = Christ's faithfulness + our faith in Christ
- freedom = freedom *from* sin and the law + freedom *to* love and be led by the Spirit

In other words, we cannot be made right by torah observance (works of the law), nor do we need to have the sign of the old covenant (circumcision) to be part of Jesus's new covenant. Instead, we are made right by Christ, whose faithful life and death are the basis of our salvation (Christ's faithfulness).[5] We are united with Christ, who saves us when we believe in him—trusting him with our minds, hearts, and bodies (our faith *in* Christ).[6] Through Jesus, we are free *from* the enslaving power of sin and free *from* having to keep all the regulations of the old covenant/law. This results in us being free *to* walk in step with the Spirit as we embody Jesus's love and goodness.

This interpretation fits much better in the overall metanarrative framework that we've looked at, and it better fits the details of Galatians. For example, Paul's issue with "works of the law" has to do with a group of people who are trying to force Gentile Christians to observe Jewish law, especially the act of circumcision (which is mentioned more than fifteen times in this letter). Circumcision symbolizes that one is a part of the covenant that God made with Abraham and his offspring. Paul responds to this pressure to make Gentiles become circumcised by making it clear that Gentiles can become Christians without having to take on the mark of the old covenant that had for so long distinguished the Jews. However, and I think this is just as important, as Paul addresses this situation, he extends this principle to torah-keeping as a whole. So, for example, Paul writes, "Every man who has himself circumcised . . . is required to do the whole Law" (5:3). Paul's point seems to be that the Jewish faith has never simply been about the covenant marker of circumcision but has always entailed faithfulness to the whole covenant. However, even if one tries to keep the entire Jewish law, it's still not enough. Sin is too pervasive: it not only corrupts us humans but it even corrupts the good that the torah was intended to achieve. What the torah *cannot* do, Christ *can* do and *has done* through his faithful life, sacrificial death, and resurrection.

As those who are united with Christ, we receive the Spirit (3:27). As Paul explains in Galatians, the indwelling of the Spirit produces a particular kind of freedom. Paul declares that one is free *from* sin and the law. The enslavement of sin, as we've seen, prevents us from being the people we were created to be. Even more, the corrosive power of sin has even perverted the goodness of God's torah, so that instead of the law being life giving, it has become burdensome and condemning.[7]

Having been freed *from* sin and the law, we are now free *to* love and serve. That's right: free to love and serve! As Paul writes, "You were called to *freedom*, brothers and sisters; only don't let this *freedom* be an opportunity to indulge your selfish impulses, but *serve* each other through *love*" (5:13). According to Paul, true freedom is expressed when humans embrace their full humanity, when humans live according to their true nature by reflecting the image of God as revealed in Christ—which means that true freedom is seen in the kind of love and service that mirrors Christ, the true image of God. Humans cannot do this on their own; they need the power of the faithful Christ to enable them. Not surprisingly, then, Paul calls the Galatians to "keep in step with the Spirit" (5:25 NIV)—the Spirit makes true freedom possible. The freedom to serve and love does not undermine Paul's teaching that we are made right by faith. Notice how faith and good deeds go hand in hand within Paul's metanarrative: "the only thing that counts is *faith working through love*" (5:6 NRSV). We are made right by Christ's faithfulness when we pledge our faith in Christ; by pledging our faith in Christ, we are committing ourselves to walk by his Spirit, who frees us to serve and love.

Ephesians 2:1–10

> As for you, you were dead in your transgressions and sins, in which you used to live when you followed the ways of this world and of the ruler of the kingdom of the air, the spirit who is now at work in those who are disobedient. All of us also lived among them at one time, gratifying the cravings of our flesh and following its desires and thoughts. Like the rest, we were by nature deserving of wrath. But because of his great love for us, God, who is rich in mercy, made us alive with Christ even when we were dead in transgressions—it is by grace you have been saved. And God raised us up with Christ and seated us with him in the heavenly realms in Christ Jesus, in order that in the coming ages he might show the incomparable riches of his grace, expressed in his kindness to us in Christ Jesus. For it is by grace you have been saved, through faith—and this is not from yourselves, it is the gift of God—not by works, so that no one can boast. For we are God's handiwork, created in Christ Jesus to do good works, which God prepared in advance for us to do. (2:1–10 NIV)

In Ephesians, Paul concisely lays out some central pieces of the Christian metanarrative. This will give us a chance to briefly clarify Paul's teaching about (1) sin, (2) God's wrath, and (3) good deeds.

1. *Humans sin and are controlled by sin.* On the one hand, sin is like a power that enslaves and corrupts ("a spirit . . . at work in those who are disobedient"). On the other hand, sin is something that we do, that we are responsible for ("gratifying the cravings of our flesh and following its desires and thoughts"). The power of sin reveals a larger reality in which real spiritual forces are aligned against God, fighting a battle for our hearts and minds. Yet sin is not just a force outside us; it is also something we find ourselves colluding with as we partner with our own brokenness. That is, we are not simply victims; we are also copartners in sin, sometimes willingly engaging in thoughts and behaviors that we know are wrong and destructive.
2. *Sin brings forth wrath.* This is uncomfortable and unpopular language, and it requires careful clarification and informed nuance. We should not consider God's wrath as we might consider human wrath, a kind of impatient and unwarranted overreaction, a "flying off the handle." It is quite difficult to reconcile the caricature of an out-of-control, angry God with the immediately following description of God we get here: "because of his great love for us, God, who is rich in mercy, made us alive with Christ even when we were dead in transgressions." As we make sense of wrath, it has to fit what we know of God's "great love" and

"rich mercy," both of which are particularly on display in God becoming human and being crucified to save broken and rebellious humankind.

One way of bringing together notions of God's mercy and wrath is to assume that God's wrath flows out of his holiness, his perfect goodness. That is, a holy God cannot abide injustice and wrongdoing. In fact, what seems at first to be a repelling characteristic—wrath—can soon become an attractive one. A God who is indifferent to injustice, who can turn a blind eye to transgression, might not be a good God. On some level we desire God to be just. Fortunately for us, God is not only just but also merciful. His ultimate response to rebellion is not a simplistic execution of justice—one where we are forced to stand alone, our imperfections judged according to a perfect standard. Instead, God reveals a merciful justice—the crimes must still be punished, but God takes that punishment on himself. He does so not by denying the damage of disobedience nor by pretending it's no big deal. Instead, God reveals the full weight of the offense, bearing it on his shoulders in the shame, brutality, and agony of crucifixion.

Another aspect of God's wrath may be felt in the natural consequences of sin. When we sin, we go against the way God has arranged the world to work. Going against the proper order of things will inevitably lead to unwanted results—natural consequences that we'd be wise to avoid. This seems implied by the description of God's wrath as God giving people over to their sins (Rom. 1:18–32).

3. *We are saved by grace (through faith), not by good deeds.* Through grace we are "saved" and "made alive" and "raised up with Christ and seated with him in the heavenly realm." We must be clear on this: our salvation relies on God's mercy and grace: "This is not from yourselves, it is the gift of God—not by works, so that no one can boast." (In Ephesians, "works" is likely a reference to "good deeds"—unlike in Galatians, where "works" referred to keeping torah.) Earlier we learned that God's grace is initiated, extravagant, unrepayable, and unrelated to status or achievements, and that it calls for response. The same view of grace fits our study here. Because God's grace is initiated, extravagant, unrepayable, and unrelated to status or achievements, "no one can boast." God's grace also calls for response: "we are God's handiwork, created in Christ Jesus *to do good works*." To connect this with what we've covered elsewhere, notice how we are saved by grace *through faith*. It is the *faithfulness of Jesus* that ultimately saves us. When we pledge our *faith in Jesus*, we are united with Christ, made alive by his saving grace,

forgiven by his mercy and sacrifice, and empowered by his Spirit to do good deeds as God's handiwork. This sounds quite similar to what we find in Paul's Letter to Titus:

> We ourselves were once foolish, disobedient, led astray, slaves to various passions and pleasures. . . . But when the goodness and loving kindness of God our Savior appeared, he saved us, not because of any works of righteousness that we had done, but according to his mercy, through . . . rebirth and renewal by the Holy Spirit. This Spirit he poured out on us richly through Jesus Christ our Savior, so that, having been justified by his grace, we might become heirs according to the hope of eternal life. . . .
>
> Insist on these things so that those who have come to believe in God may be careful to devote themselves to good works. (3:3–8 NRSV)

Colossians 1:15–23

Within his letter to the Christians in Colossae, Paul waxes eloquent about the Son of God. The words flow in a beautiful, poetic style that befits the awe-inspiring nature of Jesus and his world-changing impact.

> The Son is the image of the invisible God, the firstborn over all creation. For in him all things were created: things in heaven and on earth, visible and invisible, whether thrones or powers or rulers or authorities; all things have been created through him and for him. He is before all things, and in him all things hold together. And he is the head of the body, the church; he is the beginning and the firstborn from among the dead, so that in everything he might have the supremacy. For God was pleased to have all his fullness dwell in him, and through him to reconcile to himself all things, whether things on earth or things in heaven, by making peace through his blood, shed on the cross.
>
> Once you were alienated from God and were enemies in your minds because of your evil behavior. But now he has reconciled you by Christ's physical body through death to present you holy in his sight, without blemish and free from accusation—if you continue in your faith, established and firm, and do not move from the hope held out in the gospel. This is the gospel that you heard. (1:15–23 NIV)

Once again, we see Jesus as both God and human. He is God, for he is "the image of the invisible God" in whom "all God's fullness dwells"; he is the one "in whom" and "for whom" and "through whom" absolutely everything was created; and he holds all creation together. Implied here is that apart from the Son nothing would ever have existed or would continue to exist.

The Son is also human, for he is "the firstborn over all creation." (In this case, the language of "firstborn" does not imply that Jesus is a created being, for we just learned that he is God and the creator of all. Instead, "firstborn" here refers to him being first in "rank and status," like a firstborn son in the ancient Jewish culture.)[8] Jesus is not only firstborn over creation but also "firstborn from the dead," meaning that he is the first of a new reality—the resurrected reality where "all things" will be made whole. The phrase "all things" in this passage reminds us that God's reconciliation project is not merely human-centered but includes *everything*. If we've been paying attention, this shouldn't come as a surprise. After all, God declared creation "good," and sin distorted the created order. When Jesus conquered sin, he alleviated the broken condition of not only humans but also the created order. As "firstborn" of creation and "firstborn from the dead" we see a fascinating parallel—he represents who we are meant to be now as humans and how we will one day be restored at the resurrection.

In addition to other descriptors, Jesus is referred to as the "head of the church." There are several ways to interpret what "head" means within the ancient Greco-Roman context, and it may be that more than one meaning is intended. For example, this could mean that Jesus is the church's *source* (that is, there is no church without Jesus); and/or it could mean that Jesus is the church's *nourishment* (that is, the church can live out its purpose only through Jesus's ongoing sustaining and nourishing help); and/or it could mean that Jesus is the church's *authority* (that is, Jesus is in charge). As Jesus leads and sustains his church, as he empowers it to partner with him in the work of reconciliation, he also models how real reconciliation requires cruciform love. After all, that is how Jesus, the head of the church, made reconciliation with God possible: "he reconciled all things to himself . . . [bringing] peace through the blood of his cross" (Col. 1:20).

Last, we see again how humans found themselves "alienated from God" because of sin. And yet God did not treat all humans as rebels, as enemies. Instead, he humbled himself and took on a body so that he might redeem our bodies. He takes on our brokenness and heals it, allowing us to take on his wholeness. We who were unholy, blemished, and under accusation can now find ourselves "holy . . . , without blemish and free from accusation." This is Jesus's doing, not our own. However, a response is expected: to "continue in faith." (At this point, we should be well aware that "faith" means much more than "believing a few facts.") For Paul, this poetic passage testifies to "the gospel," the good news that God became flesh, reconciled us through his blood, rose from death, extends his wholeness to us through grace, and reigns as king. This beautiful new reality invites us all to come and find life.

Summary

I will conclude our study of Paul with Michael Gorman's insightful summary of Paul's spirituality, which he cleverly captures with several *C* words:

> The distinctive character of Paul's . . . spirituality is that it is *covenantal* (in relation to God the Father, the God of Israel), *cruciform* (shaped in accord with the cross of Christ), *charismatic* (empowered by the Spirit), *communal* (lived out in the company of other believers), and therefore *countercultural*, or alter-cultural (formed in contrast to the dominant socio-political values of the . . . world). . . . [It] is also a *creational*, or better, *new-creational*, spirituality (experienced as part of God's reconciling the cosmos to himself). Finally, this spirituality . . . has a narrative shape to it. Paul and his churches are called to tell a story with their individual and corporate lives, a story of self-giving faith, hope, and love as the means to embody and advance the story of God renewing covenant and redeeming the world through the crucified Christ. This means that Paul's spirituality is *corporeal*, bodily.[9]

Appendix B

Hell

Hell can be a troubling topic. I don't have any problem thinking that God will bring appropriate punishment on the tyrants, rapists, sex traffickers, child molesters, and others who were not appropriately punished in their earthly lives. That's probably better than the alternative—whether it's the atheistic view (there's no justice, only death) or the deist view (there's no justice because God doesn't get involved) or the "nice God" view (there's no justice because God is happy with everybody and doesn't really care if people did horrific things). I don't struggle with the doctrine of God bringing justice in the afterlife. I do struggle, however, with God sending people to a place where they will be tormented for all eternity, especially since this doesn't sound like something Jesus would do. Even more, I struggle with the notion that God condemns not just folks like child-enslavers but also folks who seem like decent people who, for whatever reason, never aligned themselves with Jesus. Is there any way to make sense of this? Let's briefly consider four ways to understand hell.

1. *Eternal conscious torment.* According to this model, hell is an experience of unceasing suffering. Those who go to hell will be there for all eternity, always conscious of their torment, without hope of escape. I have a hard time squaring this model with the justice of God—after all, how can the sins of a *finite* person merit *infinite* torment? Even though I am troubled by this model, I don't reject it as necessarily unchristian, for two

reasons. First, this view has been held by many Christians throughout the centuries; second, this view can arguably be found in Scripture.

To clarify: I think this view of hell is inaccurate, but I understand why some Christians might adopt this view. For those who hold this view, is there any way to reconcile eternal conscious torment and God's justice? We could speculate that infinite torment is a just punishment for rejecting a holy God who has made an immeasurable sacrifice on our behalf. In other words, maybe rejecting God and the sacrifice of Jesus isn't a finite sin after all. Perhaps the punishment (eternal conscious torment) does indeed fit the crime (scorning something of infinite value and cost).

2. *Annihilationism.*[1] According to this model, hell refers not to unceasing torment but to permanent destruction. In Scripture, words like "destroy" and "destruction" are the most common way to refer to punishment in the afterlife. When we think of something being "destroyed," we tend to think of it being permanently destroyed rather than being stuck in an unending process. Consequently, it could make sense to think of hell as a place of *permanent* destruction rather than *never-ending* torment. But isn't hell supposed to be "eternal"? Yes—but we can understand "eternal" to mean "permanent" rather than "unceasing." That is, to be eternally destroyed is to have no second chances, no do-overs—one's destruction lasts for all eternity. But isn't there supposed to be fire? Kind of—in this model, the references to "fire" are understood to be symbolic, capturing the permanent destruction that fire brings.[2] The references to fire occur in genres that use symbolism, so that could make sense.

Proponents of the annihilationism model argue that it's a better model than eternal conscious torment for several reasons. First, it seems to be a more natural way to interpret words like "destruction." Second, it seems more just—the punishment better fits the crime. For example, the sins of finite people are not infinitely punished but finitely punished. Further, it makes room for different levels of punishment. In eternal conscious torment, every person receives the same punishment (eternal torment). In annihilationism, some persons may receive greater punishment for greater crimes before they are annihilated whereas others may receive lesser punishment for lesser crimes before they are annihilated. Maybe the sex trafficker suffers more than the petty thief. Third, another strength of this model is that it doesn't assume that souls are inherently immortal. Instead, only God is immortal, though he may grant unending life as a gift. If unending life is a gift, it makes sense to think that

God would not grant that gift to the damned but would permanently destroy them; the awkward alternative is to imagine God perpetually giving the gift of life in order to torment a soul forever.

When I first encountered the annihilationism model, I didn't think it would hold water. But, on further research, I was surprised to find how well it aligned with both Scripture and Christian theology. Its main weakness is that it lacks much support from Christian tradition, though it is arguably present in the writings of early Christians such as Irenaeus and Athanasius.

3. *Universalism*. In this model, all persons will eventually be restored (although there may be an interim period of punishment and/or purification). It's possible to find hints of universalism in Scripture and theology. For instance, God's mercy and forgiveness are so shocking and extensive (as we see in Jesus's willing death on the cross) that it could lead one to expect God's grace and mercy to cover everyone—even those who reject him. Further, if God loves the world, is it possible for even the most obstinate sinner to exhaust God's love? And if God wills that all be saved, can anything prevent his will from being accomplished?

   Universalism does not ignore God's justice. Within this model, it's possible that some go through a period of punishment or purification before being restored. That is, finite sins might receive their appropriate consequences before the sinner's restoration. Or it might be argued that, because Jesus's sacrifice is so powerful and extensive, there's no need for further punishment, as justice has already been meted out at the cross.

   I wouldn't mind if universalism were true. However, I don't think it fits the Bible very well. Yes, there are hints of universalism in Scripture, but for the most part the Bible points to hell being eternal—which means either "unceasing" or "permanent," neither of which allows for an eventual restoration. I think the biblical picture is that God truly gives humans choices, and those choices have eternal ramifications. Similarly, I think the biblical picture is that God rarely overrides the human will, so that if our will is to reject God, then he will allow us that choice.

4. *Holistic brokenness*.[3] We can find something like this model in the writings of C. S. Lewis. Here, hell is the opposite of heaven on earth. Just as the biblical language describing heaven is full of symbolism that points to holistic restoration, so the language describing hell might carry symbolism that points to holistic brokenness—physical, social, and spiritual. Thus being in hell is something like experiencing the unrestrained consequences of sin. To paraphrase Lewis, heaven is humans

> saying to God, "Your will be done"; in contrast, hell is God saying to humans, "Your will be done."[4] In other words, for those who choose to reject God, God gives them what they want. If they don't want God, God will give them just that: an existence in which the light and life of God are increasingly overtaken by the darkness and corruption of sin.
>
> In this model, hell could be understood as eternal because it's unending and/or permanent. How might the biblical language of "destruction" fit into this model? We could imagine that the destructive impact of sin eventually annihilates all that is left of a person so that the person ceases to exist. Or perhaps the destructive, downward spiral of sin will continue eternally, as condemned people experience ever more isolation and sadness and loathing. The strength of the holistic-brokenness model is how it can be seen to fit the larger biblical vision of sin. Instead of hell being a random punishment for sins, it is the natural consequence of choosing sin. We can also notice how this model makes the reasonable assumption that hell (where God has withdrawn his presence) is like the opposite of heaven (where God is intimately present). The holistic-brokenness model seems compatible with what we know of the justice of God: God is not punishing people beyond what their sin deserves; instead, he's turning them over to the very consequences of their sin.

The doctrine of hell was at one point the most difficult thing for me to come to terms with as a Christian, especially when I was only aware of the eternal-conscious-torment model. Two things have helped me deal with my discomfort over the doctrine of hell. First, and most importantly, I assume that a God who would become human and suffer and die for sinners is a God who is trustworthy, a God who will do what is right. Whatever hell is, it won't be unjust, and it won't be contrary to the nature of God as revealed in Jesus. Second, discovering that there are other models of hell besides eternal conscious torment has helped me imagine how God's justice and the doctrine of hell could coexist.

Notes

Introduction Why Worldview Matters

1. G. K. Chesterton, *Heretics*, originally published in 1905 by the John Lane Company. Reprint available online at https://www.ccel.org/ccel/chesterton/heretics.i.html.

2. Alex Rosenberg, *The Atheist's Guide to Reality: Enjoying Life without Illusions* (New York: Norton, 2012).

3. Rosenberg, *Atheist's Guide to Reality*, vii.

4. Rosenberg, *Atheist's Guide to Reality*, vii.

5. Rosenberg, *Atheist's Guide to Reality*, ix.

6. Rosenberg, *Atheist's Guide to Reality*, 2–3.

7. This metaphor is adapted from an illustration given by Alister McGrath in *The Passionate Intellect: Christian Faith and the Discipleship of the Mind* (Downers Grove, IL: InterVarsity, 2014), 51–55.

8. Here's a bit more on the technical details of this. Let's start with Rosenberg:

> The brain is a physical system, fantastically complex, but still operating according to all the laws of physics. . . . Every state of my brain is fixed by physical facts. In fact, it is a physical state. Previous states of my brain and the physical input from the world together brought about its current state. . . . All these states were determined by the operation of the laws of physics and chemistry. These laws operated on previous states of my brain and on states of the world going back to before my brain was formed. . . . They go back through a chain of prior events not just to before anyone with a mind existed but back to a time after life began on this planet. When I make choices—trivial or momentous—it's just another event in my brain locked into this network of processes going back to the beginning of the universe, long before I had the slightest "choice." Nothing was up to me. Everything—including my choice and my feeling that I can choose freely—was fixed by earlier states of the universe plus the laws of physics. End of story. (*Atheist's Guide to Reality*, 236)

For Rosenberg, everything we think and do is the unavoidable result of physical processes that came before us, that will continue long after us, and that we have no control over. That is, free will is just an illusion.

9. James K. A. Smith, *You Are What You Love: The Spiritual Power of Habit* (Grand Rapids: Brazos, 2016), 3.

10. Smith, *You Are What You Love*, 1–25.

11. Dorothy L. Sayers, *Creed or Chaos? And Other Essays in Popular Theology* (1947; repr., London: Methuen, 1954), 1; italics original.

12. In chapter 4 we'll discuss more about what "Father" means, including how it does not indicate that God is male.

13. Forgiving someone doesn't mean we enable the person to maintain abusive patterns, but it does mean we let go of any hatred, bitterness, or desire for vengeance.

Chapter 1 The Old Testament

1. I have been particularly helped in my understanding of the biblical plotline by the writings of Richard Middleton, Scot McKnight, Tremper Longman, and N. T. Wright, as well as by conversations with my colleagues and former professors.

2. This is not to say that God's creation is in a kind of static perfection where there's no room for development and learning and growth. It's just that things are right and good.

3. We can think of the "image of God" from three complementary angles: functional, structural, and relational. The *functional* image of God is related to humanity's distinct responsibility to care for and rule over creation (Gen. 1:26–28). The *structural* image of God is related to humanity's distinct nature; according to Christian tradition, this might include humanity's distinct moral and/or intellectual abilities. Last, the *relational* image of God is related to humans' distinct ability to engage in loving relationship with God and one another. For more discussion of this, see Mark Harris, "The Biblical Text and a Functional Account of the *Imago Dei*"; Aku Visala, "Will the Structural Theory of the Image of God Survive Evolution?"; and Thomas Jay Oord, "The *Imago Dei* as Relational Love." All three essays are published in *Finding Ourselves after Darwin: Conversations on the Image of God, Original Sin, and the Problem of Evil*, ed. Stanley P. Rosenberg (Grand Rapids: Baker Academic, 2018), 48–91.

4. For an excellent discussion on this, see Tremper Longman, "What Genesis 1–2 Teaches (and What It Doesn't)," in *Reading Genesis 1–2: An Evangelical Conversation*, ed. J. Daryl Charles (Peabody, MA: Hendrickson, 2013), 103–28. See also Tremper Longman, *Genesis*, The Story of God Bible Commentary 1 (Grand Rapids: Zondervan, 2016).

5. When we are aware of the ancient context, we see how the author of Genesis might have been borrowing common creation stories and reworking them to teach truths about the one true God. As Old Testament scholar Tremper Longman writes, "[It] is important for modern readers of [Genesis] 1–2 to realize that this account of creation was not written against Darwinian but against Babylonian, Canaanite, and Egyptian claims" ("What Genesis 1–2 Teaches," 107).

6. Sometimes Scripture treats sin as if it's a personal power (Gen. 4:7), and other times it treats sin as a form of human rebellion.

7. A threefold description of physical, social, and spiritual brokenness is also present in Tremper Longman's work on Genesis.

8. See Exod. 3:1–4:17, where Moses tries to talk God into picking someone else.

9. Richard J. Middleton, *A New Heaven and a New Earth: Reclaiming Biblical Eschatology* (Grand Rapids: Baker Academic, 2014), 87.

10. For those who are uneasy about the Israelite conquest of the promised land (as well as other bothersome Old Testament accounts), a good starting point is David Lamb, *God Behaving Badly: Is the God of the Old Testament Angry, Sexist, and Racist?* (Downers Grove, IL: InterVarsity, 2011). Although Lamb leaves some questions unanswered, he nonetheless shows that much of the contemporary rhetoric that angrily denounces the Old Testament is often a distortion of the truth, based on misconceptions or mischaracterizations of the larger Old Testament story and its ancient context. See also Tremper Longman, *Confronting Old Testament Controversies: Pressing Questions about Evolution, Sexuality, History, and Violence* (Grand Rapids: Baker Books, 2019).

11. David eventually admits his guilt before God and repents, displaying something of how "a man after God's own heart" should properly acknowledge his own sin.

12. Solomon also had great wealth, though according to Scripture this was a gift from God and not something Solomon initially pursued (1 Kings 3).

13. David Nienhuis, "Reading the Bible as Story," in *A Compact Guide to the Whole Bible: Learning to Read Scripture's Story*, ed. Robert W. Wall and David Nienhuis (Grand Rapids: Baker Academic, 2015), 30.

14. The word "anointed" sounds like "Messiah" in Hebrew and "Christ" in Greek.

15. Italics in Scripture quotations have been added for emphasis, here and throughout.

Chapter 2 The Life of Jesus

1. Craig G. Bartholomew and Michael W. Goheen, *The Drama of Scripture: Finding Our Place in the Biblical Story*, 2nd ed. (Grand Rapids: Baker Academic, 2014), 22–23. There are other variations on how to divide up the "acts" of Scripture, as can be found in the writings of N. T. Wright and Kevin Vanhoozer.

2. My co-teacher, Matt Hearn (the lit scholar), deserves credit for this winsome wordplay.

3. This section borrows from a book that I cowrote with my wife, Lauren Strahan, and that was illustrated by my mother, Rebecca Strahan: *Awaiting the King: An Advent Family Devotional* (N.p.: CreateSpace, 2017).

4. Scot McKnight notes how the Gospel of John offers another angle to appreciate Jesus's work of fulfillment: "John shows how the principle institutions and feasts of Israel, those annual celebrations that told Israel's story and that shaped both memory and identity for every observant Jew, find their own completion in Jesus. Thus, we have Jesus as the *temple* in John 2, the *Sabbath* in John 5, the *Passover* in John 6, the *Feast of Tabernacles* in John 7–10, and the *Dedication* in John 10:22–39" (*The King Jesus Gospel: The Original Good News Revisited* [Grand Rapids: Zondervan, 2011], 86; italics added).

5. Keep in mind the Spirit's role in Jesus's life and ministry: "By the Spirit Jesus was conceived, anointed, commissioned, empowered, sustained, and raised from the dead" (Leonard Allen, *Poured Out: The Spirit of God Empowering the Mission of God* [Abilene, TX: Abilene Christian University Press, 2018], 107).

6. Although evil is clearly present in the Old Testament, demons are not much discussed. In the New Testament, however, they take on a more prominent role. They are apparently beings (maybe rebellious angels) who are opposed to God's purposes and seek to further corrupt the world, sometimes even inhabiting and tormenting humans.

7. Jesus's claim to forgive should shock not only an ancient audience but a contemporary one as well. I like how C. S. Lewis opens our eyes to this:

> We can all understand how a man forgives offences against himself. You tread on my toes and I forgive you, you steal my money and I forgive you. But what should we make of a man, himself unrobbed and untrodden on, who announced that he forgave you for treading on other men's toes and stealing other men's money? Asinine fatuity is the kindest description we should give of his conduct. Yet this is what Jesus did. He told people that their sins were forgiven, and never waited to consult all the other people whom their sins had undoubtedly injured. He unhesitatingly behaved as if He was the party chiefly concerned, the person chiefly offended in all offenses. This make sense only if He really was the Son of God whose laws are broken and whose love is wounded in every sin. In the mouth of any speaker who is not God, these words would imply what I can only regard as a silliness and conceit unrivalled by any other character in history. (*Mere Christianity* [1952; repr., New York: HarperOne, 1996], 51–52)

8. I like F. Scott Spencer's definition of repentance as "a change of mind . . . , will, and character in accordance with God's holy purposes" (*The Gospel of Luke and the Acts of the Apostles*, Interpreting Biblical Texts [Nashville: Abingdon, 2008], 114).

9. According to Matthew W. Bates, we should think of "belief" in terms of "allegiance." He argues that this translation makes good sense of the New Testament and the ancient

Greco-Roman usage of the term in question (*pistis*). Further, "the allegiance concept welds mental agreement, professed fealty, and embodied loyalty" (*Salvation by Allegiance Alone* [Grand Rapids: Baker Academic, 2017], 82).

10. John A. Dennis, "Death of Jesus," in *Dictionary of Jesus and the Gospels*, ed. Joel B. Green (Downers Grove, IL: InterVarsity, 2013), 173, citing Cicero, *In Verrem* 2.5.64.165–70, 2.5.66.169.

11. This quote by Seneca (*ad Lucilium* 101) is found in Joel B. Green, *1 Peter*, Two Horizons New Testament Commentary (Grand Rapids: Eerdmans, 2007), 59; the translation of Seneca is from Martin Hengel, *Crucifixion: In the Ancient World and the Folly of the Message of the Cross* (Philadelphia: Fortress, 1977), 31–32.

12. Dennis, "Death of Jesus," 174, citing Cicero, *In Verrem* 2.5.64.165–70.

Chapter 3 The New Testament Church

1. Baptism is a ritual in which people are washed with water, signifying their sins being forgiven, their rising to new lives of faithfulness to Jesus, and their being filled with and empowered by his Holy Spirit. For a concise description of baptism's significance in the New Testament, see Matthew W. Bates, *Salvation by Allegiance Alone* (Grand Rapids: Baker Academic, 2017), 174.

2. On this insight, see Earl Lavender, *Acts of the Apostles: Jesus Alive in His Church* (Abilene, TX: Leafwood, 2006), 46–47.

3. Kavin Rowe, *World Upside Down: Reading Acts in the Graeco-Roman Age* (Oxford: Oxford University Press, 2009), 5.

4. Jesus so closely identifies with his church that he considers Paul's persecution of the church as persecution of *himself*: "Why do you persecute *me*?" (Acts 9:4; 22:7; 26:14 NIV).

5. There is some debate concerning whether Paul was actually responsible for all thirteen letters, but I find the counterevidence unconvincing and question-begging, especially when one takes into account the early date of the letters' compilation and the common use of scribes, which can account for differences in style and vocabulary. This matter is not particularly relevant to our current study in this chapter, since I happen to be focusing on letters that everyone agrees are Pauline.

6. I believe that I first encountered this play on words (righteousness as "doing right") in the writings of N. T. Wright. I have found Wright's works insightful in understanding God's righteousness in Paul, although we are not always in full agreement. See especially Wright, "The Letter to the Romans: Introduction, Commentary, and Reflections," in *New Interpreter's Bible*, vol. 10 (Nashville: Abingdon, 2002).

7. Although it's a matter of some debate, there are reasons to understand Paul to be saying that God's righteousness imbues the believer, graciously giving the believer a righteous status that would otherwise be unattainable for humans. God's righteousness is revealed, then, in making us right, by gifting us with his own rightness. The best way I've found to understand this is within the context of our being united with Jesus. When we are united with Jesus, we share in his righteousness. For further discussion, see Bates, *Salvation by Allegiance*, 180–90.

8. John M. Barclay, *Paul and the Gift* (Grand Rapids: Eerdmans, 2015).

9. I'm confident that I read this threefold description of new creation somewhere, but I cannot find the source to give proper credit.

10. Specifically, Paul is referring to his mission to reconcile people to God and to one another. See David J. Downs, "2 Corinthians," in *The CEB Study Bible*, ed. Joel B. Green (Nashville: Common English Bible, 2013), 343. See also N. T. Wright, "On Becoming the Righteousness of God," in *Pauline Theology*, ed. David M. Hay (Minneapolis: Fortress, 1993), 2:200–208.

11. This insight from Irenaeus (*Against Heresies* 3.19.1) is cited in Downs, "2 Corinthians," 343.

12. This language of every knee bowing and every tongue confessing is apparently borrowed from the Old Testament prophetic book of Isaiah (45:22–24). In that context, it is before Israel's

one God that people are bowing and confessing. Here in Philippians we find an example of how the early Christians were thinking of Jesus in terms appropriate for the one God of Israel.

13. Michael J. Gorman, *Apostle of the Crucified Lord: A Theological Introduction to Paul and His Letters*, 2nd ed. (Grand Rapids: Eerdmans, 2017), 151; italics original.

14. Gorman, *Apostle of the Crucified Lord*, 84; italics original.

15. N. T. Wright, "Philippians," in *Theological Interpretation of the New Testament: A Book-by-Book Survey*, ed. Kevin J. Vanhoozer (Grand Rapids: Baker Academic, 2005), 138.

16. James K. A. Smith, *You Are What You Love: The Spiritual Power of Habit* (Grand Rapids: Brazos, 2016), 39; italics original.

17. See Richard J. Middleton, *A New Heaven and a New Earth: Reclaiming Biblical Eschatology* (Grand Rapids: Baker Academic, 2014), 109–27, 179–210, for how biblical images of cosmic razing can be metaphorical of God's judgment.

18. E.g., Jesus tells a parable that ends, "Well done, good and faithful servant! You have been faithful with a few things; I will put you in charge of many things" (Matt. 25:21 NIV). Just as the nature of reward in the afterlife is mysterious, so is the nature of punishment. Some Christians want to dismiss any notion of punishment, since it seems uncharacteristic of a loving and merciful God, but that doesn't seem to fit the biblical picture. For more on this, see appendix B (on hell) as well as chapter 5 (particularly where I discuss the line from the Apostles' Creed, "he will come again to judge the living and the dead").

19. For a brief introduction to Wright's work on this, see N. T. Wright, *Scripture and the Authority of God: How to Read the Bible Today* (London: SPCK, 2011), 122–27.

20. For more details, see Middleton, *New Heaven*.

Chapter 4 God the Father

1. The Apostles' Creed, available at http://www.anglicancommunion.org/media/109023/Apostles-Creed.pdf.

2. For a short introduction to the rule of faith, see Everett Ferguson, *The Rule of Faith: A Guide* (Eugene, OR: Cascade, 2015). The rule of faith had a consistency in the early church, even among churches separated by region and language, as Roger E. Olson points out in *Counterfeit Christianity: The Persistence of Errors in the Church* (Nashville: Abingdon, 2015), 26.

3. For more on the Apostles' Creed, including its background and its interpretation, see Alister E. McGrath, *I Believe: Exploring the Apostles' Creed* (Downers Grove, IL: InterVarsity, 1998); Michael Bird, *What Christians Ought to Believe: An Introduction to Christian Doctrine through the Apostles' Creed* (Grand Rapids: Zondervan, 2016); and Luke Timothy Johnson, *The Creed: What Christians Believe and Why It Matters* (New York: Doubleday, 2003). I will be drawing on these authors' insights throughout the next three chapters.

4. On the critique of dualism that follows, see C. S. Lewis, *Mere Christianity* (1952; repr., New York: HarperOne, 1996), 42–46.

5. "[The] words 'God is love' have no real meaning unless God contains at least two Persons. Love is something that one person has for another person. If God was a single person, then before the world was made, he was not love" (Lewis, *Mere Christianity*, 174).

6. For these and other Gospel references to Jesus's unique relationship with the Father, see Johnson, *Creed*, 79–80.

7. See Bird, *What Christians Ought to Believe*, 60–62.

8. Bird, *What Christians Ought to Believe*, 62.

9. For what follows, see Bird, *What Christians Ought to Believe*, 66–67.

10. C. S. Lewis, *The Problem of Pain* (1940; repr., New York: Simon & Schuster, 1996), 24.

11. Lewis, *Problem of Pain*, 25.

12. I appreciate Mark Harris's study in which he convincingly shows that even though the language of Genesis 1 isn't definitive on this matter, the larger biblical witness makes it clear

that all of creation finds its origin in God (*The Nature of Creation: Examining the Bible and Science* [Bristol, CT: Acumen, 2013], 123).

13. "The biblical creation motif does not consist of a single concise and well-defined concept or principle . . . [for] it is simply too varied in genre, aim, and content" (Harris, *Nature of Creation*, 79). See also Tremper Longman, "What Genesis 1–2 Teaches (and What It Doesn't)," in *Reading Genesis 1–2: An Evangelical Conversation*, ed. J. Daryl Charles (Peabody, MA: Hendrickson, 2013), 112–19.

14. Richard J. Middleton, "Reading Genesis 3 Attentive to Human Evolution: Beyond Concordism and Non-overlapping Magisteria," in *Evolution and the Fall*, ed. William T. Cavanaugh and James K. A. Smith (Grand Rapids: Eerdmans, 2017), 78.

15. Longman, "What Genesis 1–2 Teaches," 103–28.

16. To complicate matters further, another well-respected scholar, John Walton, argues that Genesis 1 is focused more on functional creation than on material creation. He also claims that Genesis 1 resembles ancient accounts of temple construction. If he's correct, Genesis 1 might not be intending to offer an account of material creation; rather, it would be teaching that God's temple is the earth, where God has brought order and where humans are to be his priests (representatives) who carry out the sacred task of caring for creation. I'm not sure Genesis is as narrowly focused on functionality as Walton claims; however, we certainly find Walton's ideas in Scripture, where the earth resembles a temple (Isa. 6:3; 66:1–2) and where humans are to function as God's priests ("images of God" and "kingdom and priests"). If Walton is right, then Genesis is not in conflict with science, because Genesis is concerned with teaching truths about how things were *made to function*, not how things were *made*. See Walton, *Lost World of Genesis One: Ancient Cosmology and the Origins Debate* (Downers Grove, IL: InterVarsity, 2009).

17. Longman, "What Genesis 1–2 Teaches," 108.

18. For a more detailed explanation, see my article, "How in Hades Do We Teach Genesis 1–3?" *Perspectives on Science and the Christian Faith* 71 (2019): 119–22.

Chapter 5 Jesus Christ

1. This messianic expectation can be found in Isa. 11:1–9; 42:1–4; 61:1–4, as cited in Leonard Allen, *Poured Out: The Spirit of God Empowering the Mission of God* (Abilene, TX: Abilene Christian University Press, 2018), 65, 88.

2. The Greek word for "Lord" (*kyrios*) can alternatively be translated as "God," "ruler," or "master"—and, as we'll see, the New Testament makes use of all these possibilities.

3. In a rewrite of history, it's sometimes suggested that the doctrine of Jesus's divinity came late and that the earliest Christians thought of Jesus as just a great teacher or prophet. As Roger Olson says, "Anyone who has studied second-century Christian writings and anti-Christian writings knows better" (*Counterfeit Christianity: The Persistence of Errors in the Church* [Nashville: Abingdon, 2015], 72). For evidence, he references Celsus, Justin Martyr, Irenaeus, Origen, and Tertullian.

4. To confess Jesus as Lord has public, political implications; it's not merely a private and internal thing: "Keep in mind that Nero did not have Christians thrown to the lions because they said, 'Jesus is Lord of my heart'" (Michael Bird, *What Christians Ought to Believe: An Introduction to Christian Doctrine through the Apostles' Creed* [Grand Rapids: Zondervan, 2016], 93).

5. For examples of this balance in the Gospels, one might discern Jesus's divinity in his unusual birth, his authority to forgive sins, and his receiving worship, whereas the greatest example of Jesus's humanity would be his suffering and death.

6. Luke Timothy Johnson, *The Creed: What Christians Believe and Why It Matters* (New York: Doubleday, 2003), 141–42.

7. Bird, *What Christians Ought to Believe*, 77.

8. David J. Downs, "2 Corinthians," in *The CEB Study Bible*, ed. Joel B. Green (Nashville: Common English Bible, 2013), 343.

9. For this and more on Jesus as mediator, see Bird, *What Christians Ought to Believe*, 77–78.

10. God makes people right both legally (forgiving our guilt and sparing us from its due consequences) and vocationally (freeing us from sin so we can live as we were meant to). As we study the effects of the cross, we also learn something about the human condition. As Joel Green writes, "We find in the New Testament an abundance of terms and phrases for conceiving the human condition that characterizes human existence apart from God: slavery, hard-heartedness, lostness, friendship with the world, blindness, ungodliness, living according to the sinful nature, the reprobate mind, the darkened heart, enemies of God, dead in trespasses and more" ("Kaleidoscopic View," in *The Nature of Atonement: Four Views*, ed. James Beilby and Paul R. Eddy [Downers Grove, IL: InterVarsity, 2006], 167).

11. Scot McKnight, *A Community Called Atonement* (Nashville: Abingdon, 2010), 69; italics original. McKnight explains that we must understand God's wrath in light of God's love in two ways. First, we must remember that it is God who initiates the work of healing and forgiving us (lest we misconstrue things by envisioning a loving Jesus who steps in the path of a rage-fueled God). Second, God's wrath flows from his love for his creation, a love that naturally works in tandem with justice—a seeking to make things right, which sometimes involves consequences for injustice.

12. Johnson, *Creed*, 167.

13. Green, "Kaleidoscopic View," 168–70.

14. Johnson, *Creed*, 173–74.

15. Alister E. McGrath, *I Believe: Exploring the Apostles' Creed* (Downers Grove, IL: InterVarsity, 1998), 55–56.

16. See Johnson, *Creed*, 165.

17. Bird cleverly writes, "That 'Jesus was crucified, died, and was buried' is probably the only line of the Apostles' Creed that even atheists could confess with a clear conscience" (*What Christians Ought to Believe*, 111).

18. In some translations of the Apostles' Creed, the term "dead" is translated "hell," which I believe is a mistake. More likely, this is about Jesus descending to "the dead" (or "Hades"), not hell. "Hades" or "the dead" is commonly understood as something like the waiting place of the dead, in contrast to "hell," which is more like separation from God (Bird, *What Christians Ought to Believe*, 144). As for the hows and wheres of Hades, Scripture is vague. Apparently we don't need to know, or we are incapable of comprehending.

19. For a more detailed examination of this line of the creed and its background, see Bird, *What Christians Ought to Believe*, 143–54. For an argument that this line doesn't belong in the Apostles' Creed (because it's found only in later versions of the creed and because its New Testament support is weak), see Wayne Grudem, "He Did Not Descend into Hell," *Journal of the Evangelical Theological Society* 34 (1991): 103–13.

20. McGrath, *I Believe*, 62.

21. Johnson, *Creed*, 175.

22. Bird, *What Christians Ought to Believe*, 146.

23. Bird, *What Christians Ought to Believe*, 165–66.

24. Jesus's sitting at God's "right hand" is explicitly mentioned twice in this section (Heb. 8:1; 10:12).

25. Bird, *What Christians Ought to Believe*, 163.

26. C. S. Lewis, *Miracles* (1947; repr., New York: Touchstone, 1996), 194.

27. McGrath, *I Believe*, 74.

28. Especially helpful is Dallas Willard, *Divine Conspiracy: Rediscovering Our Hidden Life in God* (New York: Harper, 1998), 67–73, 257.

29. For more on this question, see Lewis, *Miracles*, 204–8.

30. McGrath writes, "We are being judged by someone who knows us totally . . . , who is passionately committed to us . . . , [and] whom we know and trust" (*I Believe*, 76–79).

31. Bird, *What Christians Ought to Believe*, 170. Bird cites other New Testament references that show the joy and excitement of Jesus's return (Phil. 3:20–21; Col. 3:4; Titus 2:13; Heb. 9:28).

32. C. S. Lewis, *Mere Christianity* (1952; repr., New York: HarperOne, 1996), 31.

33. Especially insightful on this topic is Matthew Bates's *Salvation by Allegiance Alone* (Grand Rapids: Baker Academic, 2017), esp. 107–25, 165–92.

34. What about those who have never heard about Jesus or had any real chance of knowing him? The short answer is: I don't know. The slightly longer answer is: I believe Scripture teaches (1) that Jesus is the only way to salvation and (2) that God deals more leniently with those who sin in ignorance. Consequently, I believe that the only route to salvation passes through Jesus, but I suspect that, in God's mercy, he may choose to extend the saving impact of Jesus to those who never had a chance to know him. We could get a whole lot more complex and play out several what-if scenarios, but I think it all boils down to Jesus as the only way and God doing what is just and merciful—whatever that may be.

35. Bates puts it together this way: "Initial declared allegiance . . . to Jesus the king causes a union with the king and his body, and the maintenance of this union is an embodiment of allegiance, a lived allegiance that includes good deeds" (*Salvation by Allegiance*, 121).

Chapter 6 The Holy Spirit and the Church

1. See Luke Timothy Johnson, *The Creed: What Christians Believe and Why It Matters* (New York: Doubleday, 2003), 220–23, for how the New Testament characterizes the Spirit as both person and power.

2. By "person" I don't mean a human with a physical body but, as Michael Bird puts it, "someone who is self-aware, capable of cognition, has a capacity to relate to other beings, and possesses recognizable traits of character" (*What Christians Ought to Believe: An Introduction to Christian Doctrine through the Apostles' Creed* [Grand Rapids: Zondervan, 2016], 186).

3. Alister E. McGrath, *I Believe: Exploring the Apostles' Creed* (Downers Grove, IL: InterVarsity, 1998), 79–81. The same holds true when we consider Bird's observation that the Holy Spirit plays a role "in creation, revelation, salvation, and empowerment" (*What Christians Ought to Believe*, 189).

4. For other places where the New Testament implies God is triune, see Leonard Allen, *Poured Out: The Spirit of God Empowering the Mission of God* (Abilene, TX: Abilene Christian University Press, 2018), 60–62.

5. The Nicene Creed, available at https://www.anglicancommunion.org/media/109020/Nicene-Creed.pdf.

6. Bird, *What Christians Ought to Believe*, 183.

7. Bird, *What Christians Ought to Believe*, 190.

8. Johnson, *Creed*, 223.

9. C. S. Lewis, *Mere Christianity* (1952; repr., New York: HarperOne, 1996), 175.

10. Johnson, *Creed*, 252.

11. As Johnson rightly points out (*Creed*, 252), Genesis claims God made "them" in his image, "male and female" (Gen. 1:26).

12. Bird, *What Christians Ought to Believe*, 199–200. The Nicene Creed makes the church's unity explicit by confessing "one" church. In the Apostles' Creed, "this is implied by the creed's reference to 'church' rather than 'churches'" (McGrath, *I Believe*, 92).

13. One thing that made the church distinctive in the first century was its diversity. But that does not mean it got this right 100 percent of the time. The New Testament is full of examples where believers are chastised for being divisive. But even in its imperfection, the church stood out from its culture for being unconventionally diverse.

14. Humility was not a virtue in the first-century world, since the culture was largely one of honor and shame, wherein a person was always looking to improve one's status. Notice how worldview shapes values: if Jesus reveals what humans are to be about, then humility is

a virtue; if Caesar reveals what humans are to be about, then humility is a vice; and if nature alone determines what humans are to be about, then humility is a virtue when it helps one survive and a vice when it hinders survival.

15. Even when all is set right, humans still have a purpose to reflect God's holiness in their love for one another and their care for creation.

16. I hope it's clear by now that I'm using "Christian" to refer to those who have accepted God's grace and seek to live as his people, which would exclude those who might identify as "Christian" simply because of their national, cultural, or familial upbringing.

17. The Macedonian church also helped the Jerusalem church, even though the Macedonian church itself was quite poor (2 Cor. 8:1–2).

18. John Mark Hicks, *Come to the Table: Revisioning the Lord's Supper* (Orange, CA: Leafwood, 2002), 148–49.

19. The New Testament isn't always clear on the precise timing of forgiveness (at confession, at repentance, or at baptism) or the method of baptism (immersion or sprinkling). Not surprisingly, churches have different opinions on these matters. Nevertheless, almost all churches regard confession, repentance, and baptism as critical steps for Christians. In the New Testament it's simply taken for granted that all Christians confess, repent, and are baptized. The Nicene Creed also assumes Christians are baptized: "We confess one baptism for the forgiveness of sins." For more on this, see Johnson, *Creed*, 276–81.

20. McGrath, *I Believe*, 98–102.

21. In this book, I interact with two types of dualism. One type is cosmic dualism, which is the view that there are two supreme powers—one good and the other evil. The other type of dualism, which we're currently considering, is something like substance dualism. This view posits that humans are composed of two independent substances: the material and the immaterial (mental/spiritual). Throughout the book, context should make clear which type of dualism is under consideration.

22. Bird, *What Christians Ought to Believe*, 215.

23. For a thorough introduction to the whole topic of restoration and renewal in Scripture, see Richard J. Middleton, *A New Heaven and a New Earth: Reclaiming Biblical Eschatology* (Grand Rapids: Baker Academic, 2014).

24. As to the foreverness of eternal life, the Nicene-Constantinopolitan Creed (AD 381) confesses that "[Jesus's] kingdom will have no end." As to the quality of eternal life, Jesus declares, "I came so that they could have life—indeed, so that they could live life to the fullest" (John 10:10).

25. Johnson, *Creed*, 295.

Chapter 7 The Distinctiveness of the Christian Faith

1. Larry W. Hurtado, *Destroyer of the Gods: Early Christian Distinctiveness in the Roman World* (Waco: Baylor University Press, 2017).

2. Alister E. McGrath, *Heresy: A History of Defending the Truth* (New York: HarperOne, 2009).

3. Iain Provan, *Seriously Dangerous Religion: What the Old Testament Really Says and Why It Matters* (Waco: Baylor University Press, 2014).

4. Hurtado, *Destroyer of the Gods*, 183–88.

5. Hurtado, *Destroyer of the Gods*, 21.

6. Hurtado, *Destroyer of the Gods*, 22.

7. Hurtado, *Destroyer of the Gods*, 29.

8. Christianity was diverse with regard to ethnicity (Jews, Gentiles, Samaritans), gender (male, female), social status (slave, free, rich, poor), and location (Judea, Samaria, Rome, etc.). Becoming a Christian didn't mean abandoning one's ethnicity, gender, social status, or location; these just ceased to have the same impact on one's identity and practice.

9. Hurtado, *Destroyer of the Gods*, 33.

10. Certainly the Christian notion of a personal and loving God can also be found in Judaism, but once again the general ethnic exclusivity of Judaism limited its impact in contrast to the transethnic nature of Christianity.

11. Hurtado has an interesting chapter on early Christianity's well-documented and peculiar fondness for books. Hurtado writes, "The place of books in early Christianity, so remarkable in the ancient Roman setting, is another example of influence upon notions that we take for granted today. We expect religion to involve some sort of scriptural writings, and we assume that the practice of religion will typically include reading these writings, whether in corporate worship or in private devotion" (*Destroyer of the Gods*, 188).

12. Hurtado, *Destroyer of the Gods*, 144–45. Hurtado is citing a letter from a certain Hilarion dating to 1 BC, which is found in P. Oxyrynchus 4.744. Greek and English translation in A. S. Hunt and C. C. Edgar, *Select Papyri I: Private Affairs* (Cambridge, MA: Harvard University Press, 1932), 294–95.

13. As was typical in the ancient world, there was a double standard: a wife was to sleep only with her husband.

14. Pieter van der Horst, "How the Poor Became Blessed," *Aeon*, March 14, 2019, https://aeon.co/essays/the-poor-might-have-always-been-with-us-but-charity-has-not. This is a fascinating article written by an expert in early Christianity. Here's his summary: "So in spite of any relativising observations, it remains an indisputable fact that organised charity in the sense of a communal obligation towards the needy, which was by and large unknown in Greco-Roman culture, was created by the Jews and adopted by the Christians. And one can hardly deny that these developments were inspired by the sincere conviction that humankind should imitate God's special concern for the most vulnerable among humans—the poor."

15. Hurtado, *Destroyer of the Gods*, 15.

16. Pliny the Younger, *Letters* 10.96–97, www.earlychristianwritings.com/text/pliny.html.

17. Kavin Rowe, *World Upside Down: Reading Acts in the Graeco-Roman Age* (Oxford: Oxford University Press, 2009), 5.

18. McGrath, *Heresy*, 2–3.

19. McGrath, *Heresy*, 78.

20. Athanasius—the great defender of orthodoxy and opponent of Arianism—was exiled five times by Emperor Constantine "for stubbornly resisting any compromises with Arianism" regarding the full divinity of Jesus. See Roger E. Olson, *Counterfeit Christianity: The Persistence of Errors in the Church* (Nashville: Abingdon, 2015), 78.

21. McGrath, *Heresy*, 81–82.

22. Provan, *Seriously Dangerous Religion*, 30; italics original.

23. E.g., when God creates the sky, sun, and moon, it is clear in Genesis that he has created impersonal objects—unlike in Egyptian writings. Egyptians thought of the sky, sun, and moon as deities (Provan, *Seriously Dangerous Religion*, 50).

24. Richard J. Middleton, *A New Heaven and a New Earth: Reclaiming Biblical Eschatology* (Grand Rapids: Baker Academic, 2014), 44.

25. Evil is difficult to define, as it doesn't easily fit neatly into any categories. On the one hand, there is a personal force behind it (especially as associated with Satan), and evil can also function as a power (especially when we think of sin). On the other hand, evil can be something of a vacuum—the emptiness that is the opposite of God's goodness and love and creative will.

26. Roger E. Olson, *The Essentials of Christian Thought: Seeing Reality through the Biblical Story* (Grand Rapids: Zondervan, 2017), 212.

Chapter 8 Christianity and Life's Big Questions

1. Alex Rosenberg, *The Atheist's Guide to Reality: Enjoying Life without Illusions* (New York: Norton, 2012), 2–3.

2. While writing this chapter, I found Roger E. Olson's book, *The Essentials of Christian Thought: Seeing Reality through the Biblical Story* (Grand Rapids: Zondervan, 2017), to be very informative.

3. For further study on this topic, see Olson, *Essentials of Christian Thought*.

4. If we insist that God is love but not three in one, it creates a major problem that is ultimately incompatible with the biblical metanarrative. Specifically, it seems to make God *dependent* on creation and therefore not self-sufficient. As Olson writes, "If God were not [three in one], however, then creation would be necessary for God insofar as God is conceived as a God of love" (*Essentials of Christian Thought*, 169).

5. Olson, *Essentials of Christian Thought*, 145.

6. Olson, *Essentials of Christian Thought*, 53. Olson also helpfully explains that, unlike some philosophical concepts of God (such as Aristotle's Unmoved Mover), the Christian God is capable of truly being in relationship with his creation, the kind of relationship in which God's actions are not wholly fixed. God can respond to human decisions and actions. This is not to say that God can be controlled or manipulated; God cannot be controlled, and his character and nature are unchanging. However, in God's unchanging character and nature he still engages us in a real relationship, which means that he still can shape his actions to properly respond to our choices (*Essentials of Christian Thought*, 60, 166–67).

7. In humans it's hard—maybe impossible—to separate what's spiritual from what's physical. We experience the spiritual (whether sin or the Holy Spirit) in our physical bodies (addictions, sickness, etc.); and what we do with our physical bodies (whether good or evil) shapes our spirits/souls.

8. Richard J. Middleton, *A New Heaven and a New Earth: Reclaiming Biblical Eschatology* (Grand Rapids: Baker Academic, 2014), 40.

9. Middleton also points out that when "we look at the biblical texts that explicitly address the creation and purpose of human beings—Genesis 1–2, or Ps. 8, or even Ps. 104—not one of them says that we are created to 'worship God'" (*New Heaven*, 40–41).

10. For more discussion on this, including Scripture references, see Middleton, *New Heaven*, 133–34.

11. Is Jesus's parable offering a literal description, or is he just using a popular motif? When Jesus speaks to the man crucified next to him, what does he mean by "today" and "paradise"? In what sense is Paul "with Christ" in death? And is the vision in Revelation meant to be read literally or symbolically?

12. Roger Olson helpfully notes that "discerning the biblical metaphysic is a matter of looking behind the narrative at what it *assumes*" (*Essentials of Christian Thought*, 141; italics original).

13. C. S. Lewis, *The Problem of Pain* (1940; repr., New York: HarperOne, 1996), 99.

14. For a more technical and robust defense of this position, see Joshua Marshall Strahan, "Free Will, God's Providence, and Quantum Entanglement," *Theology and Science* (forthcoming).

15. Some might debate Rosenberg here based on quantum physics and/or the notion of emergence. For instance, the indeterminacy of quantum physics might allow for a certain indeterminacy in our lives. Or, while molecules and atoms might follow deterministic patterns, the complex combination of molecules and atoms might open up new possibilities that allow a measure of freedom to emerge within the complex system. I find these attempts unconvincing. Rosenberg himself anticipates those who want to suggest that quantum indeterminacy might allow for free will by simply pointing out that we cannot control what happens at the quantum level either. These quantum events still control us; we don't control them (*Atheist's Guide to Reality*, 237).

16. Rosenberg, *Atheist's Guide to Reality*, 115.

17. For an eye-opening look at pride as the "essential vice," see C. S. Lewis, *Mere Christianity* (1952; repr., New York: HarperOne, 1996), 121–28.

18. For a more detailed version of the following critique, see C. S. Lewis, *Miracles* (1947; repr., New York: Touchstone, 1996), chaps. 2–4.

Chapter 9 Challenges to the Christian System

1. Unintentionally, the structure of my next two chapters parallels Timothy Keller, *The Reason for God: Belief in an Age of Skepticism* (New York: Dutton, 2008). Keller starts his excellent book also by addressing obstacles to Christian faith (including the same four issues I treat in this chapter), and the second half of his book addresses evidence for Christian faith (as does my subsequent chapter). We take a similar approach in part because I've found Keller's work beneficial over the years and in part because we are influenced by many of the same authors, such as C. S. Lewis, Alvin Plantinga, Alister McGrath, and N. T. Wright.

2. In preparation for this section, I found William Lane Craig's concise and thoughtful discussion of this topic very helpful (*On Guard: Defending Your Faith with Reason and Precision* [Colorado Springs: David C. Cook, 2010], chap. 7, "What about Suffering?"). My approach to this topic parallels and is informed by Craig's work, though my first exposure to a similar line of thought came years earlier from C. S. Lewis, *The Problem of Pain* (1940; repr., New York: HarperOne, 1996), and *A Grief Observed* (1961; repr., New York: HarperCollins, 1994).

3. Technically, what we do is not under the foster-care system, but it's functionally very similar, as we partner with a Christian organization that puts at-risk or vulnerable children in the homes of safe families.

4. Lewis, *Grief Observed*, 6–7, 25, 29–30.

5. See, e.g., the psalms of lament and the book of Job.

6. "They say of some temporal suffering, 'No future bliss can make up for it,' not knowing that Heaven, once attained, will work backwards and turn even that agony into glory." In C. S. Lewis, *The Great Divorce* (1946; repr., New York: HarperOne, 2001), 69.

7. Alister E. McGrath, *If I Had Lunch with C. S. Lewis: Exploring the Ideas of C. S. Lewis on the Meaning of Life* (Carol Stream, IL: Tyndale, 2014), 180.

8. C. S. Lewis, *Mere Christianity* (1952; repr., New York: HarperOne, 1996), 47–49.

9. Craig humorously writes, "If [one] insists that an all-powerful being *can* do the logically impossible, then the problem of suffering evaporates immediately, for then God can bring it about that He [an all-good and all-powerful being] and suffering both exist, even though this is [suspected to be] logically impossible" (*On Guard*, 155).

10. Craig, *On Guard*, 156–60.

11. "Charles Darwin: Scientist and Writer," https://www.westminster-abbey.org/abbey-commemorations/commemorations/charles-darwin#i1165.

12. Georges Lemaître disliked speculation about the theological implications of his work, saying, "As far as I can see, such a theory remains entirely outside any metaphysical or religious question" (quote found, without citation, in Simon Singh, *Big Bang: The Origin of the Universe* [New York: Harper Perennial, 2005], 362). In his study of the big bang, Singh reminds readers that it's not only religious folks who sometimes allow their presuppositions to influence their scientific leanings. After all, the big bang was not initially embraced by scientists, who preferred to take a "leap of faith" and believe the "quite flimsy evidence" for an eternal universe (since it seemed to remove the need for a creator); nor was the big bang initially accepted by the Soviets, who found that the theory conflicted with Marxist-Leninist ideology (*Big Bang*, 79–80, 363).

13. It is noteworthy that the Roman Catholic Church later admitted its error regarding Galileo. As Singh recounts, "Cardinal Paul Poupard reported that theologians at the time of Galileo's trial 'failed to grasp the profound non-literal meaning of the Scriptures when they describe the physical structure of the universe'" (*Big Bang*, 485).

14. Alister E. McGrath, *Enriching Our Vision of Reality: Theology and the Natural Sciences in Dialogue* (West Conshohocken, PA: Templeton, 2017), 117.

15. Sean Carroll makes a nicely nuanced case for why scientific evidence renders faith claims unlikely (*The Big Picture: On the Origins of Life, Meaning, and the Universe Itself* [New York: Dutton, 2016]). He argues not that science definitively disproves such claims (which are beyond the reach of science) but that scientific evidence gives us strong reasons to reject such claims. The strength of his case rests on his assertion that there is no scientific evidence that anything interacts with or manipulates the natural order of things. (So, to his point, if there is a reality beyond nature, it would be irrelevant to us since it is neither accessible to us nor interfering with us.) I might counter his thoughtful argument with the following:

- The evidence Carroll points to strikes me as too narrow, not adequately accounting for the complexity of the subject in question (see, e.g., Karl W. Giberson and Francis S. Collins, *The Language of Science and Faith: Straight Answers to Genuine Questions* [Downers Grove, IL: InterVarsity, 2011], 118–20; and John Polkinghorne and Nicholas Beale, *Questions of Truth: Fifty-One Responses to Questions about God, Science, and Belief* [Louisville: Westminster John Knox, 2009], 41–43).
- It's possible that interference with the natural order could be more the exception than the rule (so that it would be unlikely to be demonstrated by experiment).
- Our deep instincts about morality, purpose, free will, personhood, and wonder seem to point beyond scientific explanations—as evidenced by Carroll's own labored, and I think unsuccessful, attempt to hold together naturalism alongside objective morality, ultimate purpose, and true free will. He contends for a "poetic naturalism," where he seems unwilling to play by his own metaphysical rules. It leads him to make frustrating, nonsensical claims (e.g., "Ideas like 'meaning' and 'morality' and 'purpose' are nowhere to be found in the Core Theory of quantum fields, the physics underlying our everyday lives. . . . That doesn't prevent these ideas from being real" [*Big Picture*, 389]).
- It may be that God—being beyond nature—interacts with nature in a way that is often invisible to and/or undetectable by natural instruments (see, e.g., C. Michael Williams, "Recontextualizing an Interventionist God: Finding Room for God at the Intersection of Science and Faith," *Journal of Faith and the Academy* 10 [Fall 2017]: 58–83).

16. As C. S. Lewis so nicely puts it,

> If you are a Christian you do not have to believe that all the other religions are simply wrong all through. If you are an atheist you do have to believe that the main point in all the religions of the whole world is simply one huge mistake. If you are a Christian, you are free to think that all those religions . . . contain at least some hint of truth. When I was an atheist I had to try to persuade myself that most of the human race have always been wrong about the question that mattered to them most; when I became a Christian I was able to take a more liberal view. But, of course, being a Christian does mean thinking that where Christianity differs from other religions, Christianity is right and they are wrong. (*Mere Christianity*, 35)

17. For a readable discussion on this topic, see Keller, *Reason for God*, 3–21. For something a bit more philosophical, see Harold Netland, "Jesus Is the Only Way to God," in *Debating Christian Theism*, ed. J. P. Moreland, Chad V. Meister, and Khaldoun A. Sweis (Oxford: Oxford University Press, 2013), 497–508.

18. In Alister E. McGrath, *The Passionate Intellect: Christian Faith and the Discipleship of the Mind* (Downers Grove, IL: InterVarsity, 2014), 147–68. In this essay, McGrath is responding to atheistic criticisms of religion, such as can be found in Christopher Hitchens's book *God Is Not Great: How Religion Poisons Everything* (New York: Twelve, 2007).

19. McGrath, *Passionate Intellect*, 148–49. I am reminded of C. S. Lewis's classic book *The Screwtape Letters*, in which demons try to discourage thoughtful reasoning with half-baked

evidence, like "everyone knows that . . ." or "any right-thinking person can see . . ." (*Screwtape Letters* [1942; repr., New York: HarperOne, 1996], 2–4).

20. McGrath, *Passionate Intellect*, 165–66.

21. Friedrich Nietzsche, *The Antichrist*, trans. H. L. Mencken (New York: Alfred A. Knopf, 1918). Available online at https://www.gutenberg.org/files/19322/19322-h/19322-h.htm; italics original.

22. Lewis, *Screwtape Letters*, 39.

23. The bird/egg analogy is adapted from Lewis, *Mere Christianity*, 198–99.

24. See Lewis's helpful discussion in *Mere Christianity*, 207–17.

25. I visited Ireland recently, and up to that point I had understood that the violent conflict in Ireland was primarily religious—Catholics against Protestants. As I toured Ireland and read the history, I was surprised to discover that the conflict seemed more politically than religiously motivated, with those in the South (primarily Catholics) fighting for Ireland's independence from the UK, and those in the North (primarily Anglican Protestants) wanting to remain part of the UK.

26. McGrath points out, "One of the greatest tragedies of this dark era in human history is that those who sought to eliminate religious belief through violence and oppression believed they were justified in doing so" (*Passionate Intellect*, 158).

27. Michael Shermer, *How We Believe: Science, Skepticism, and the Search for God* (New York: Freeman, 2000), 71, quoted in McGrath, *Passionate Intellect*, 167.

28. For more, see John Ortberg's *Who Is This Man?* (Grand Rapids: Zondervan, 2012). Ortberg overstates his case, but even with a healthy dose of nuancing Ortberg's numerous examples show how Christianity had a great deal of positive influence throughout Western cultures.

29. Andrea Palpant Dilley, "The World the Missionaries Made," *Christianity Today* 58 (January/February 2014): 34–41.

Chapter 10 Not Blind Faith

1. C. S. Lewis, *The Weight of Glory, and Other Addresses* (1949; repr., New York: HarperOne, 2001), 140.

2. C. Stephen Evans, "Are We Hardwired to Believe in God: Natural Signs for God, Evolution, and the *Sensus Divinitatis*," in *Knowing Creation: Perspectives from Theology, Philosophy, and Science,* ed. Andrew B. Torrance and Thomas H. McCall (Grand Rapids: Zondervan, 2018), 205–6.

3. If the atheist has hope, it is most likely a hope in humanity's unaided ability to solve the problems facing our world. Not only do humans have a less-than-stellar track record in this category but also, according to Alex Rosenberg, humans have no real freedom to change the course of events anyway.

4. N. T. Wright, *The Resurrection of the Son of God* (Minneapolis: Fortress, 2003). For a concise coverage of many similar points, see William Lane Craig, *On Guard: Defending Your Faith with Reason and Precision* (Colorado Springs: David C. Cook, 2010), 219–62.

5. Wright, *Resurrection of the Son of God*, 718.

6. "Outside Judaism, nobody believed in the resurrection" (Wright, *Resurrection of the Son of God*, 35).

7. Wright, *Resurrection of the Son of God*, 205; italics added. To be clear, Jews might believe that someone could be temporarily raised from the dead (such as when the Old Testament prophet Elijah healed the widow's son), but these would be instances of something closer to resuscitation from death to normal life with a mortal body—that is, these individuals were not experiencing God's resurrection from death to eternal life with an imperishable body.

8. Wright, *Resurrection of the Son of God*, 276.

9. "[The] Jewish and pagan worlds of late antiquity were . . . full of speculations about life after death, covering a wide spectrum of opinion inside Judaism as well as outside. Though the

early Christians came from many different backgrounds . . . there is virtually no such spectrum in the New Testament" (Wright, *Resurrection of the Son of God*, 477).

10. See Craig, *On Guard*, 228. Craig also quotes the first-century Jewish historian Josephus: "Let not the testimony of women be admitted, on account of the levity and boldness of their sex" (*Antiquities* 4.8.15).

11. Examples include the disciples on the road to Emmaus not immediately recognizing Jesus in Luke's Gospel (24:13–35) and Mary Magdalene thinking Jesus was the gardener in John's Gospel (20:11–18).

12. Wright, *Resurrection of the Son of God*, 680.

13. To speculate that the disciples got the idea from pagan mythology seems historically off base given that first-century Jews were known for their monotheism and their disdain for idolatry and also that "there's no trace of cults of dying and rising gods in first-century Israel" (Craig, *On Guard*, 248).

14. Craig, *On Guard*, 221.

15. For further detail on the insufficiency of these rival explanations, see Craig, *On Guard*, 245–61.

16. For those skeptical about the Bible's accuracy, notice that this argument doesn't require one to assume that the Gospels are completely accurate in every historical detail. The historical reporting of the Gospels is a topic for another book. Here I'm simply pointing to recurring themes in independent historical sources (empty tomb, resurrection appearances, disciples' unprecedented beliefs that they are willing to suffer for)—themes that are present throughout these accounts, even when the details aren't always easy to line up. If one dismissed all historical documents that have potentially inconsistent details, we'd have very little ancient history (Craig, *On Guard*, 243).

17. C. S. Lewis, *Mere Christianity* (1952; repr., New York: HarperOne, 1996), 52. Some would say that we should add "legend" to this list. That is, the disciples simply made up these things about Jesus that Jesus never actually said or did. Such claims, in my opinion, have not taken seriously the early and consistent witness of the Gospels along with most early Christian writings.

18. What follows is like a modest version of the Kalam argument that William Lane Craig has popularized. See, e.g., William Lane Craig, "The Kalam Argument," in *Debating Christian Theism*, ed. J. P. Moreland, Chad V. Meister, and Khaldoun A. Sweis (Oxford: Oxford University Press, 2013), 7–19. I find Craig's argument to be clear, thoughtful, and fairly compelling, though not as airtight as he presents it.

19. Stephen Hawking, *The Illustrated A Brief History of Time*, rev. and enlarged ed. (New York: Bantam, 1996), 160.

20. Alister E. McGrath, *The Big Question: Why We Can't Stop Talking about Science, Faith and God* (New York: St. Martins, 2015), 90.

21. Wes Morriston, "Doubts about the Kalam Argument," in Moreland, Meister, and Sweis, *Debating Christian Theism*, 21.

22. Sean Carroll, *The Big Picture: On the Origins of Life, Meaning, and the Universe Itself* (New York: Dutton, 2016), 307–9.

23. Simon Singh writes, "As Alan Guth, the father of inflationary theory, put it: 'It's often said there is no such thing as a free lunch. But the universe itself may be a free lunch.' Unfortunately, the scientific community has to admit that all these possible answers [for the origin of the universe], from rebounding universes to spontaneous quantum creation, are highly speculative and do not yet properly address the ultimate question of where the universe came from" (*Big Bang: The Origin of the Universe* [New York: Harper Perennial, 2005], 492).

24. Carroll, *Big Picture*, 311–12.

25. Alvin Plantinga argues that purely naturalistic explanations for this phenomenon are unconvincing (*Where the Conflict Really Lies: Science, Religion, and Naturalism* [Oxford: Oxford University Press, 2011], 271–91); see also McGrath, *Big Question*, 83–89.

26. If survival is the main drive in the evolution of the human brain, then perhaps we should be surprised that the human brain is capable of such complex and theoretical thought, which seems less important for survival. As Plantinga cleverly writes, "It is only the occasional assistant professor of mathematics or logic who needs to explain Gödel's first incompleteness theorem in order to survive and reproduce" (*Where the Conflict Really Lies*, 286).

27. Albert Einstein, "Physics and Reality," in *Ideas and Opinions* (New York: Bonanza, 1954), 292, quoted in McGrath, *Big Question*, 85.

Appendix A More about Paul's Theology

1. Richard B. Hays, *1 Corinthians*, Interpretation (Louisville: Westminster John Knox, 1997), 252–82.

2. Hays, *1 Corinthians*, 266.

3. Hays, *1 Corinthians*, 269.

4. Especially helpful for understanding this reading of Galatians are Richard B. Hays, "The Letter to the Galatians," in *New Interpreter's Bible*, vol. 11 (Nashville: Abingdon, 2000), 181–348; and Scot McKnight, *Galatians*, New International Version Application Commentary (Grand Rapids: Zondervan, 1995).

5. Numerous passages clearly show that Jesus's faithfulness makes humanity's justification possible: "he gave himself for our sins so he could deliver us" (Gal. 1:4); "God's Son . . . loved me and gave himself for me" (Gal. 2:20); "if we become righteous through the Law, then Christ died for no purpose" (Gal. 2:21).

6. The references to "faith/belief" in Gal. 2:16 are somewhat ambiguous, except for the second reference, wherein the *believer's* faith is clearly indicated by the Greek grammar: subject (we, *hēmeis*), preposition (in, *eis*), and object (Christ, *christon*).

7. The law itself isn't the real problem: sin is. For example, Paul writes, "Is the law, therefore, opposed to the promises of God? Absolutely not!" (Gal. 3:21 NIV). We find a similar teaching in Romans 7.

8. Nijay K. Gupta, *Colossians*, Smyth & Helwys Bible Commentary (Macon, GA: Smyth & Helwys, 2013), 55.

9. Michael J. Gorman, *Apostle of the Crucified Lord: A Theological Introduction to Paul and His Letters*, 2nd ed. (Grand Rapids: Eerdmans, 2017), 141; italics original.

Appendix B Hell

1. I've learned about this view primarily from Edward Fudge, *The Fire That Consumes: A Biblical and Historical Study of the Doctrine of Final Punishment*, 3rd ed. (Eugene, OR: Cascade, 2011); and Glenn Peoples, "Fallacies in the Annihilationism Debate: A Critique of Robert Peterson and Other Traditionalist Scholarship," *Journal of the Evangelical Theological Society* 50 (2007): 329–47.

2. See, e.g., Ezek. 20:47–48. See also Peoples, "Fallacies in the Annihilationism Debate," for thoughtful responses to several supposed biblical problems with annihilationism.

3. To my knowledge, there is not a technical name for this view, so this is my descriptive name for it.

4. C. S. Lewis, *The Great Divorce* (1946; repr., New York: HarperOne, 2001), 75.

Scripture Index

Subject Index